Dickens's London

Edinburgh Critical Studies in Victorian Culture

Series Editor: Julian Wolfreys

Volumes available in the series:

In Lady Audley's Shadow: Mary Elizabeth Braddon and Victorian Literary Genres
Saverio Tomaiuolo
978 0 7486 4115 4   Hbk

Blasted Literature: Victorian Political Fiction and the Shock of Modernism
Deaglán Ó Donghaile
978 0 7486 4067 6   Hbk

William Morris and the Idea of Community: Romance, History and Propaganda, 1880–1914
Anna Vaninskaya
978 0 7486 4149 9   Hbk

1895: Drama, Disaster and Disgrace in Late Victorian Britain
Nicholas Freeman
978 0 7486 4056 0   Hbk

Determined Spirits: Eugenics, Heredity and Racial Regeneration in Anglo-American Spiritualist Writing, 1848–1930
Christine Ferguson
978 0 7486 3965 6   Hbk

Dickens's London: Perception, Subjectivity and Phenomenal Urban Multiplicity
Julian Wolfreys
978 0 7486 4040 9   Hbk

Visit the Edinburgh Critical Studies in Victorian Culture web page at www.euppublishing.com/series/ecve

Also available:
Victoriographies – A Journal of Nineteenth-Century Writing, 1790–1914, edited by Julian Wolfreys
ISSN: 2044-2416

www.eupjournals.com/vic

Dickens's London

Perception, Subjectivity and Phenomenal
Urban Multiplicity

Julian Wolfreys

EDINBURGH
University Press

© Julian Wolfreys, 2012

Edinburgh University Press Ltd
22 George Square, Edinburgh

www.euppublishing.com

Typeset in 10.5/13 Sabon
by Servis Filmsetting Ltd, Stockport, Cheshire, and
printed and bound in Great Britain by
CPI Group (UK) Ltd, Croydon, CR0 4YY

A CIP record for this book is available from the British Library

ISBN 978 0 7486 4040 9 (hardback)
ISBN 978 0 7486 5603 5 (webready PDF)
ISBN 978 0 7486 5605 9 (epub)
ISBN 978 0 7486 5604 2 (Amazon ebook)

The right of Julian Wolfreys
to be identified as author of this work
has been asserted in accordance with
the Copyright, Designs and Patents Act 1988.

Contents

Alternative Contents

Enargia

List of Illustrations and Maps

Series Editor's Preface

'Victorian' is a term at once indicative of a strongly determined concept and an often notoriously vague notion, emptied of all meaningful content by the many journalistic misconceptions that persist about the inhabitants and cultures of the British Isles and Victoria's Empire in the nineteenth century. As such, it has become a by-word for the assumption of various, often contradictory habits of thought, belief, behaviour and perceptions. Victorian studies and studies in nineteenth-century literature and culture have, from their institutional inception, questioned narrowness of presumption, pushed at the limits of the nominal definition, and have sought to question the very grounds on which the unreflective perception of the so-called Victorian has been built; and so they continue to do. Victorian and nineteenth-century studies of literature and culture maintain a breadth and diversity of interest, of focus and inquiry, in an interrogative and intellectually open-minded and challenging manner, which are equal to the exploration and inquisitiveness of its subjects. Many of the questions asked by scholars and researchers of the innumerable productions of nineteenth-century society actively put into suspension the clichés and stereotypes of 'Victorianism', whether the approach has been sustained by historical, scientific, philosophical, empirical, ideological or theoretical concerns; indeed, it would be incorrect to assume that each of these approaches to the idea of the Victorian has been, or has remained, in the main exclusive, sealed off from the interests and engagements of other approaches. A vital interdisciplinarity has been pursued and embraced, for the most part, even as there has been contest and debate amongst Victorianists, pursued with as much fervour as the affirmative exploration between different disciplines and differing epistemologies put to work in the service of reading the nineteenth century.

Edinburgh Critical Studies in Victorian Culture aims to take up both the debates and the inventive approaches and departures from convention that studies in the nineteenth century have witnessed for the last half-century at least. Aiming to maintain a 'Victorian' (in the most positive sense of that motif) spirit of inquiry, the series' purpose is to continue and augment the cross-fertilisation of interdisciplinary approaches, and to offer, in addition, a number of timely and untimely revisions of Victorian literature, culture, history and identity. At the same time, the series will ask questions concerning what has been missed or improperly received, misread or not read at all, in order to present a multi-faceted and heterogeneous kaleidoscope of representations. Drawing on the most provocative, thoughtful and original research, the series will seek to prod at the notion of the 'Victorian', and in so doing, principally through theoretically and epistemologically sophisticated close readings of the historicity of literature and culture in the nineteenth century, to offer the reader provocative insights into a world that is at once overly familiar and irreducibly different, other and strange. Working from original sources, primary documents and recent interdisciplinary theoretical models, Edinburgh Critical Studies in Victorian Culture seeks not simply to push at the boundaries of research in the nineteenth century, but also to inaugurate the persistent erasure and provisional, strategic redrawing of those borders.

Julian Wolfreys

Abbreviations

Throughout, I have cited the Penguin editions as amongst the most generally available and reliable of scholarly editions. However, I have also consulted certain of the Oxford editions, particularly with reference to the editorial apparatus, and bibliographical details of these are also given below. Where I have cited the Oxford editions, this is made clear in the endnotes.

AP   *Dickens' Journalism Volume 2: 'The Amusements of the People' and Other Papers: Reports, Essays and Reviews 1834–51.* Ed. Michael Slater. London: J. M. Dent, 1996.

BH   *Bleak House.* Ed. Nicola Bradbury. Preface Terry Eagleton. London: Penguin, 2003. *Bleak House.* Ed. and Int. Stephen Gill. Oxford: Oxford University Press, 1996.

DC   *David Copperfield.* Ed. and Int. Jeremy Tambling. London: Penguin, 1996. *David Copperfield.* Ed. Nina Burgess. Int. Andrew Sanders. Oxford: Oxford University Press, 1997.

DS   *Dombey and Son.* Ed. and Int. Andrew Sanders. London: Penguin, 2002.

GA   *Dickens' Journalism Volume 3: 'Gone Astray' and Other Papers from* Household Words *1851–59.* Ed. Michael Slater. London: J. M. Dent, 1998.

GE   *Great Expectations.* Ed. Charlotte Mitchell. Int. David Trotter. London: Penguin, 2003.

HT   *Hard Times.* Ed. and Int. Paul Schlicke. Oxford: Oxford University Press, 1989.

LCD v. I House, Madeline, Graham Storey, et al, eds. *The Letters of Charles Dickens Volume One 1820–1839.* Oxford: Clarendon, 1965.

LD   *Little Dorrit.* Ed. and Int. Stephen Wall and Helen Small. London: Penguin, 1998. *Little Dorrit.* Ed. and

	Int. Harvey Peter Sucksmith. Oxford: Oxford University Press, 1999.
MC	*Martin Chuzzlewit.* Ed. and Int. P. N. Furbank. London: Penguin, 1986. *Martin Chuzzlewit.* Ed. and Int. Margaret Cardwell. Oxford: Oxford University Press, 1998.
MED	*The Mystery of Edwin Drood.* Ed. and Int. Arthur J. Cox. Int. Angus Wilson. London: Penguin, 1985.
MHC	*Master Humphrey's Clock and A Child's History of England.* Int. Derek Hudson. Oxford: Oxford University Press, 1958.
MJG	*Memoirs of Joseph Grimaldi.* Ed. and Int. Richard Findlater. New York: Stein & Day, 1968.
NN	*Nicholas Nickleby.* Ed. and Int. Michael Slater. London: Penguin, 1986.
NT	*No Thoroughfare* (with Wilkie Collins). Newcastle upon Tyne: Cambridge Scholars, 2008.
OCS	*The Old Curiosity Shop.* Ed. Angus Easson. Int. Malcolm Andrews. London: Penguin, 1985.
OMF	*Our Mutual Friend.* Ed. and Int. Adrian Poole. London: Penguin, 1997. *Our Mutual Friend.* Ed. and Int. Michael Cotsell. Oxford: Oxford University Press, 1989.
OT	*Oliver Twist.* Ed. Peter Fairclough. Int. Angus Wilson. Harmondsworth: Penguin, 1986.
PP	*The Pickwick Papers.* Ed. and Int. Mark Wormald. London: Penguin, 2003. *The Pickwick Papers.* Ed. and Int. James Kinsley. Oxford: Oxford University Press, 1998.
SB	*Dickens' Journalism Volume 1: Sketches by Boz and Other Early Papers 1833–39.* Ed. Michael Slater. London: J. M. Dent, 1994.
SJ	*Selected Journalism 1850–1870.* Ed. and Int. David Pascoe. London: Penguin, 1997.
TTC	*A Tale of Two Cities.* Ed. and Int. Richard Maxwell. London: Penguin, 2000.
UT	*Dickens' Journalism Volume 4: 'The Uncommercial Traveller' and Other Papers 1859–70.* Ed. Michael Slater and John Drew. London: J. M. Dent, 2000.

Advertisement

– The familiar city beckons to the *flâneur* as phantasmagoria – now a landscape, now a room.

– The reader must not expect to know where I live.

– Much of our modern difficulty, in religion and other things, arises merely from this, that we confuse the word 'indefinable' with the word 'vague'.

– My dear, you never have found number eighty-one Norfolk Street, Strand, advertised in Bradshaw's *Railway Guide*, and with the blessing of Heaven you never will or shall so find it.

– Literary critics do not take into account that such a work like this constitutes a scientific exploration in the same category as the work of Freud or Newton.

– You might have some difficulty in penetrating the arcana of the Modern Babylon in the direction of the City Road.

– The most distinctive cities bear within them the capacity of being nowhere.

– From the windows of my room I saw all London lying in the distance like a great vapour, with here and there some lights twinkling through it.

– He did not go in for 'observation', a priggish habit; he did not look at Charing Cross to improve his mind or count the lamp-posts in Holborn to practise his arithmetic.

– And that explains the mystery of the key!

– His passionate power of expression makes him the most important representative of modernity at the present time.

– I can tell you best what he is, by telling you what Doctors' Commons is.

– There is no such place as London after all.

– We must not lose sight of you. We must not let you pass out of our knowledge. We must know all about you.

– And I am now reduced to a mere wayward memory, losing itself in street after street as far as the dazzling lights of the bridges, among passers-by dreamt up by the winter sun.

– Appearance is an intrinsic determination of being. But it is immediately evident that since the localisation of being, which constitutes its appearance, implies another particular being – its site or situation – appearance as such is what binds or re-binds a being to its site. The essence of appearance is relation.

– Why, highty tighty, sir!

– An image presented to us by life brings with it, in a single moment, sensations which are in fact multiple and heterogeneous.

– The walls of my lodgings might have something to tell if they could tell it. The dear boy was always fond of story books. I am sure this house – his own home – might write a story or two for his reading one day or another.

– even supposing –

For
Hillis

Acknowledgements

I would like to thank:

- Elaine Hobby, on behalf of the Department of English and Drama at Loughborough University, for providing a small grant from the Head of Department Discretionary Fund towards the completion of this project.
- Alyson Rogers, on behalf of English Heritage, for permission to reproduce the illustration of the Adelphi; reproduced by permission of English Heritage. NMR.
- Mark Annand, of Bath Spa University and site author of the Greenwood's Map, and the University, for permission to reproduce plates from Greenwood's Map of London 1827.

I would, also like to thank the following, who, in some measure, have had a beneficial effect on my thinking in the conception and development of this project: Megan Becker-Leckrone, Anne-Marie Beller, Catherine Bertrand, Christoph Bode, Carol Bolton, John Brannigan, Ian Buchanan, Frederick Burwick, Torsten Caeners, Thomas Docherty, Nick Freeman, Jean-Michel Ganteau, Jens Gurr, Julia Kuehn, J. Hillis Miller, Bill Overton, Tatiana Pogossian-Michoud and Frank Pointner.

Jackie Jones, at Edinburgh University Press, has, as ever, offered unstinting support for, and faith in, this project; her critical appreciation is without peer, and I thank her once again.

Preface

Everybody thinks that they know Dickens's London or, if you prefer, 'Dickensian London'. The distinction is worth making at the outset, even though I will not have explicit recourse to the differentiation again. 'Dickensian London' is a fiction, a constellated matrix of images, tropes and other rhetorical or visual keys, which, occasionally synonymous with 'Victorian London' (it has become this, at least), is neither more nor less 'true', as far as representations go, than any other. 'Dickensian London' is a fictional topography doubling as a stage, on which appear eager and hopeful young persons, middle-aged or cynical men of business, lawyers, criminals, dependent women, people who are perpetually disappointed, those who daily expect something to turn up, children, adolescents, the homeless, street-wise characters and so forth. Such a London is a fixed and fictive place, the setting of which allows for incongruous or chance meetings, life-changing events and unexpected reversals of fortune.

Such a London – *Dickensian* London – is that simulacrum produced in the words of Josiah Bounderby, of Coketown, who, after a fashion, claims that London made him what he is, first in Chapter 4 and then, from the seventh chapter, in a rejoinder to Mrs Sparsit:

> 'Josiah Bounderby of Coketown learnt his letters from the outsides of the shops, Mrs. Gradgrind, and was first able to tell the time upon a dial-plate, from studying the steeple clock of St. Giles's Church, London, under the direction of a drunken cripple, who was a convicted thief, and an incorrigible vagrant.' (*HT* 21)

> 'People like you, ma'am, accustomed from infancy to lie on Down feathers, have no idea how hard a paving-stone is, without trying it. No, no, it's of no use my talking to you about tumblers. I should speak of foreign dancers, and the West End of London, and May Fair, and lords and ladies and honour-ables.' (*HT* 60)

A 'big, loud man, with a stare, and a metallic laugh' (*HT* 18), a 'man made out of coarse material' (*HT* 18) and, moreover, a 'man who could never sufficiently vaunt himself a self-made man' and who 'was always proclaiming', as a result, his 'old ignorance and his old poverty' (*HT* 18), Josiah Bounderby is also a self-perjuring fictionaliser. He invents himself, creating the image of his being and his identity as having sprung from the very paving stones of the capital. Having triumphed over homelessness and illiteracy, Josiah Bounderby is 'self-made' but only to the extent that his autobiography is an invention of a few of the stereotypes and clichés that come, so often today, to stand in for the idea of 'Dickensian London' in the minds of many readers. In just these two quotations, the reader is confronted with not only the pavements, but also the outsides of stores, as well as a clock on a church steeple, which introduces sound to the visual image. London's demi-monde is signalled synecdochally here through the West End and Mayfair, and a sense of place is evoked through the figures of tumblers and 'foreign dancers' (a neat economy of conflation is to be noted). Such figures belong, it might be suggested in passing, to Wordsworth's confused and often anxious lists of simulacra, which, refusing any representational order or control, distress both the subject during his 'Residence in London' (1995, 250–96) and the subject of urban representation itself. Whether or not such a resonance is to be read, returning to Bounderby there is, inevitably one feels, a cripple who also happens to be an alcoholic *and* thief, as well as a vagrant. This tutelary and anonymous phantasm of Bounderby's imagination is a virtual portmanteau character, so replete is he with 'types', and having sprung not so much from the streets of London as from the pages of Newgate novels and penny-dreadfuls. Here, in Bounderby's imagination, is captured, as if from a magic lantern show or a BBC period drama of the early twenty-first century, *Dickensian London*. All human life is here – or near enough.

Everything in the two self-advertising and defensive, bombastic expositions relies on polarisation, extremes of the urban figure in the popular imagination. There is criminal life *and* a world of opulence, one of poverty *and* also one of the social elite. There is entertainment *and* suffering. Bounderby's affirmations of the self refigure, in extracted and condensed form, material not that far removed from some of the detail to be read in certain of the *Sketches by Boz*. There are differences, however, not least in the fact that Boz, as the titular narrator, hardly ever speaks of himself, save as a medium or conduit for whatever is gathered in the proper name 'London', its scenes, events, places, architecture and people, and the subjective experience of these translated as perception, memory, observation and transcription. Bounderby, on the other hand, speaks only of himself through the stock rhetoric, as is clear. In the *Sketches* there is to be read humour, compassion, sorrow and amusement. In *Hard Times* Bounderby's narrative of individualistic triumphalism lacks any of those qualities, unless it be that, through his words, the reader is afforded entertainment at what turns out to be perfidy and mendacity. That the self-making man lies to such an extent might be apprehended in the coarseness of the representations, at least indirectly.

That Josiah Bounderby is able to generate himself through storytelling by recourse to what were already overly familiar elements of urban narrative, fictional or real, by the 1850s suggests the power that London had over the imagination. Bounderby's fiction of the self relies on the *locus classicus* of the capitalist individual, in which London is a place where the streets are paved with gold for those who can drag themselves out of the mire – literally as well as metaphorically, this being mid-nineteenth-century London (see the opening pages of *Bleak House*). He is a fictional testament to the equally fictional urban myth of surviving the city's 'hard times', so to speak. Bounderby cannot make as much of himself as he does, and cannot invent his fictive image quite so convincingly, without the fictions of the city: those, on the one hand, which he reiterates and which are given form by numerous novelists, and those, on the other, which the city itself engenders, out of its complex quotidian existence and the need on the part of some to reduce, make manageable and so control the material of London in the imagination. Regardless of the crudity of Bounderby's London images, and regardless of the shamelessness of his 'literary plagiarism' in drawing on the clichéd urban narrative, its poetics and rhetoric, thereby smelting and recasting what is already, by the mid-Victorian moment, stale and adulterated material, one thing becomes clear: as soon as there is London, as soon as London is *there*, in the imagination, in the memory, or before one, *there is* 'more than one voice in a voice' (Derrida 2002, 166). And this 'implicit multiplicity of the authorizing source', or 'polyology' (Miller 1998, 149), *forges* the image, even as any origin becomes dispersed so as to make available to our comprehension a sense 'at the unfathomable depths of an abyssal staging' (Derrida 2002, 166) that occurs every time London is written or writes itself through the momentary gathering of its traces in any narrative of place, fictional or real; so here we get a sense, we receive, 'the beating heart of what is blithely called literary fiction' (Derrida 2002, 166). To put this differently, as soon as there is London, fiction, narrative, storytelling take place.

A difficulty thus arises in this abyssal complication of the presumption of a boundary (that Bounderby, I fancy, seems partly to name, in passing) between the fictional and the real, and the difficulty is there in the name, the narration, the memory, the very idea of London. London displaces itself from itself and from within itself, giving us to apprehend how there is no final identity or meaning, no *there* there, not as a discrete, complete ontological phenomenon or object. Dickens appears to comprehend this, or at least he receives it in this spirit, in his efforts to reiterate, trace and translate 'London' from the materiality of the world to that of the letter. For Dickens, there is no ultimately justifiable distinction between the fictive and the real, the imaginary and the material. There is no absolute separation between lie and truth (hence the doubleness *and* duplicity implicit in my choice of the word *forge*, above), only the trace and play of a third term, and this is the pulse, the rhythm and flow we call 'literary', which serves to deconstruct the boundary. In this, Bounderby thus comes to be figured as the most typical narrator of the city. For Bounderby exists as a 'state of mind' predicated on a fiction, a state of mind, like any other, 'made or altered by language'; and this 'possibility appears in all those forms of language pervasive in novels, that cannot be made to correspond to any single unified consciousness' (Miller 1998, 152). The Dickensian narrator of the city reads what he is given, that which is also the matter by which he is written, that which the city writes on him, writing him as its subject, inscribing his subjectivity as a reading / writing of the always already 'more than one voice in a voice'. He gives us a clue to reading London, therefore, as well as to the ways in which London writes the subject, and so makes it possible to begin a reading without ever to have done with that act of reading, but to remain with a reading of London to come, even as London remains – and remains other to any reading in which are marked, desired or implied, finite limits. Dickens knows this, apprehending also that the enigma called the 'literary' is nothing other than the 'task' of responding and being open to this other, and of 'interpret[ing] the given sensations as signs of so many laws and ideas' (Proust 1996, 232).

A Note on the Text

The contents page is divided. There are the principal contents, and then a list of the *enargia*, the scenes and images to which I refer throughout the present volume. In the majority of cases, a discussion and reading follow each sketch; with a very small number of examples, though, I have presented an extract simply for the purpose of illustration, and for the reader to reflect on the image of London in the light of the other considerations throughout the book. If the reader expects there to be an entry under Z, however, he or she will be disappointed. If London is a city where someone may walk for hours on end, without reaching the beginning of an ending, to paraphrase Friedrich Engels, then it seems inappropriate to include a 'final' entry under the last letter of the alphabet. Dickens's London, like the list of entries one can only begin to imagine under such a title, never reaches an end, any more than Engels's imagined pedestrian. The other thing the reader may wish to note is the absence of an introduction. If there is no conclusion to London, equally there can be no 'introduction' if by this one intends or suggests an overview or model by which the eye can take in everything at once, so as to gain a perspective. London proves repeatedly that such a wish is idle, the very idea impossible. One can only arrive in, or return to, the city and reflect on what is before one. In lieu of an introduction, however, I would refer the reader to the chapter that stands alone after the alphabetical entries, under the heading, 'Dickens, our Contemporary'.

Dickens's London

The Adelphi (1780)

The Adelphi

Arrivals (and Returns)

London

Nicholas Nickleby

They rattled on through the noisy, bustling, crowded street of London, now displaying long double rows of brightly-burning lamps, dotted here and there with the chemists' glaring lights, and illuminated besides with the brilliant flood that streamed from the windows of the shops, where sparkling jewellery, silks and velvets of the richest colours, the most inviting delicacies, and most sumptuous articles of luxurious ornament, succeeded each other in rich and glittering profusion. Streams of people apparently without end poured on and on, jostling each other in the crowd and hurrying forward, scarcely seeming to notice the riches that surrounded them on every side; while vehicles of all shapes and makes, mingled up together in one moving mass, like running water, lent their ceaseless roar to swell the noise and tumult.

As they dashed by the quickly-changing and ever-varying objects, it was curious to observe in what a strange procession they passed before the eye. Emporiums of splendid dresses, the materials brought from every quarter of the world; tempting stores of everything to stimulate and pamper the sated appetite and give new relish to the oft-repeated feast; vessels of burnished gold and silver, wrought into every exquisite form of vase, and dish, and goblet; guns, swords, pistols, and patent engines of destruction; screws and irons for the crooked, clothes for the newly-born, drugs for the sick, coffins for the dead, and churchyards for the buried—all these jumbled each with the other and flocking side by side, seemed to flit by in motley dance like the fantastic groups of the old Dutch painter, and with the same stern moral for the unheeding restless crowd.

Nor were there wanting objects in the crowd itself to give new point and purpose to the shifting scene. The rags of the squalid ballad-singer fluttered in the rich light that showed the goldsmith's treasures, pale and pinched-up faces hovered about the windows where was tempting food, hungry eyes wandered over the profusion guarded by one thin sheet of brittle glass—an iron wall to them; half-naked shivering figures stopped to gaze at Chinese shawls and golden stuffs of India. There was a christening party at the largest coffin-maker's and a funeral hatchment had stopped some great improvements in

the bravest mansion. Life and death went hand in hand; wealth and poverty
stood side by side; repletion and starvation laid them down together.
    But it was London. (*NN* 488–9)

So, Nicholas Nickleby, entering the city for the second time, that second
time being both an arrival and a return, in which the urban world makes
an impression, gathering itself before the subject. The coach rattles,
and in doing so augments the initial aural experience and image. More
than this, the vehicle's resonance implies its motion also, whilst both
standing against *and* commingling with the noises already underway.
Here is sound for specific subjects, for both the reader and Nicholas and
Smike as well. The reader encounters that which is experienced by the
occupants of the coach. Nicholas and his fellow passengers are all but
immersed in motion, noise and a fleeting series of successive fragmentary visual images added to the aural figures. However, reverberation
precedes vision initially, even though one slides into the other; noise
becomes bustle, which suggests both rapid motion and sound, the two
becoming enfolded in the momentary definition of the London street in
the extract's first sentence, which is crowded: with sound, with sight.
The narrating mechanism's lens mediates between what the passengers on the coach witness and what is given the reader to see, through
the medium. We are directed 'now' to this, 'here and there' to that,
in clausal modifiers that map both temporal and spatial co-ordinates;
which points, though concealing nothing, do little, if anything, to construct a stable or complete vision or representation of the urban world.
Indeed, the impression is one simultaneously of both too little and too
much, mere fragments of information or a sensory overload, grasping
after the merest detail, the most minimal of phenomena available to the
senses, as they seek a sense of the world of London. There is so much,
and the inhabitants of London are so habituated to this kaleidoscopic
mêlée, that the sense one has of the 'streams of people' is that they barely
appear to notice ('scarcely seeming') much at all in the 'shifting scene'
constituted through 'the quickly-changing and ever-varying' 'procession' of phenomena. Interestingly, those people who coalesce into a
stream, and are elsewhere figured by the motion of 'pouring', thereby
losing solidity and individuality in the process, are dissolved into a collective phenomenal city-effect. Their fluidity defines street life, but is also
a phenomenon of the streets, as is illuminated by the 'brilliant flood' of
lights and lamps, this liquid solution of the urban becoming the medium
by which modes of transport are transformed: 'vehicles of all shapes and
makes, mingled together in one moving mass, like running water' in a
'ceaseless roar'. The expression of London appears as the experience

of a waterfall, the urban sublime approached through the translation of what strikes the eye and other senses in the *en passant* gesture of immanent analogy. Not only do the city's inhabitants become dissolved into the flow, so too vehicles are seen to deliquesce in the urban solution – and this, of course, is figured in the dissolution of representation into alliteration and other formal effects in the transcription of experience and perception. Additionally, so indistinct are the people rendered in their aqueous condition that the narrator can only observe semblance rather than fact. It is not that the 'people' scarcely notice; rather, they scarcely seem to take account of what takes place around them. The reading of experience, and with that the perception on which reading relies, is rendered, if not problematic, then, at the least, limited in its efficacy and certainty. The narrator's perception is challenged through the limit imposed on it by the unknowability concerning collective perception of others. London thus confronts the subject's perception with an experience of the aporetic.

Of the many effects concerning perception in this passage, there is therefore the curiosity of a double effect, which, seemingly paradoxical, both draws the subject into the experience with a startling immediacy and, in prohibiting settled reflection or comprehension, maintains a distance between subject and experience. This is replicated to some degree when one tries to describe what takes place here, for there is so much, there is such an overflow in all directions, that it becomes difficult to decide which details to stress, what to repeat, where to alight so as to consider reflectively, or what to offer to a reading as a result of the anxiety that something of equal significance might be omitted, occluded or otherwise given too little emphasis. Returning, therefore, to the beginning of the passage excerpted, and starting again with sound: rattle is both noise and motion. The transitive form of the verb involves someone, it takes him or her up as if in a vehicle, which of course this particular trope is. It is both the vehicle, obviously, in which the passengers are conveyed, but it is also the vehicle of re-presentation, having a performative tropic dimension, in which the reading subject is transported, as it were. This motion – by which language performs the action it describes – places the reader in the experience whilst witnessing that experience, albeit in a virtual form.

While the question of how to define, where to direct one's attention, remains therefore, as a result of performative slippage, and seemingly endless re-direction and reiteration, adumbration of phenomena, effect and trope might serve to an extent in apprehending how the Dickens-machine reproduces the city and, more importantly, the idea of the subject's impression of London, his or her sense of the world. Noise is, as has been observed, the principal medium of urban perception: 'rattle', 'noisy', 'bustling', 'ceaseless roar', 'noise and tumult'. More than that, sound serves as the formal framing device for the first of the three paragraphs cited. Noise surrounds what one sees, it is all around, and thus serves to create the impression that the reading subject is being immersed in the solution of the city and its motility. In this, and, of course, elsewhere, both in this passage and throughout his text, Dickens apprehends what Herbert Read defined in the paintings of Cézanne as the 'surface sensuousness'[1] of objects (Read 1988, xviii), as this is given to the subject's perceptual experience as the 'constitutive eidos of the given' (Williams 1993, 169), to express this in phenomenological terms. Dickens's writing is informed neither by an attempt to impose his own self on the city, nor by attempt to render London merely in an 'impressionistic' manner. Rather, it is a matter of inventing a writing of the city that attends both to the singular and the iterable, re-presenting in turn that which is imprinted on memory, through attendance on 'invariant structures' (Williams 1993, 167), thereby opening a reading / writing of the forms of objective reality received as phenomena. Dickens does not give an impression; he writes the visual and aural as they strike one. If we allow aurality as image into the definition of the painting, or if we admit an expanded sense of writing to include the idea of painting as a modality of the written, then it might be said it is the figure of Boz / Dickens who, as much as Constantin Guys,[2] is the 'painter' of modern life *par excellence*. Like Baudelaire, and in anticipation of, not impressionism, but the post-impressionism of Paul Cézanne, Dickens is the 'profound *painter* of appearing objects of perception' (Williams 1993, 168). The sound of London serves, in this apprehension, as the parergon of the image, but also, crucially, that which is given to perception as that which, in memory, frames the re-presented image; hence its priority in Nicholas's return to London, a second entrance to the city in which London returns to the subject with a reality that exceeds mere impressionism, with the force of proximity and intimacy, which no mere impression can conjure. In order that *all* London is figured, though not through the desire for an impossible totality, fully realised, it is to the welter of detail, time and again, that the reading / writing subject has recourse.

Moving from sound to motion, then: bustling, streaming, pouring, jostling, mingling, moving, swelling, dashing, quickly changing, ever-varying, procession, jumbling, flocking, flitting, dancing, restless, shifting, fluttering, hovering, wandering, shivering. Everything that there is found in play, in concert and separately, independently, unconscious of every other movement, but all caught in the image as the machinic-organic operations of the city. As experience reads so writing takes place, which conveys that experience for the reading of another, in the rhythms and forms where the world becomes text, placing the reader both in, and before, this experience, and, in the process, in the virtual encounter with the phantasm of London of the 1830s. Each motion reiterates every other, even as movement is of the essence of both London and the passage, without being an object in itself. In those movements, and in their inflections of one another, we are given to read that tropological work and mode of perception that becomes the play of reflection in the passage from *Our Mutual Friend* discussed elsewhere. Action and activity are the conditions of the objects available to perception, without being objects themselves. Through this mode of production, the Dickens-machine generates the sensate experience of that which is the concrete, to cite Herbert Read, of the image (Read 1988, xix). Perception is thus accorded a primacy in the text of Dickens, through the narrating act of reading / writing. This primacy, however, is not to be taken as the sign of intellectualism, of a perception that is purely one of consciousness, thereby rediscovering a mind / body dualism. Perception, and the experience from which it springs with an immediacy signalled through the shifts, the jumps, the fragmentation, the iterability, and the avoidance of absolute definition that make up the performative dimension of Dickens's text, takes place within a 'living bodily system' (Johnson, 1993, 8). In this, a Dickensian phenomenology of the urban anticipates not the phenomenology of Husserl, but that of Maurice Merleau-Ponty, whose understanding of phenomena was from 'the worldly standpoint of bodily incarnation and intersubjective, historical situation' (Johnson 1993, 8). This is what is given us to read through the details of sound, motion and so forth in the interplay invented by the narrator and experienced in performative fashion through the reading subject, in a fusion of 'self and world' (Johnson 1993, 12).

Which leaves us with what is given to see. One needs light in order to perceive and this is provided by those 'long double-rows of brightly burning lamps' that arrive *now* in order to be seen and to allow us to see; additionally, there is the periodic presence of chemists' 'glaring lights', and the accumulated brilliance flooding from the shop windows. Perception becomes taken over by sparkle, colouration, richness, glitter, and a general vibrancy equal to the work of noise and play of motion. This triadic relationship is then transformed into a somewhat hallucinatory procession, strange, curious and exotic as a result of volume, density, excess, passing 'before the eye'. Objects vie for the eye's attention, as the second paragraph moves with the illusion of increasing rapidity, alighting only to name one detail after another. The word supplements the sensory, phenomenal trace. Hand-worked gold and silver, vases, vessels, weapons, 'engines of destruction', opiates, coffins: all tumble and jostle, replacing and displacing one another, both in temporal sequence and, at the same time, vying for space, alongside one another, and assuming to the eye – which in truth is the roving camera rather than the objects having any vitality of their own – the appearance of a macabre early modern dance, as captured by 'the old Dutch Painter'. Arguably, it is the act of painting which imposes meaning, and which suggests interpretation for the narrating, viewing subject. What is of primary significance throughout, though, is the reminder that there is always perception for some *one*, for a subject in the world, whether it be Boz, the imagined painter, the anonymous figures looking in windows, as a reader looks at the page attempting to consume the details and digest the surfeit, or Nicholas and Smike, along with the other passengers on the coach. Dickens privileges the sensory qualities throughout. In doing so, and thereby in giving attention to the 'sensible properties of the world' (Johnson, 1993, 12), we have returned to us a sense not only of the world, but of the immediacy of our involvement in, and perception of that world. 'Quality, light, color, depth, which are there before us, are there only', as Maurice Merleau-Ponty argues, 'because they awaken an echo in our bodies' (1964b/1993, 22/125)[3] of what is shared with the other. When we read in this manner, attending to the primacy of perception, and that which we apprehend as a result, such 'correspondences in turn give rise to some tracing rendered visible again ... Rather than seeing [the scene] ... I see according to, with it' (23/126).[4] In arriving, London thus returns, as if its coming were for us, as if the arrival were ours.

The narrating spectator is thus in part an optical, if not a reflecting device: a 'mirror as vast as the crowd itself; [comparable to] a kaleidoscope endowed with consciousness, which, with every one of [the crowd's] movements presents the multiplicity of life and the flickering grace of all the elements of life' (Baudelaire 1992, 400). This will doubtless be familiar to some as the definition of the *flâneur* by Charles Baudelaire, who continues: 'He is an *I* insatiable for the *non-I*, which, at every instant renders and expresses it in images more living than life itself, always unstable and fugitive' (1992, 400). But as we have argued, the narrating subject in Dickens is no mere consciousness any more than he is just an eye or lens; he is a figure – on occasions named Boz – who is both *in* and *of* the crowd, and whose ability is to transport the reader to that place, on to those streets.

It may be objected, though, that to read a page is *not* the same as standing in the place about which one reads. I am at a remove from any 'real' person corresponding more or less with the fiction, the idea, of 'Boz'. Yet, to argue this is, implicitly, at the least, to decide on the image, whether in words or as a drawing or painting, to be just a 'tracing, a copy, a second thing ... the mental image [being] such a drawing' (1964b/1993, 23/126). It is to keep the image at a remove, in place-holders, and thus to replicate that scientific distance between consciousness and the world, which the literary breaks down repeatedly through the *as if* of fictional and virtual realities of narrative. One does not 'look' at a scene or image in a text as one would look at a thing, certainly. Instead, rather than looking at or seeing a building, a door, a room, the furniture in the scene, as if these were the real things, I see with, according to, the narrative 'eye'; but the eye, in reading, comes to belong both to the phantom narrator and to 'I' as the reader, by virtue of the fact that, in reading the narrator's re-presentation, I come to be *in* that place, seeing from that perspective, and given perception that is no longer solely that of the narrator, but equally not only, originarily, my own. I haunt the place of the "narrator", the other, even as this figure of the other comes to haunt me[5]; in this, as a result of the phantom effects of the narrating machine, reading and the narrator-effect put back in place, re-present-ing, the 'unoccupied' space that was filled by the painter. There is still, there remains, implicitly, a 'painting subject' with any painting, but 'nar-ration', 'narrating-effect' and 'narrator' all serve to make more explicit that which is omitted or absent, even as these figures are not wholly as absent as the 'author' or the present 'reader', belonging to or compris-ing a third term. What we 'see' then, in entering London with Nicholas and Boz, along with whoever else might be looking from the coach, is not composed of things borrowed from the real world. Instead, we enter into an imaginary, which is simultaneously very close and further away from the 'actual' (23–4/126). The imaginary, which escapes definition even as one reaches the conclusion 'But it was London' as a result of the combinatory effects of sound, motion and visual image, offers 'traces of vision' from within the real; Dickens's narration 'gives vision ... the imaginary texture of the real' (24/126).

> Whitechapel, Blackheath, Blackfriars, Windsor Terrace, City Road, The Strand, Drury Lane, Fleet Street, Buckingham Street, the Adelphi, Custom House [Lower Thames Street], the Monument, Fish-Street Hill, St Paul's Cathedral

David Copperfield

What an amazing place London was to me when I saw it in the distance, and how I believed all the adventures of all my favourite heroes to be constantly enacting and re-enacting there, and how vaguely I made it out in my own mind to be fuller of wonders and wickedness than all the cities of the earth, I need not stop to relate. We approached it by degrees, and got, in due time, to the inn in the Whitechapel district, for which we were bound. I forget whether it was the Blue Bull, or the Blue Boar; but I know it was the Blue Something, and that its likeness was painted up on the back of the coach. [. . .] More solitary than Robinson Crusoe, who had nobody to look at him and see that he was solitary, I went into the booking-office, and, by invitation of the clerk on duty, passed behind the counter, and sat looking at the parcels, packages, and books, and inhaling the smell of stables (ever since associated with that morning), a procession of the most tremendous considerations began to march through my mind. (*DC* 73, 74–5)

Murdstone and Grinby's warehouse was at the water side. It was down in Blackfriars. Modern improvements have altered the place; but it was the last house at the bottom of a narrow street, curving down hill to the river, with some stairs at the end, where people took boat. It was a crazy old house with a wharf of its own, abutting on the water when the tide was in, and on the mud when the tide was out, and literally over-run with rats. Its panelled rooms, discoloured with the dirt and smoke of a hundred years, I dare say; its decaying floors and staircase; the squeaking and scuffling of the old grey rats down in the cellars; and the dirt and rottenness of the place; are things, not of many years ago, in my mind, but of the present instant. They are all before me, just as they were in the evil hour when I went among them for the first time, with my trembling hand in Mr. Quinion's. (*DC* 150–1)

'There is a furnished little set of chambers to be let in the Adelphi, Trot, which ought to suit you to a marvel.'
    With this brief introduction, she produced from her pocket an advertisement, carefully cut out of a newspaper, setting forth that in Buckingham Street in the Adelphi there was to be let, furnished, with a view of the river, a singularly desirable and compact set of chambers, forming a genteel residence for a young gentleman, a member of one of the Inns of Court, or otherwise, with immediate possession. [. . .] They were on the top of the house . . . and consisted of a little half-blind entry where you could see hardly anything, a little stone-blind pantry where you could see nothing at all, a sitting-room, and a bedroom. The furniture was rather faded, but quite good enough for me; and, sure enough, the river was outside the windows. [. . .] I saw [my aunt] safely seated in the Dover Coach . . . and when the coach was gone, I turned my face to the Adelphi, pondering on the old days when I used to roam about its subterranean arches, and on the happy changes which had brought me to the surface. [. . .] It was a wonderfully fine thing to have that lofty castle to myself, and to feel, when I shut my outer door, like Robinson Crusoe. (*DC* 331–3)

I landed in London on a wintry autumn evening. It was dark and raining, and I saw more fog and mud in a minute than I had seen in a year. I walked from the Custom House to the Monument before I found a coach; and although the very house-fronts, looking on the swollen gutters, were like old friends to me, I could not but admit that they were very dingy friends.

> I have often remarked—I suppose everybody has—that one's going away from a familiar place, would seem to be the signal for change in it. As I looked out of the coach window, and observed that an old house on Fish-street Hill, which had stood untouched by painter, carpenter, or bricklayer, had been pulled down in my absence; and that a neighbouring street, of time-honoured insalubrity and inconvenience, was being drained and widened; I half expected St. Paul's Cathedral looking older. (*DC* 753–4)

If every arrival or return, and the experience this implies, is singular, then the vision narration gives to the *imaginary texture of the real* must in some manner be marked by difference and repetition, of necessity. In part, what makes the experience, and the perception, singular is the fact that I stand in this place, and no other. And when someone – David Copperfield in this instance – arrives four times at least, each is as haunted by the others as it displaces them. In *David Copperfield* there are four arrivals into London for David; or, to turn this around, London arrives for its principal, reading / writing subject, to his experience, perception, consciousness and memory. London insists in *Copperfield*. That the older Copperfield narrates each of these occasions makes explicit the work of memory in narration as re-presentation, and complicates, if I can use this phrase, the number of arrivals, as well as the number of Copperfields. Additionally, because there is the figure of the narrating narrator, David Copperfield, whose perception of the city is re-presented as both perception of event and memory of those earlier perceptions, it is not enough to think the various arrivals as being simply sequential in the history of the subject. To begin to grasp how the function of first-person narrator operates in re-presenting London; and, in order that we can, if not account, then apprehend the effect of the arrivals of London to its subject figured through the agency of the first-person narrative (the example of David being only Dickens's second attempt at a first-person narration, the first – if we discount the Boz of *Sketches* – being Master Humphrey, and the third, Esther Summerson), we need to account for the play between sense and idea; and, more than this, it is necessary to perceive how 'the very subtle and complex difference between the memory of sensation and the memory of idea emerges', as Sarah Winter argues, 'in the additional step of being conscious not only of the past self's presence at an event . . . but also of the past self's original conception of the complex ideas' (2011, 68) involved in apprehending the city for a first time, and subsequent times. The role of reading the city, and memory's revisions, indicate that 'reading produces a mediated memory that also permits self-reflexivity and a[n...] awareness of personal identity as a series of past states of consciousness leading up to the present' (Winter 2011, 68). From the very first words of the novel, such self-reflexivity is always already a constituent element of David's identity and selfhood; Being is self-reflexive by virtue of the fact that one knows one *is* and that one is in the world, even if that perception is marked by a limit of not knowing. London gives to David a particular sense of self, even as, in the various encounters with the city, David's sense of the world is modified by the challenge to his previously held ideas, and the subsequent reflection on the memory of the tensions between anticipation and retrospect. As Peter Ackroyd avers, *Copperfield* is 'a novel of memories and a novel about memory' (1990, 606).

Before considering the various arrivals or returns, and reflecting on the various convolutions of the city and the subject, I wish to address the way in which certain problems can arise if one treats the subject's encounters with the urban space in straightforward historical or contextual terms, seeking in the process to relate the fictive or imaginary vision to that which is real, historically speaking. Jeremy Tambling observes how David arrives in London 'on three separate occasions': the first when he is sent to Salem House school, at Blackheath, the second when he is sent by Mr Murdstone to Murdstone and Grinby's, not far from Blackfriars, and the third when he comes up by coach from Canterbury, as a young man, staying at the Golden Cross (2009, 122–4). There is also a fourth, cited as the last of the passages on which the present essay focuses. Each of David Copperfield's arrivals in London is markedly different from that of Nicholas Nickleby's entries into the capital. No Boz or Master Humphrey conducts the tour while maintaining the pretence that they are either wholly or partially outside the places and events they are directing us to consider. I raise this point because it is important to understand Copperfield *as* Copperfield, a singular creation, as distinct from other narrators as 'he' can be said to be from the author Charles Dickens. Given that there are biographical aspects of Dickens's life to be found in the narration of Copperfield, playing hunt the biographical allusion is diverting as a pastime but it does not serve in reading either the narrator or the fictive subject's[6] relation to place accurately, and certainly fails in apprehending the sense of London that each narrator or narrating effect produces. Prior to considering the passages in question, therefore, I wish to illustrate a couple of local difficulties in Tambling's reading of London in *David Copperfield*, generated in part by the constraints of a biographical-historical reading.

It can be no surprise, surely, as the critic claims, that either David Copperfield or *David Copperfield* speaks, in Jeremy Tambling's words, 'about the place [Warren's Blacking Factory] where Dickens worked: 30 Hungerford Stairs, near Hungerford Bridge, off the Strand, on the east side of Craven Street, in a position which has entirely disappeared, owing to the remodelling of Hungerford Market, and the building of the Embankment' (Tambling 2009, 123). As detailed and engaging a piece of biographical-cultural-historical material as this is, all of it only points to what is no longer there. Tambling's historical precision is marked because of the surprise he manifests in relation to those biographical and memorial traces on which Dickens drew in giving the sense of place to the young Copperfield's experience of living in London, with the Micawbers, and having to work at Murdstone and Grinby's. The sentence I have cited begins, 'Yet the text refuses to speak', while the next starts 'The evasion allows . . .'. Is this, really, an 'evasion'? What evidence, other than the desire of the reader, is there? Correlates between the imaginary and the real notwithstanding – as soon as there is a 'London' in a novel, there is a relation between the two, and to name streets, boroughs, buildings and so on is only to align the imaginary map with that in the 'real world' in order to call up the sensibility of a location – to assume surprise and suspect the author of evasion or obfuscation, merely because Forster employed a fragment of autobiography Charles Dickens had written 'preceding beginning *David Copperfield*', is, to say the least, suspect in the force it seeks to apply in making one narrative mode couple with another, or the one to fit precisely with the other. Certainly, David Copperfield's initials are those of Charles Dickens reversed, but to move from this, abbreviate them into a supposedly encrypted siglum that stands in for the author – *DC* – and then connect this, in passing, on the fly, in parentheses, to the inverted coffee shop sign (Tambling 2009, 122) is, if not a fancy too far, then at least open to a psychoanalytic reading of transference on the part of the critic, whose historicist will might be read as desiring to fix the Dickens text in place a little too hurriedly.

That sense of what is missing, the implicit accusation of omission, is signalled elsewhere in Tambling's reading, in the observation on David's first entrance to the city. Although Tambling has begun Chapter 6 of *Going Astray* by stating, as have others, that *David Copperfield* is set in the London of the 1820s (as are, most obviously, *Pickwick* and *Little Dorrit*; see Tambling 2009, 121),[7] when writing of Copperfield's arrival from Suffolk, 'having spent time at Great Yarmouth, in Norfolk, 120 miles away from London', Tambling initially suggests that Great Yarmouth might be connected to Chatham (Dickens having lived in the latter between 1815 and 1823, a period coinciding roughly with that of *Copperfield*'s setting), and that the former was the first to erect a memorial to Nelson. Immediately after this concatenated series of real–fictional relations, the critic notes that

[w]hen Dickens wrote *David Copperfield*, Nelson's column, planned in 1838, had been completed in Trafalgar Square (1843), one of the principal sites in London which was to impose a way of seeing London as monumental, and mapping everything in relation to it . . . But there is no mention of Trafalgar Square in this text. (Tambling 2009, 122)

Given the historical moment of the novel, this can hardly be surprising. Why mention a location that is not yet a significant site, which is, in fact, a non-place in the time of *David Copperfield*, its symbolic mapping and perceptual determination not having been planned? And, surely, Tambling's associations beg the question, would David have known about the memorial to Nelson, assuming, again, that the real and the fictive are simply interchangeable?

David's early memories of the city govern the narratives we receive. It might seem too obvious a remark to make, so obvious in fact that it verges on the glib, but the older narrator omits all but the most cursory, telegraphic signposting of the city's topography, often employing only place names and streets to identify place. Such naming occurs only as it is pertinent to the re-presentation of the perceptions of the younger self, and that David's past experience of the city, concerning hunger and the acquisition of food. We must distinguish briefly, of course, between topography and architecture as discourses of the urban subject, and the narrating narrator recollects vividly the details of Murdstone and Grinby's, as can be seen in the second of the four passages above. But regarding specific sites in London for the younger David, place is only usually accorded recognition if it is remembered in relation to food, as we have said. Consider, in this light, those two 'first' entries into London: the earlier when David is sent to attend Salem House, Blackheath, the latter when Mr Murdstone dispatches the boy to work in his business at Blackfriars. Before considering the role of food for the younger Davids in the recollection of the experience of London, we have to comprehend the mode of the Davids' arrivals, and, through these, the arrivals of London.

Initially, the youngest David conjured to memory attempts to perceive London as it might be apprehended through the heroic adventures of his favourite literary figures. London is thus a fiction rather than a reality. As such it is given to a poetics of expression, the city being a place, David imagines, of 'amazing . . . adventures' or 'wonders and wickedness'. Such alliterative possibilities continue in the adult's imagined childlike perception through the name of the inn, which is either the 'Blue Bull' or 'Blue Boar', or indeed, 'Blue Something', as the precise name can no longer be remembered, it being the idea of a phantastic creature more than the proper name that registers longest. However, while the narrating narrator maintains the passage through alliteration, the device modulates from fantasy to the more prosaic recollection / perception, or rather the perception of that earlier perception (reading / writing) of 'parcels', 'packages' and 'procession' to the distinctly mundane 'smell' and 'stables'. There is something deliberate in the alliterative construction, signifying the artistic intervention of Copperfield the novelist in the writing of his younger, past self's perceptions, given in this first encounter with the city as an alphabet of idea and sense, anticipation and experience, moving from A to S. London is 'made out' in David's mind as having more wonders and wickedness than any other city on earth. This 'making-out' is the memory of that initial perception, with the image of London apprehended at a distance, and the reflection on measuring the difference between the imaginary and real, the distant and the immediate, the general and the specific is determined as that procession of 'most tremendous considerations'. The older Copperfield thus constructs the memory of perception that engages in both a narrative and epistemological 'movement of recovery, of recuperation, of return to self, the progression [described as that mental procession which displaces the imaginary life of the city in fiction, with which the passage gets underway as London is approached in the morning] toward internal adequation' (Merleau-Ponty 1968, 33).

An important process is witnessed in play here, one which is as temporal as it is spatial in the reconstitution of the self and the subject's sense of the world through the interrelated accommodations of experience, anticipation, retrospect, memory, narrative, and the perception of perception distinct from the perception of event. Arriving in London is not at this moment a question of taking note of, and giving name to, landmarks, locations, streets and so forth. How can it be, when this younger David, in his relation to the city and his re-presentation of himself as being in the process of determining his selfhood in relation to place, does not yet know anything concrete of London? What is revealed, however, through the older narrative replay of the younger self is a displacement of assumptions concerning *how* the world is understood. 'Objective thought', Merleau-Ponty argues, is 'unaware of the subject of perception. This is because it presents itself with the world ready made, as the setting of every possible event, and treats perception as one of these events' (Merleau-Ponty 1962, 207). That 'objective thought' is what the older Copperfield shows to us apropos the younger David's perception of London at a distance, albeit an objective thought mediated through the phantasms of fiction. This in itself is a nicely rhetorical convolution of process, inasmuch as it implies, on the one hand, that the idea of the city perceived as totality is only ever a fiction, while, on the other hand, suggestively positing 'objective thought' as itself a childish fantasy

– which fantasy is subsequently concretised, however, through that first, and the subsequent references to the self compared with Robinson Crusoe (which references are themselves subject to modulation and perceptual transformation, given their different times). But 'objective thought' is displaced; it is made to give way, as the image of an indistinct, yet whole London gives way to sensory apprehension, the world no longer being 'ready made' but in the making, always unfolding before the subject, whose mind has to accommodate itself and its relation to the world in the authentic registration of process, motion and phenomenal detail. Perception is unveiled through the narrative of reading / writing and the endlessness of the dialectic of 'narrating-narrated' Being not as something in the world; rather, the 'perceiving subject is the place where these things occur'. David Copperfield would have us know – hence the necessity here of a first-person narrative machinery – that '[t]here can be no question of describing perception itself as one of the facts of the world, since we can never fill up, in the picture of the world, the gap which we ourselves are, and by which it comes into existence for someone' (Merleau-Ponty 1962, 207). That interpolation of the 'fictional' Robinson Crusoe – a phantom image projected not by the younger but by the older Copperfield, not merely *an* older Copperfield, we should remember, but the author Copperfield – thus serves to offer a comparison between the imaginary and the real, by which the distinction in terms of perception of the real and the fictional illusion of objectivity breaks down; importantly, though, the fictional 'whole' subject momentarily creates the illusion of closing the gap, 'which we ourselves are', whilst intimating that a 'whole' subject is as much a fiction belonging to the imaginary as the idea of a London envisioned in totality. The question remains: for whom is the fiction of Crusoe the image that fills the absence in the self? The older, narrating or younger, narrated Copperfield? The phantom of the lonely self – the self becomes the island on which the castaway is shipwrecked – is perceived, and perceives himself, to be more alone than the original Crusoe, precisely because Copperfield 'had nobody to look at him and see that he was solitary'. Yet, did the child in his first encounter with London feel this, does the older figure remember this reflexive perception of the self seen by others, or is the man-become-author fictionalising? Not one of the possibilities excludes the others. The reader is left within the experience of an undecidability that is also Copperfield's own – which undecidability, in this event, along with the abyss of perception and experience it opens and to which one is opened in reflection and re-presentation, becomes the expression of the gap in the world we are.

The first arrival of London and arrival in London, already complicated by fictional projection, thus makes plain a number of matters concerning the self and the city. Arriving at the coaching inn in Whitechapel, David is then taken through the city to Salem House and Blackheath. Like Oliver Twist before him, though, whose own initial journey across central parts of the city lack much specificity, the young Copperfield notices little by way of district, topography, architectural singularity or other detail. He does not notice, obviously, because his selfhood is still accommodating itself to seeking a grounding in the place, which gives himself to himself, as it were. His senses are too confounded, but the sense that predominates is that of hunger. What David does observe is a 'baker's window' and a 'grocer's shop', from purchases in which, and the change David receives, the older Copperfield reports of his younger self that the latter developed ('made me consider') the idea of London as a 'very cheap place'; but also, subsequently, a place of 'great noise and uproar' through which one must pass, and which confuses the boy's 'weary head beyond description' (*DC* 77). As with arrival at the inn, in Whitechapel, the sense of London is precisely that, a sensate apprehension, from without and within. Hunger, economic exchange, shop fronts, the visual, noise and motion: all come together in the movement from north to south, a distance of approximately 6 miles, as David is told. Though the boy notices little specifically, and memory shaped by narration either cannot or will not give more detailed information, choosing only to affirm the limits of knowledge and recollection, the details of monetary exchange and distance remain, as the principal 'co-ordinates' and phenomena of the city. There is, then, what might be called a broad or general specificity, as detail of experience appears through the miasma of initial reception.

This is in marked contrast to the second arrival in London, where the ten-year-old David's knowledge of the city and his awareness of his surroundings are more studied, more precise. There is the initial impression of Murdstone and Grinby's cited above, followed by the meeting with Micawber, lodgings, work and, once more, the search for food on a daily basis. The experience of the workplace – the second passage, above –not only is for David a shocking encounter but its mode of appearance is in stark contrast to other, more nebulous perceptions. As Dickensian descriptions of architecture and topography go, this particular passage is notable for the relative shortness of its sentences and clauses. Typically, detail accumulates, semi-colon coming to substitute for the final completion of a sentence, as clause after clause accretes for the reader's eye, inviting the imaginary reconstruction of place through the serial succession of detail. But the detail is traced in what might be called, in comparison with the Dickensian observation of architectural form or topographical recollection, a certain attenuated adumbration of the elements. Though the locale is given – Blackfriars – definition is sparse, controlled. This is a liminal location, a limit-site, as much of the river as of the land, but also at various 'edges': the last house in the street, at the bottom of that street, the final construction on land and at the bottom of the hill, which trajectory the street follows and maps. There is no motion in this passage, aside from the memory of the rats' endless occupation, and the implicit rhythm of the tide. Nor is there a great deal in this image of sound, save for the aural omnipresence of the rats, whose noise accompanies their movement. Of detail, there is recalled an apprehension of architectural craziness and, with more precision, panels, while the place is recalled through the sense of discolouration, decay, dirt and rottenness, the material decomposition anticipating the moral corruption suggested in the idea of an 'evil hour'.

The memory is vivid, not to say traumatic. The trauma is attested to inasmuch as this is an image, with the subject now in its disruptive revenance. This is the very nature, the definition of the traumatic phantasm, it being that which returns as, and in, the imaginary *as if* for a first time. Indeed, the traumatic is just this phantasmal re-presentation of experience and perception through memory's recurrence. Thus trauma is tropic, rhetorical, phenomenal rather than merely physical or empirically experiential. This is borne out in that temporal recurrence where the past does not simply return in a present, but in effect *is* the present; it consumes the present for the subject. This is seen, whether one considers this immediate passage or that scrap of autobiography concerning Warren's Blacking Factory, to which Tambling alludes, and from which Dickens edits so as to produce the Copperfield version (2009, 124).[8] It is worth mentioning this, only so as to have done with the reductive, not to say facile comparison made by a number of critics, between Murdstone and Grinby's and Copperfield's experience on the one hand, and Warren's and Dickens's experience, on the other, once and for all. Unlike Tambling (whose commentary, to be fair, is neither reductive nor facile, but who, in his mapping 'real' London on to the fictional counterpart, does seek, unreasonably in my opinion, to make one the image of the other too hurriedly, in a manner that conflates the phenomenal with the empirical), I have no desire to conflate – if not confuse, or at least *fuse* – the two, and I mention the edit of the autobiographical fragment in order to consider briefly the rhetorical, aesthetic and phenomenal aspects of the transition between the author, the narrator and, in this case, the principal subject, David Copperfield.

Copperfield and Dickens, though, it has to be stressed, are not the same. To quote Andrew Sanders, while certain of the fragments of the autobiographical manuscript printed in *The Life of Charles Dickens* [by John Forster] clearly bear a . . . verbatim relationship to David's account of himself . . . especially . . . the sixth paragraph of Dickens's description of his time at Jonathan Warren's Blacking warehouse . . . Readers should not confuse fact and fiction, or equate living with telling.[9]

They should not; but they do, and this despite the 'fact' that while Warren's was situated at 'Hungerford Stairs, Charing Cross', Murdstone and Grinby's is at Blackfriars, approximately 1 mile east of Warren's location. Dickens excises from the autobiographical fragment a number of small but telling details, in order to give to the act of telling, the voice of another. If David is a sharp observer, as is remarked, and as he observes reflectively of himself, at various junctures in the narrative, his memory of the Blackfriars workplace is just such an example of acute experience and observation (to use two terms from the novel's full title), and subsequent mental registration of the initial perception. Dickens's account of Warren's is adverbially and adjectivally 'richer' (though not by a great deal), and thus arguably more 'typical' of representations of architecture and place that are found in the author's other novels. But what is significantly absent from the Copperfield vision when compared with Dickens's account is Copperfield himself. The work of this passage is to re-present the place to the subject *now*, as the phantasm of place that all but consumes, and certainly encompasses, the ten-year-old. While Dickens can remark that '[t]here was a recess . . . in which I was to sit and work.'[10] going on to describe the work in some detail, as part of, and belonging to, the description of the workplace, David does not enter into a recollection of the work his younger self was expected to perform in this initial paragraph. Indeed, as I have suggested, his own earlier self is barely 'there'. There is the hint of imaginative interpretation ('I dare say') regarding the accumulated dirt, which arrives only after several sentences of apparently objective description in which no overt expression of self is to be read. This is followed by the insistence, twice, that the 'things' are before the mind's eye with a painful proximity, in the 'present instant'. Only in the last sentence of the paragraph does the 'I' of the younger David come to be remembered, going among the things, in imaginary imitation, we might argue, of the experience, much as the reader goes amongst the dirt, the rottenness, the decay, and the sound of the rats. 'David' is barely a body here, only that perception translated in motion just described, and reduced to a 'trembling hand' held by another's.

Of significance, then, is not just the re-presentation but also the persistence of the initial perception, for everything that is of the imaginary texture of the real, its phantom power, does not belong as objective fact, nor in the past as mere memory. To reiterate and insist on the modality of the textual work: everything, each detail, is 'not of many years ago, in my mind, but of the present instant'. Every aspect is 'all before me, just as they were'. The initial experience defines the self, or some significant aspect of one's Being, to the extent that the temporal space between the two selves suffers erasure, if not collapse. Memory and writing collude, for representation and re-presentation become mutual palimpsests of one another in, and framed by, the subject's sensory apprehension – and it is the self's apprehension which is paramount here, not the objects, as that last-cited observation serves to remind us – so that, as elsewhere in the writing of the city and the subject's relation to London, the extract moves from being mere observation (if it is ever just this), in a performative staging 'before' the reader who comes to stand in for the younger and older Davids.

What we should observe here, before passing to the ten-year-old Copperfield's association of London and hunger in the second example, concerns the process that the Dickens text generates across *David Copperfield* in a manner that is nowhere else presented in any Dickens text – certainly not with the immediacy or sustained intensity that we find in this novel. The process is one of the self coming, through reflection, to know that which Merleau-Ponty describes as the 'unreflected' prior to any reflection (1964a, 152–3), a subjectivity not yet conscious of itself. The novel charts retrospectively, through the filter of the phenomenological narrative, the journey from '*pre-reflexive cogito*' (Merleau-Ponty 1964a, 152) to a self unveiling to itself a return of selfhood the temporality and spacing of which do not guarantee an absolute or totalised knowledge, but which in its reflectiveness apprehends its being in the world and the intimate extent to which selfhood is part of the world, even as the world is given to it through the subject's appearance in that world. In each moment of retrospect the world appears to the subject and determines, simultaneously, the subject's being and, with that, the specificity of site and self in relation. Retrospective re-presentation by the narrating, older David works through the narrating self withholding and shaping knowledge and information particular to the singularity of relation between site and self, and self as a place within place, and employing those traces that compose memory as they make clear the relation, whether experience of a given locus is traumatic or not. Hence, the significance of the search for food, as this always relates to place names. David's memory and narrative reconstruction function as a mapping of the co-ordinates that connect sensory need and locale, as given in place.

In contrast to David's early paucity of urban knowledge – or perhaps a knowledge that admits its own limits through exposing itself as being on the 'outside' of a world of phenomena and signs too vast, initially, to grasp – there is the modern Babylon of Wilkins Micawber and its 'arcana' (*DC* 153). Micawber's ripe discourse negotiates between the hieratic and quotidian, the resistance to immediate access and the specificity of place, rendered through reference. It is therefore unwise to write off Wilkins Micawber as merely someone who succumbs to rhetorical flourishes, the baroque turn of phrase and observational hyperbole. His apprehension of London, as presented to David in his inaugural statements, demonstrates that Micawber is someone who knows not only how to move through the city but also, importantly, how to read it, and to respond to the play, always in place between the local and the unknowable, the fixed point and the limit of knowledge. In short, Wilkins Micawber sees London as it is. His projections enable us, to paraphrase Henri Lefebvre, to 'identify those relations but not to grasp them' (Lefebvre 2003, 47), at least not directly, for perception only comes through individual experience. Here, then, is a subject of the city, someone who grasps, if not the city in its totality, then the means by which any topoanalysis, reliant on apperception and indirection, might be most efficaciously articulated.

For, unlike other Dickens characters, Micawber apprehends this at least: that 'it is not enough to define the urban by the single fact that it is a place of passage and exchange' (Lefebvre 2003, 47), by the urban subject. Something other revealed in the imaginary texture of the real that the subject's perception and memory bring to the encounter gives access to 'urban reality' (Lefebvre 2003, 47). Thus, while Lefebvre, wishing to move beyond such apprehension as is opened to the reader in the Dickens text, and which subsequently has become explicated in phenomenological discourse, argues that, in order to grasp that reality, 'we should abandon phenomenology for analysis' (Lefebvre 2003, 47), this is to engage in a fundamental misperception grounded in a desire to know absolutely the totality of phenomena rendered as the totality of objects, and thus miss what is authentic in the experience, remaining outside the urban. Analysis must return to the phenomenological experience of the urban in order that one comprehend in a pre-theoretical manner the relation between being and experience, perception and event. Micawber may not know what he does; he should not be received by readers, though, as merely a figure of fun. For, in his address to the ten-year-old Copperfield, his language offers an explanation of the way the London subject inhabits a space where relation between self and space are intimately and inextricably interwoven. Hence, his address, which fixes self to place, as the site of a landing place in the otherwise endless motions of London's fluid rhythms.

Naming an address gives one little if any immediate access to place, save perhaps through imaginative association of pronouns. Such naming does not, however, provide any more than a co-ordinate awaiting decryption. It belongs initially, then, to the 'arcana', despite its apparent transparency, and this initial inaccessibility for David is maintained, for he is unable to give any sense of the journey there. 'Windsor Terrace, City Road' (*DC* 153) is the home of Wilkins Micawber and his family, and remains initially secreted, unavailable to any approach. Though Micawber gives no details about the house, other than the intimation that, to the London uninitiated such as David it might be difficult to find, David does recollect that he noticed, once arrived, that the house was 'shabby, like himself [Micawber], but also, like himself, made all the show it could' (*DC* 153). House and self are interchangeable to a degree, therefore; that they are reciprocal figures makes their status as phenomena explicit to the subject learning to read the city. For the older David, there is what Husserl describes as '*explication in memory*' (Husserl 1973, 129). That which was first grasped in perception is made clear once the intuition is encountered as 'simple apprehension'. The older David's memory gives nothing away, other than the explication in memory of the simple apprehension, and thus fills in for that which Micawber can only intuitively register: re-presentation must return to the phenomenological ground, reflexively coming to terms with the experience as such in order that the subject can give place to both himself and that which takes place in the specific locus, with the singularity of the authentic apprehension in its historicity, as this encounter has left its trace.

All of which brings me to the question of David, London and food. Lodging with the Micawbers, David's memory of working life is interspersed with only a sketchy sense of place, announced through the punctuation afforded by place names – St Martin's Church, the Strand, Drury Lane, Fleet Street, Covent Garden Market, the Adelphi, all of which are associated principally with food: stale pastry, rolls, pudding, saveloy, a penny-loaf, a 'fourpenny plate of red beef', bread and cheese 'and a glass of beer', 'ready-made coffee and a slice of bread-and-butter', a venison shop, 'pine-apples' (155–6). The linear succession of place names is purely an after-effect, rather than a historical route, of course, but it does offer an interesting virtual 'tour' between church and areas in which London's theatres are to be found, through significant thoroughfares and across Covent Garden Market, a principal site belonging to the first chapter – 'The Streets-Morning' – of the 'Scenes' from *Sketches by Boz* (*SB* 49–54). There is something of a parallel to be drawn between the relation of names and that of food. As David's locations move from the church to theatre, so the food he recalls goes from daily stale pastry and bread to the more costly venison and exotic pineapples. Moreover, the range of food suggests an experience of involvement and of being returned to an outside, a place merely of observation. David's observation of pineapples recalls his first London memory of hunger and looking in shop windows; whereas before he had surmised London an inexpensive place to live, he now understands differently.

Returning to those place names, were we to map these, we would find David's London world a somewhat tightly circumscribed area; with the exception of the Adelphi development (just south of the Strand and abutting the river; Fig. 1), bounded by what are now Shaftesbury Avenue and High Holborn to the north, Tottenham Court Road to the west, the Strand to the south and Farringdon Street to the east, and with the City Road just under 1.5 miles north-east from Fleet Street, David's movements and his memory of the search for food, between work and lodging, cover relatively little ground. In crossing and re-crossing the same streets in search of food in those moments not defined by the workplace or the Micawbers' world of debt, enforced secrecy and misplaced optimism, David comes to be defined through the search after food and the awareness of that which is beyond his immediate experience. He glimpses a world within but other than the world he encounters at hand. Our sense of London as we read is given a sense of immediacy through the constant return of the search for food, but equally we remain at a distance, by virtue of the fact that the labyrinth of lanes and alleys, passages and streets connecting the place names are not figured in any detail, if at all. The names merely trace a map without giving access to any sense of place, except that the sensate apprehension is always tied to food.

London is thus both source of meagre nourishment and threat to life. It is a prison and a labyrinth, a Babylon, having its very own 'Tower of Babel' (*DC* 779). The city is only transformed for David on his third arrival / return, the occasion being taking up with Mr Spenlow and moving into 'a furnished little set of apartments', as seen in a newspaper advertisement by Betsy Trotwood, located in 'Buckingham Street in the Adelphi'. Reading and writing precede location, the newspaper cutting offering to both David and the reader simultaneously an image of the furnished 'compact set of chambers'. What we see *of* the Adelphi here, or previously in the novel in the ten-year-old's reference, is very little, and with good reason. In the present scene, we move from the advertisement to the interior, of which little more is revealed. The faded furniture and the 'stone-blind pantry' aside, there is, 'sure enough, 'the river . . . outside the windows'. In all, this is, as David recalls, a 'wonderfully fine thing to have that lofty castle to myself, and to feel, when I shut my outer door, like Robinson Crusoe' (*DC* 332–3). However, of the Adelphi there is little by way of concrete or objective detail. Once more, what David sees, that which is David's perception and experience, these are everything. He places himself in his world through the present imaginative comparison with Robinson Crusoe and with the memory of his previous experience when working at Murdstone and Grinby's. His younger self therefore comes back to him as he ponders 'on the old days when I used to roam about its subterranean arches, and on the happy changes which had brought me to the surface' (*DC* 332). Self and place, being and memory are significant; the world as concatenation of objects is given little account, the emphasis being on the manner in which the reception of the world as phenomena determines selfhood, once again. It is instructive to compare this moment with Copperfield's re-presentation of his younger self's experience of the Adelphi arches: 'I was fond of wandering about the Adelphi because it was a mysterious place, with those dark arches [which, according to historical accounts, were the dwelling places of criminals and the homeless]. I see myself emerging one evening from some of those arches, on a little public house close to the river' (*DC* 157). Once more, as elsewhere, we encounter the doubling of the self, imaginary vision closing the space between selves in a perception of experience, a memory of the initial perception given narrative manifestation. The arches, in their imagined mystery, obscure any sense of danger present in the reality of the location, and extend architecturally the exoticism of the pineapples. Beyond the plural noun, there is no other visual or material detail, any more than the Adelphi's material or objective presence is described later. The world is there for both Davids almost exclusively as received phenomena. Space and place are produced only to the extent that they give access to David's different, temporally bound moments of being, and we are forced to conclude that the

> relationship between the imaginary and the real is therefore quite unrelated to that of an alleged tracing of the real. In a sense, the imaginary is even closer to the real than a duplicate . . . In another sense, the pictorial image [such as it is in either perception of the Adelphi] is more distant from the real . . . since it is only an expression of it . . . and is not intended to set us back before pragmatic reality. (de Waehlens 1993, 181)

The vision David has of this part of London is one governed by personal change over time, and also of a certain vertical ascent: from an underground labyrinth in which little is to be seen, to an elevated position, occupying a 'castle', from which the river is visible. Growth of reflective consciousness, or otherwise a coming to consciousness of oneself, is thus charted by a temporal passage that has a particular axis related to a movement from invisibility given in the form of unawareness to a self-consciousness given in the sense of vision. It is important that we note while the younger David had been hungry and found his work a source of misery, he had been 'fond' of wandering through the arches underneath the Adelphi Terrace; and, while the singularity of the experiences remains marked, what threads together the Davids is that iterable reference to the fiction and image of Crusoe. This had initially appeared on David's first arrival in London, at the coach inn before the journey to Salem House.

There is, then – significantly in the formation of David's reflective selfhood – both the sense of seeing himself as an other to himself, whether temporally or through comparative analogues between traces; or through the iterability of apprehensions concerning others seeing him, where perception shifts to become reflection of self and other. The older David asks himself, without being able to answer, what others made of the 'strange, little apparition'. The city is thus mapped through various manifestations of memory, of taste, of watching others and of self-reflection: 'I can see him now, staring at me'; 'I see myself emerging one evening'; 'I wonder what they thought of me!' (*DC* 156). These last comments offer a complex image. The belated, narrating narrator imagines his other younger self, at given points in place and time, being observed, though at the time not obviously conscious of being observed, or, if conscious, then not yet capable of articulating the perception in a manner given to the narrating, later self. Reflection and re-presentation are the conditional co-ordinates of mnemotechnic topoanalysis, a mapping of place in which self, place and others return to figure the poetics of urban identity. Reflection affords a momentary aestheticisation of the phenomenological mode, or perhaps a making modern of Romantic aestheticisation of the individual through a revelation of the phenomenological basis of reflection on one's being in relation to specific sites at given times.

With this, what we are given to read through the returns and arrivals in London, as we read, is a sense of an elucidation, the explication, of self, and with that, a perception that one's being is never totalisable, never finished, any more than the concatenated phenomena of the modern city are available to knowledge in a totalised form. Self is revealed in its reflection to itself as a distinctly modern phenomenon. Unlike a Tom Jones, perhaps, or any other fully formed narrative subject belonging to more traditional novelistic forms; or belonging, say, to the conventions of the *Bildungsroman*, David is an unformed project, and a projection also of what I have called elsewhere the Dickens-machine.

If it takes Dickens seven novels and fifteen years of writing to find the appropriate 'voice' for a first-person narrator (Boz remains implicit in 'his' narrations, Master Humphrey more mechanically a device for 'viewing' the world of London), this must have to do, surely, with the time needed to shift to an elucidation, an exposition or, more accurately, explication in relation to the world, where reflection makes possible 'the actual clarification which reveals what was meant in advance with a distinctness which delimits it' (de Waehlens 1993, 186). Self and world are never separable; both are unfinished projects of modernity and narrative writing has to respond to and map this, with a degree of fidelity, if the historicity of the moment is to be registered fully. The Dickens-machine thus produces a distinctly different mode of being and subjectivity, the truth of which is a product of the need to respond appropriately – that is to say, through a mode of narrative marked by an authentic historicity. 'David' is therefore the subject of, as well as subject to, the modernity of the city. His being is constituted through a reading / writing of London, with which being's appearances to itself are intimately bound, and re-bound.

I will come back to these issues regarding the form of the novel in relation to selfhood, place, perception and memory in the conclusion of this essay, but we must turn to David's fourth entrance into the capital, his last significant arrival and return to London; or, to insist on this inversion, we must recognise how London arrives for its subject, how it returns. This is, of course, still an act of re-presentation, but that of an adult David, whose memory and experience unfold comparatively: to begin with the obvious, in this passage, there are co-ordinates, pronouns giving location, four to be exact. While those street names and places which had been associated with food had been given in no especial order, here a route is mapped: Custom House – the Monument – Fish-Street Hill – St Paul's Cathedral (this last more in expectation of its transformed appearance). What the eye rests on initially, though, is an immensity of fog and mud, as if to signify a changed world, one already signalled as moving into a 'wintry autumn'. There is rain and it is 'dark', so that whatever perspective there might be, whatever light is available, whatever horizon is available to the eye, all must be limited in the extreme. With David, in David's mind's eye, what the reader 'sees' is the limit to perception. Perception is attenuated, restrained. This is what memory re-represents, a minimally visible and knowable world. Evening is also announced, so that the various atmospheric, material and meteorological together inform the seasonal and diurnal temporal phenomena, as these appear to the subject's apprehension. Whereas the younger Copperfield was presented by his older self as barely noticing the city, here the narrating Copperfield's older, narrated self, notices, experiences and recollects in detail that which cannot be seen through, or got around, so to speak, epistemologically, as well as experientially.

David thus sees and immediately reflects on the limits of visibility – at least he re-presents his other self as being suspended momentarily in this process. What the eye also observes is change. First-person narration, we should remind ourselves, strengthens once again the illusion, on the one hand, that there is someone there, while on the other, the 'I' of the narrator and the 'I' of the reader are, if not the same, then, substitutable in the act of perception, the one elided or supplemented by the other in the work of reflection. Equally, the reader is involved in the perception of perception; I know I am reading someone's 'reading', I see what another chooses I should see, and chooses how I should see what the other's other self had seen, and which is selectively constructed through the linguistic formulation of memory in narrative form.

Most significantly, then, there is the inescapable presentation of the sense that there is always a *someone* and always, equally, a *there*. The self is in the place, and the place is for that someone. Paradoxically, perhaps, this perception on the part of the reader is strengthened by the self-consciousness of a narrator who chooses to confront the limits of representation aesthetically and mimetically, through the stress on limit and phenomena, rather than on an urban reality comprised solely of objects. This is the world of early nineteenth-century London, but it is also, always a world of phenomena, with a sense of the world mediated in a self who is *in* the appearance of the world, simultaneously close and also at a remove. The memory of perception illuminates that of the self's others, which remain as the trace of relations in between a body 'fully in the world' (see immediately below). Narrative mode helps us grasp that mind, body and world are not separable, that there is not a consciousness on one side of a barrier, on the other side of which there is a corporeality. Moreover, 'the relation between the things and my body is decidedly singular':

> it is what makes me sometimes remain in appearances, and it is also what sometimes brings me to the things themselves; it is what produces the buzzing of appearances, it is also . . . what casts me fully into the world. Everything comes to pass as though my power to reach the world and my power to entrench myself in phantasms only came one with the other . . . The world is what I perceive, but as soon as we examine and express its absolute proximity, it also becomes, inexplicably, irremediable distance. (Merleau-Ponty 1968, 8)

This *is* David Copperfield, entrenching himself in phantasms, as Merleau-Ponty describes the self's relation to appearances, one's being in the world, but also at a distance. Such doubleness, of relation spatially and temporally, of self to place, and older to younger self; of the subject apprehending himself as both other *and* himself, through the transformation of the city; this is given directly in the intimation of architectural dilapidation, all the more noted in its disrepair and decay for being anthropomorphised in memory as 'old' but 'dingy friends', in the disappearance of the old house on Fish-Street Hill, 'pulled down in my absence, in the draining and widening of a 'neighbouring street', and in the expectation of Wren's cathedral having aged. There is a curiousness here, a sense of melancholy and irony, in the perception of aging for the city as the sign of alteration, transfiguration or reconstruction, which 'again' is a displacement of the subject's sense of time passing, inflected through his own remembrances of times past and lost as such, and only available in their phantasmic revenance. What is 'time-honoured' is the sense of place being unhealthy, difficult of ingress and egress, as though architectural, urban 'improvement' were a subject of ambiguity, if not ambivalence. And while the appearances of the past crowd the vision of the present, in lieu of clarity of perspective (emotionally as well as atmospherically) with a noticeable intimacy tantamount to a sense of *Sehnsucht*, the world David perceives is announced in its distance, both by change and disappearance, but also through the 'vehicle' of the coach ride, which serves to keep the subject off the street, and seeing a world both his and not his, through the frame of the coach window.

The area of London through which David travels in this arrival covers little more than a mile, if that, but in that mile the history of the city is opened, not least in the references to the Monument and St Paul's, both of which recall the Fire of 1666, inevitably. Less obvious to the modern reader, but not necessarily to a London subject of David's age and acuity of observation, is the implied history of alterations to the Custom House, on Lower Thames Street. Risking speculation, the ten-year-old Copperfield may have seen David Laing's New Custom House, built between 1813 and 1817, the old Custom House having been destroyed by fire in February 1814. In 1825, the year following construction of the new London Bridge – not the old one, on which the young David used to sit in its recesses – part of the floor of the Long Room in Laing's building collapsed, due to subsidence. Reconstruction work was begun, overseen by Sir Robert Smirke, who also transformed the façade. This would have been what greeted the older David on his fourth arrival in London, even though detail is not given. The point to be made is that London is mutable, its identity and meaning unstable, and this is part of the condition of both its existence and any authentic historicised perception or memory of it. To comprehend this is to perceive – perception as reception – consciousness of one's Being, one's becoming. Both David Copperfield and *David Copperfield* announce this in numerous ways, not only in those details we have already considered,[11] apropos arrival and return, and by extension singularity and iterability, but also in the relation the self is perceived, and perceives himself as having, to his other selves and his other, the modern Babylon, a trope that is worked simultaneously as an architectural and textual figure, an imaginative figure of construction both architecturally and in a multiplicity of voices or writings. The urban subject only comes to apprehend itself in seeing itself as other and therefore mutable also. If London is a site, or more precisely a composite and constellation of sites, traced and re-presented through transformation and loss, through phantasmic proximity and, equally, 'irremediable distance', then so also is the modern subject, subject to, and projection of, the modernity of difference rather than sameness.

In conclusion, David's arrivals in and returns to London – and the city's many, not always happy returns in *David Copperfield* – determine his being in relation to place, to which he is at once intimately bound, but from which, perhaps, he longs to maintain a distance. Arrival is, from the first, marked by anxiety, which subsequently modulates through unhappiness, elevation and, finally, melancholy. If there is an ambivalence to be read in David's memories of the city and the subjective reconstructions and re-presentations, then it is not unreasonable to speculate that there is in London for David a 'melancholy' bound up with the sense 'that it must always be in change' as Jeremy Tambling argues (2009, 138). Whether this is to be read, in Tambling's terms, as expressive of a desire on David's – or Dickens's – part to stay 'with the other, repressed areas of London' is, for me at least, questionable (2009, 138); there is here possibly the sign of a Foucauldian recuperation too far. With the exception of the first and final arrival, all other experience of London, and memory of that experience in its re-presented form, concerns the growth, if not of a poet's mind, then that of a novelist (to borrow a Wordsworthian formula). But as the persistence of hunger shows in the childhood and adolescent experiences of London, the mind, or consciousness, is never divorced from the corporeal singularity that repeatedly experiences the sensory experience of the world acutely. Nor are misery and joy purely intellectual perceptions but are also connected to the body for David. It is only in the self become novelist – one fiction or phantasm of the self as other – that some other perspective is afforded to perception, as memory and narrative come to co-operate in the re-presentation of the urban reality, in the telling and showing, occasionally the performing, of being and event in close relation.

Additionally, though, something else is taking place here in the formation of the narrative history, which has to do, it can be argued, with the historicity of the novel as genre, and concomitantly with a radicalisation, if not, finally, a subversion, and thus a modernisation of the novel, narrative history and the *Bildungsroman* apropos urban modernity and its intimate relation to the self. There is a growth in the apprehension of modernity modulated through Being's ability to reflect and re-present itself through the apprehension of its different, singular selves temporally given and spatially placed. And this in turn may help explain, or at least open an hypothesis on to, both the form of *David Copperfield* and its proto-modernity as a novel, as well as its distanced setting, its being placed a generation before the novel's publication.

To put this differently, and so expound the point through returning to the idea of the two Davids, the narrating narrator and the narrated narrator: as there are at least two Copperfields, so there are two *David Copperfields*. There is one novel embedded in another, framed by the other. This framed narrative is the more conventional, not to say Romantic tale of growth and education, both psychological and moral, which does not see that it sees (any more than its protagonist), but which engages in the use of Romanticism's vehicle of the isolated individual whose experiences are aestheticised through the formalisation of experience in a narrative.

The other novel, the modern narrative which frames the conventional tale and which is a narrative of modernity, is reflexive, open-ended from its very first sentence. It rejects convention and closure, reminding the reader that what is 'just' aesthetic for the Romantic, and therefore the formal working through of a constellation of devices, tropes and rhetorical exteriorisations of the self, is undeniably phenomenological to the modern subject, to the subject produced by modernity – and a modernity, moreover, inescapably defined by the modern Babylon. The younger, narrated David has to come of age, fully in possession of a certainty equivalent to blindness, a lack of insight, only afforded later, and this is figured as much in the younger David's not seeing the city as it is in his choice of first wife, Dora Spenlow. Reader, he married her. Such a narrative belongs to the past, however; its perception is made inauthentic by that later implicit perception of its earlier counterpart. Modernity makes it impossible to believe in such a narrative and the conventions of closure by which it is structured. So, Dora must die, in a traumatic reiteration of David's own mother's death, which, we might say, releases David or at least splits David in two.

David is released both from the fictional world in which he has lived from the time he learned to read, and from the London that is, on the one hand, that of imaginary and fictive characters, and on the other, an immersive labyrinth that constantly brings home want, hunger, debt and unhappiness. Though *David Copperfield* arrives finally at another, second marriage, and thus accommodates a moment of closure which recuperates it within the conventions it exposes, it does so only in admitting both the reformation of form and the impossibility of defining the self in isolation. Being is always a 'being-there'. Always traced by the signs of its historicity, Being can only be read, after *Copperfield*, as defined in singular but iterable manner, by a world of phenomena, and by places which give place to perception of experience, thereby inscribing on to memory those traces which return through re-presentation. *David Copperfield* thus concludes, if this is the right word, in a final chapter, called a 'retrospect', which, anachronistically – at least with regard to that term – maintains a present tense that can only end when reading comes to an end. In that illusion of a perpetual present tense, that which David writes is, here, a matter of perception, and thus a translation of what he sees. Having begun the final chapter by 'look[ing] back, once more' (*DC* 802), the phantasm that is David Copperfield records that he sees: 'I see myself . . .'. He asks, though, 'What faces are the most distinct to me in the fleeting crowd?' which are 'all turning to me as I ask my thoughts the question?' (*DC* 802). The image of the phantom crowd whose faces turn, causing self-reflection, illuminates both the persistence of the urban in that figure of the crowd, and in the self being with others, in the experience of the world and reflective memory of that. As if to emphasise vision as the dominant trope of the chapter but also as the medium bringing the past into the present as a phantom presence, and with that, the relation of self to others in the world, both Betsy and Peggotty return the gaze through spectacles (*DC* 803). David imagines he sees himself being seen, and so is both within and at a distance from the world perceived. To repeat the words of Merleau-Ponty, '[e]verything comes to pass as though my power to reach the world and my power to entrench myself in phantasms only came one with the other.' Even the eye of Micawber appears to sight, reaching in writing across the world to see Copperfield, whose vision, and reading of the letter, cause it to be transcribed, given a writing that in turn opens it to the reader's view (*DC* 802). And all this is confessed, as 'faces fade away' (*DC* 805), realities 'melt' and 'shadows' are dismissed late at night when the world is no longer available to simple vision (*DC* 806), in 'our house in London' (*DC* 795). Thus Dickens loses David, even as David had lost himself 'in the swarm of life' (*DC* 776) on those occasional visits to London before marrying Agnes and moving back to the city for a final return.

Banking and Breakfast • Gray's Inn Square, Temple Bar, Strand Lane

Temple Bar

Banking

A Tale of Two Cities

Tellson's Bank by Temple Bar was an old-fashioned place, even in the year one thousand seven hundred and eighty. It was very small, very dark, very ugly, very incommodious. It was an old-fashioned place moreover, in the moral attribute that the partners in the House were proud of its smallness, proud of its darkness, proud of its ugliness, proud of its incommodiousness. They were even boastful of its eminence in those particulars, and were fired by an express conviction that, if it were less objectionable, it would be less respectable. This was no passive belief, but an active weapon which they flashed at more convenient places of business. Tellson's (they said) wanted no elbow-room, Tellson's wanted no light, Tellson's wanted no embellishment. Noakes and Co.'s might, or Snooks Brothers' might; but Tellson's, thank Heaven!—

[. . .] Tellson's was the triumphant perfection of inconvenience. After bursting open a door of idiotic obstinacy with a weak rattle in its throat, you fell into Tellson's down two steps, and came to your senses in a miserable little shop, with two little counters, where the oldest of men made your cheque shake as if the wind rustled it, while they examined the signature by the dingiest of windows, which were always under a shower-bath of mud from Fleet-street, and which were made the dingier by their own iron bars proper, and the heavy shadow of Temple Bar. If your business necessitated your seeing 'the House', you were put into a species of Condemned Hold at the back, where you meditated on a misspent life, until the House came with its hands in its pockets, and you could hardly blink at it in the dismal twilight.

Your money came out of, or went into, wormy old wooden drawers, particles of which flew up your nose and down your throat when they were opened and shut. Your bank-notes had a musty odour, as if they were fast decomposing into rags again. Your plate was stowed away among the neighbouring cesspools, and evil communications corrupted its good polish in a day or two. Your deeds got into extemporised strong-rooms made of kitchens and sculleries, and fretted all of the fat out of their parchments into the banking-house air. Your lighter boxes of family papers went up-stairs into a Barmecide room, that always had a great dining-table in it and never had a dinner, and where, even in the year one thousand seven hundred and eighty, the first letters written to you by your old love, or by your little children, were but newly released from the horror of being ogled at through the windows, by the heads exposed on Temple Bar with an insensate brutality and ferocity worthy of Abyssinia or Ashantee.

But, indeed, at that time, putting to Death was a recipe much in vogue with all trades and professions, and not least of all with Tellson's. Death is Nature's remedy for all things, and why not Legislation's. Accordingly, the forger was put to Death; the utterer of a bad note was put to Death; the unlawful opener of a letter was put to Death; the purloiner of forty shillings and sixpence was put to Death; the coiner of a bad shilling was put to Death; the sounders of three-fourths of the notes in the whole gamut of Crime, were put to Death. Not that it did the least good in the way of prevention . . . Thus, Tellson's, in its day, like greater places of business, its contemporaries, had taken so many lives, that, if the heads laid low before it had been ranged on Temple Bar instead of being privately disposed of, they would probably have excluded what little light the ground floor had, in a rather significant manner.

Cramped in all kinds of dim cupboards and hutches at Tellson's, the oldest of men carried on the business gravely. When they took a young man into Tellson's London house, they hid him somewhere till he was old. They kept him in a dark place, like a cheese, until he had the full Tellson flavour and blue-mould upon him. Only then was he permitted to be seen, spectacularly poring over large books, and casting his breeches and gaiters into the general weight of the establishment. (*TTC* 55–7)

Every idea, writes Walter Benjamin, 'contains the image of the world'. The 'purpose of the representation of the idea', therefore, is 'nothing less than an abbreviated outline of this image of the world' (Benjamin 1998, 48). Benjamin's is a not unreasonable proposition, allowing as it does for an attenuated definition of aesthetic and, therefore, phenomenal perception. It insists on the singular in the notion of the idea, and from that suggests the link between abstraction and representation, which figure, mimetic or otherwise, is always pragmatic, always in service to thought in order that the idea be 'embodied', given manifestation as the phantasmic translation in material guise through a perceivable form. Yet, accepting this, we must also account for the fact that there is no such thing as a simple or, by implication, complete image. In the words of Marcel Proust, the image is always, already, multiple: 'An image presented to us by life', remarks Marcel in *Time Regained*, 'brings with it, in a single moment, sensations which are in fact multiple and heterogeneous' (1996, 245). 'Life' presents its subject – its reader, if you will – with a complex self-differentiated image, made 'rhetorical' or 'poetic' by virtue of perception and comprehension. Thus, any image of 'life' is also, too, a poetic and phenomenal figure, a trope giving meaning, shading in the figure with the 'idea', as Benjamin terms it, the idea being that which is other than the material, and which finds spectral form in the image.

Therefore, any representation of an idea, in which is contained the image of the world, comprises the traces of those multiple and heterogeneous sensations, which it is the purpose of the image and its representation to read, write, translate and communicate to the reader of the image, and thereby the constelled idea immanent within the equally constelled image. To read those traces is to reduce the image and its representation to that which makes the image or re-presentation play on the sensations of the reader, his or her experiences and perceptions of the phantom figure for the material world, to play on the apprehensions of the subject, as if the image and its idea were both for the reading subject and that 'subject' effect by which the idea of a narrator comes into being. In engaging in this phenomenal reduction, we thus make possible access to an authentic reality beneath the surface of the material, empirical and mimetic in any representation, those effects, aspects and traces once again, by which apperception may have taken place at an intuitive or pre-theoretical level.

This being so (and this is much, for it implies the proper work of all literary fiction, if not all art), what world is shown the reader in the representation of Tellson's Bank, by Temple Bar? What is the idea within which this image is contained, which comes to be represented in this striking and singular manner? Who is that 'you' to whom this passage comes to be addressed by the second paragraph, and who gives us insight into the secret, yet patently visible condition of Tellson's? And what *is* a 'Barmecide' room?

Amongst the many oddities of this representation of a banking institution, the idea of the Barmecide room is not the least odd. Imaginary, unreal, illusory, a fiction – a fictive figure for the work of all fictive figures, for the play of fiction itself, as that which, neither lie nor truth, neither fact nor fiction exactly, none the less is invested with an authenticity in its formal presentation – involving the willing suspension of disbelief between two parties: Tellson's makeshift storage area doubles as a(n equally 'fictive') dining room where dinner is never served, hence the noun, and thus serves only as a storage facility for documents on the tacit understanding that the room itself already has about it the idea of a fictional pretence. Nothing is as it seems and everything makes do, stands in for something else which it is not, *even*, as the narration observes on more than one occasion, in the year one thousand, seven hundred and eighty. This spelling out of the numerical representation of the year and its subsequent reiteration has a purpose. We are reminded, through that spelling out and the idiom by which it is introduced, that we are *not* in the presence of fact or history; we are, however, complicit in a narrative, data rendered as rhetoric, in the play of the image. To round off the image, and furthermore the representation of an idea through the non-simple image, the figure of 'Barmecide' (coming from the *One Thousand and One Nights*) is completed by the allusion to 'the heads exposed on Temple Bar' which 'ogle' the room with 'an insensate brutality and ferocity worthy of Abyssinia or Ashantee'. The initial and final images having to do with the particular room in question frame the 'reality', revealing in the process not merely the surface reality but an authentic or essential reality that is available only through the framing devices of the fictional figures. Fiction frames and so deconstructs reality here, rather than the 'real' being the ground for a mimetically or empirically slavish representation. Perception re-presents, and determines for the good reader this singular instance of London's banking world.

From the sentence, it is not easy to tell initially whether the word 'Barmecide' is adjective or noun if one is not familiar with the word; one cannot say whether it is the room which is illusory or an architectural structure for the manufacture and maintenance of illusions and the imaginary. The institutional, it might be hinted, is 'barmecidal', this is the authority that institutions wield. However, in that this room contains a dining-table on which dinner is never served suggests two things: that the room itself is not a chimera but, from an architectural point of view, real or material enough, certainly as solid as the dining-table; the other intimation here, particularly as we are invited to imagine a table on which no food is served, is that Dickens was aware of the word having come into English from *One Thousand and One Nights*, or indeed that he had recalled the figure of the prince who served a feast to a beggar on dishes that were empty. There is ambiguity, if not irony, to be read in what this literary intertext has to say about the banking institution. This single detail is worth considering for it touches on the relationship in the passage between materiality or solidity and the persistent-evanescent, to which matters of death and darkness prevalent in the passage may be read as belonging.

This apparent dichotomy – perhaps incongruity is a better term, or paradox – appears to reveal the heart of banking practices, at least as far as Tellson's is concerned, to the extent that a degree of belief in solidity and reliability is required in practices and institutional forms which rely on creating the illusion of stability, strength and permanence, whilst dealing with its customers principally in terms of trust. Banking, supposed as a matter of material conditions, is shown to the reader, exposed before our eyes, as engaging in pretence, in convenient fictions of trust, security, confidence and all those other coded fictions by which banking maintains itself, and the workings of which 'modes of semiotic efficiency' (Guattari 2011, 304), in an ironic and fictionalised-demystified manner of presentation, it is the purpose of a passage such as this to put into play. In effect, the Dickens-machine engages in giving to 'your' vision 'essential realities' (2011, 302) in institutional operation beneath the 'world of *habit*' (2011, 302) through a function described by Félix Guattari in his reading of Proust as 'discernibilization' (2011, 302–6).

Such an operation, peeling back the mystification that supports the world of habit, is made to work through particular devices, tropes and effects common to the work of the Dickens-machine in its technology of re-presentation and projection. There is, for example, alliteration from the very first sentence: T[ellson's] B[ank], T[emple] B[ar].[12] Alliteration requires but also, in this case, inaugurates iterability, in this case both phonic and graphic. Repetition and iterability then come into their own: very, very, very, very; old-fashioned, old-fashioned, wanted no, wanted no, wanted no; put to Death, put to Death, put to Death, put to Death, put to Death, put to Death – banking, it would seem, is a process of execution, the bank, despite its appearance, a machinery for decapitation, if the heads on Temple Bar are anything to go by. Then there are comparisons, which themselves form both pairs and opposites: less objectionable, less respectable, passive belief, active weapon; a door has uncannily human qualities; anthropomorphised – and therefore having its 'authentic' reality laid bare from beneath its merely material surface and habitual function – the door is apprehended as idiotic, obstinate and as having a weak rattle in its throat. More excessive than metaphor, the door is thus a figure of catachresis, drawing attention to its impossible fictionalisation. Everything in or about Tellson's is touched with hyperbole: the employees are the oldest, windows are the dingiest, though capable of being made dingier. 'Proper' iron bars find their metaphorical iteration in Temple Bar, as if to signal, once more, that all the world is available for narrative, rhetoric and the poetic 'making' that takes place in re-presentation. That inhuman, yet living door is merely the forerunner of the House itself, which has its hands in its pockets. Following the first two paragraphs about the House, 'you' become the focus, the House has greeted you, as a customer. But you are always connected to your money, you being nothing but an extension of capital. Returning to the architectural and formal accents: drawers are wormy and old. Money is musty, it decomposes into rags; there is corruption as well as decomposition and worm-eaten wood. Documents are rendered, as if so much dead flesh. All tends, as we have implied, towards execution by the house, Death being a 'recipe', but also a 'remedy'. Death is everywhere, reiterated seven times, as successive 'executions' are, well, executed on anyone doing anything illegal in relation to money and law, the law of money, the law of the house: in short, economics. Heads are laid low or exposed, as if on spikes. In what must be a pun, business is carried on 'gravely'.

There is a paradox here, which tends towards the revelation of the power of the fictive and the nature of the imagination in transforming experience into perception, and thence into memory or narrative. Dickens's reading and writing of specific locations, architectures, details of structure, their daily and habitual functions and what causes the functions to operate without being understood directly discerns what is beneath the ideological work invested in quotidian habit. Thus, what Guattari theorises and explicates from the reading of Proust may be perceived as being already underway in Dickensian modes of perception, presentation and re-presentation, through those suspensions of narrative in order that someone looks at the scene before an otherwise unseeing subject. Tellson's Bank is exposed to an illumination of its Gothic aspects; or rather that it is only available to be read authentically, beneath its machinic unconscious operation, through a Gothic architextural tropology. The narrating effect is to unveil, cause to appear what lies beneath in phantastic terms, hyperbole and excess, iterability and related formal devices heightening so as to make plain what is true.

What such scenes effect in their seemingly needless detail (mimetically understood, so much detail and concomitant effect can only be misrecognised as 'creating atmosphere', as it were) is to put the brakes on plot development and narrative flow. We have entered the chapter and also a given building in London simultaneously. It is therefore necessary that we are immersed in place, made subjects to it, given a vision of what is there, as if we were close to the location ourselves. That pause or hiatus in narrative flow in favour of the intensification of presentation and re-presentation specifically for some subject, for the purposes of explication, analysis and demystification, is focused in this passage in the sustained apostrophe to the second person, whether singular or plural. That each of us is addressed as 'you' or 'your' fully realises the encounter, whilst also allowing for the explication of chance experiences. Had a narrative not led us to this place, we would not consider it. As we are now here, let us consider it fully, in order to 'see' what is 'really' occurring. This is what Félix Guattari encourages as a mode of perception and engagement, although, of course, Dickens has anticipated him. Guattari's approach to an 'armed' alliance between the 'empirical apperception of the Kantians' and the 'eidetic reduction of phenomenologists' that involves simultaneously an 'abandon to fortuitous encounters and to the bareness of the real, and to a greater sophistication of the mode of semiotization' (Guattari 2011, 302) is thus fully evident throughout Dickens in general, and in the presentation of the bank in particular.

Readers of Dickens will immediately recognise that which is typical of Dickensian narrators in and of the city: abandonment to the apparently fortuitous encounter. While this might be seen as poor plotting, an aesthetic over-reliance on the rhetorical possibilities of chance in order to further narrative or effect, such misperception fails to consider, and therefore see, the extent to which the abandonment to chance is part of a deliberate technique for the purpose of making available an essential reality irreducible to mere empirical fact. To put this differently, and to borrow from Proust – as does Guattari – in coming to terms with the manner in which the Dickens text would have us see what is underway in an idea such as banking, and make available a necessary apperception, the 'writer's work' has to be understood, as Proust presents it, as 'merely a kind of optical instrument which he offers to the reader to enable him to *discern* what, without this book, he would perhaps never have perceived in himself' (1996, 245). But the writer is also – always – a reader, the two, as we have argued, fused, albeit maintaining their differences, in the figure of the narrating effect, the technology of

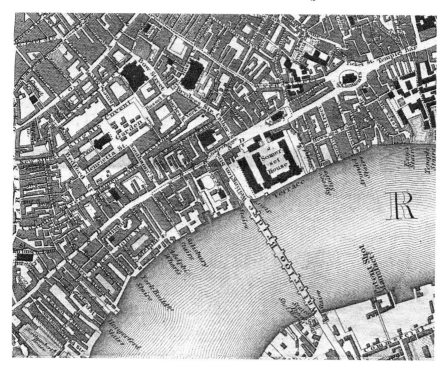

Temple Bar, Buckingham Street, the Adelphi

image projection that grounds impressions, to which reading / writing responds. Thus, London is made available as that which, through its tropological and architectural convergences, produces a subject capable of reading otherwise, of reading the impression. Pausing to notice, the Dickensian narrator forces on us a 'certain poetic passivity' (Guattari 2011, 305), in which 'the machinic rhizome does the rest' in making available for perception via the 'micropolitics of assemblages of enunciation' (Guattari 2011, 305), in which the narrator device as subject of the city is revealed in the process as 'nothing more, as an individual, than the catalyst of such an assemblage' (Guattari 2011, 305). Such a subject catalyses our ability to 'recapture' an impression we never knew we had received.

Breakfast • Gray's Inn Square, Temple Bar, Strand Lane

'The Steam Excursion', *Sketches by Boz*

He dressed himself, took a hasty apology for a breakfast, and sallied forth. The streets looked as lonely and deserted as if they had been crowded overnight, for the last time. Here and there, an early apprentice, with quenched-looking sleepy eyes, was taking down the shutters of a shop; and a policeman or milkwoman might occasionally be seen pacing slowly along; but the servants had not yet begun to clean the doors, or light the kitchen fires, and London looked the picture of desolation. At the corner of a by-street, near Temple Bar, was stationed a 'street-breakfast'. The coffee was boiling over a charcoal fire, and large slices of bread and butter were piled one upon the other, like deals in a timberyard. The company were seated on a form, which, with a view both to security and comfort, was placed against a neighbouring wall. Two young men, whose uproarious mirth and disordered dress bespoke the conviviality of the preceding evening, were treating three 'ladies' and an Irish labourer. A little sweep was standing at a short distance, casting a longing eye at the tempting delicacies; and a policeman was watching the group from the opposite side of the street. The wan looks and gaudy finery of the thinly-clad women contrasted as strangely with the gay sunlight, as did their forced merriment with the boisterous hilarity of the two young men, who, now and then, varied their amusements by 'bonneting' the proprietor of this itinerant coffee house.

Mr Percy Noakes walked briskly by, and . . . turned down Strand Lane . . . (*SB* 376)

Stepping back from the intensity of scrutiny demanded by the detail of such images as are offered by arrival in London or the inner realities of a place such as Tellson's Bank, and taking as a cue the idea of the chance encounter and the lingering gaze it can engender, consider the title of Charles Dickens's first published book, as it appeared in February 1836, in two volumes: *Sketches by 'Boz', illustrative of Every-day Life and Every-day People*. Disarmingly straightforward, it offers much of significance for our understanding of Dickens and London. In its mode of commentary, this title gives much in miniature to be read in anticipation of Dickens's acts of reading and writing of the city. The 'sketch' as mode of presentation is comprehended in general as that which is, if not unfinished, then an image executed on the fly, something brief, an outline, rather than a complete or finished image. From the Greek, meaning that which is executed in an extemporary manner, the idea of the sketch suggests something both pictorial and written, a preliminary rather than a final execution. In literary terms, the sketch, popular during the nineteenth century, implies brevity and adumbration, without substantial plotting. Suggestive rather than explicit, it is, as Boz's title has it, 'illustrative' of, and therefore illuminating, the quotidian. There is in the title in question the promise of something fleeting, occurring repeatedly. On the surface, this would appear to be what takes place throughout *Sketches by Boz*.

Yet, there is to be read, again and again, the gesture of the pause, the gaze turned in another direction, the contemplation or reflection of a narrating subject, who serves to place the reader in proximity to the otherwise unnoticed moment, experience or event. Considered otherwise, the 'sketch', in its brevity, offers to its reader a double time. On the one hand, something comes to pass, the moment there and gone, and with it, the perception. But at the same time, in the fleeting encounter – from the corner of the eye, as it were – time slows, to take in, however sketchily, outlines, cultural 'gestures' of 'everyday people' and 'everyday life' as these are determined by the moment in London, and as these gestures, therefore, in being otherwise unobserved, define the city. The subject pauses in a hurry and, in hurrying, is momentarily brought to a halt. The temporality of the instant of the sketch is thus hurried and leisurely; out of this tension, an image arrives. The 'spatial and temporal unity' (Barbaras 2006, 130) given in a moment of perception returns to the subject a sense of the world, in which he or she takes part, the 'everyday' emerging from within itself and inviting a second look, a look in which consciousness and reflection, judgement, translation occur. The idea of the 'sketch', then, in its impossible double tempi, marks the text in a manner that implicitly dismisses the 'propriety' of well-tempered representation in relation to plotting. Both less and more than mimetic realism, it involves its subject in an impressionistic intimacy that the distance of complete representation and measured time would keep at a distance. In the play of representation and perception with which the sketch engages, there is a making-visible in the adumbration of the everyday, which would otherwise remain invisible. Such a provisional privileging of phenomena, captured in passing, 'exposes us' in its 'serious game' – the sketch as *scherzo*, the jest as social gesture in all its historicity – the 'vision of what does not at all rise to the level of objectivity' (Marion 2004, 42), but which none the less requires that we involve ourselves in the vision.

A 'substantial selection of Dickens's previously published pieces (with three new items), later known as the First Series' (*SB* ix), *Sketches by Boz* was reprinted in 1839 and divided by the author in the volume publication into four sections – 'Seven Sketches from our Parish', 'Scenes', 'Characters' and 'Tales'. Together, these offer the reader, if not an encyclopedia, then a miscellany of London life and scenes in the early nineteenth century that is simultaneously idiosyncratic and exemplary. Moving from apparently detached observation with interjected, subjectively rendered perceptions to fictive reinvention reliant on an eye for the comic, grotesque, pathetic and, in general, any thing, person, phenomenon or event susceptible to supplement, hyperbole, satire, parody or pastiche, *Sketches by Boz* registers as it mediates the various and diverse worlds of the pre-Victorian capital. It traces the signs of place

and its people, on the verge of an unanticipated modernity of existence and being. It marks in a sketched manner a mobile, fluid, often
chance concatenation of elements (as we have already implied), aspects,
attributes, features and characteristics, to which form is given, a frame
is rendered through the rapid yet detailed transcription of architecture,
scene, place and architectonic relation in the constitution of a moment at
once ephemeral and yet all too materially there. Each short piece, and the
'Scenes' in particular, register and present with a vitality and immediacy
more analogous to photographic media rather than the more leisured
and stable representation available to the painter. Hence, that all-
important first word of the title, *sketches*, which are *illustrative of everyday life and every-day people*, and which inaugural title captures what is
to come, with an economy and suggestive plenitude in inverse proportion
to the brevity, the hurriedness that the idea of a sketch implies.

In these sketches there is a precision, an accuracy or exactness of perception, as well as exaggeration or distortion; indeed, it can be argued
that perception is so thorough, so scrupulous in the marking of particulars and the greater whole they signify, which is always more in Dickens
than the sum of those parts, *because* of exaggeration. Perception and
translation of the world effect in translation the truth of that world
precisely through, on the one hand, controlled embellishment, over-
emphasis and elaboration and, on the other hand, a celerity of eye and
pen that, in its motions, offers something more than a skiagraph and
less than fully rendered mimetic representation. No mere reflection of
early nineteenth-century London scenes, *Sketches by Boz* is not simply
'concerned with the phenomena but the mode of their givenness . . . not
with what appears but with [the manner of] appearing' (Henry 2008, 2).

That *Sketches* is, then, properly a miscellany – a gathering or pastiche
of diverse, apparently random events, subjects and phenomena without
the necessary transcendent organisation that the notion of an anthology
implies – is verifiable through merely listing the titles of the 'Scenes':
'The Streets-Morning', 'The Streets-Night', 'Shops and Their Tenants',
'Scotland-yard', 'Seven Dials', 'Meditations in Monmouth-street',
'Hackney-coach Stands', 'Doctors' Commons', 'London Recreations',
'The River', 'Astley's', 'Greenwich Fair', 'Private Theatres', Vauxhall-
gardens by Day', 'Early Coaches', Omnibuses', 'The Last-Cab-driver,
and the First Omnibus Cad', 'A Parliamentary Sketch', 'Public Dinners',
'The First of May', 'Brokers' and Marine-store-Shops', 'Gin-shops', 'The
Pawnbroker's Shop', 'Criminal Courts', 'A Visit to Newgate'. Other
than the common denominator, 'London', which defines provisionally chance concatenation rather than determinate meaning, such titles
and the topics, scenes, people and events to which they refer have only

random and passing relation. Certainly there is a degree of frequency – there are types of shop, forms of transport – and particular local overlaps – Doctors' Commons, Criminal Courts, Newgate, or Astley's, Greenwich Fair, Vauxhall-gardens – suggestive of societal and cultural commonality, correlation or association, as well as of discursive or institutional correspondence or alliance. However, what the titles give us to understand is that London, taken as a whole, cannot by definition be defined. It resists totalisation or homogeneity. Its 'identity' is determined by difference, by relation-without-relation. The scenes are, of course, not the only sketches of everyday London (and, it should be noted, not all of the pieces published as *Sketches* have the metropolis as their specific location). As the title of the collection indicates once more, all the pieces gathered together provide instances and glimpses, and therefore insight into, the way we lived then in the city. Urban moments are recorded as incidentals rather than serving primarily as framing devices or simple context for the principal narrative.

One such passage is found in 'The Steam Excursion', a sketch first published in October 1834, in the *Monthly Magazine* (SB 369–87). The tale concerns a law student, Mr Percy Noakes, who was 'generally termed—"a devilish good fellow"' (*SB* 369), which translates as having an extensive and busy social life, and someone who 'inhabit[ed] a set of chambers on the fourth floor, in one of those houses in Gray's Inn Square which command an extensive view of the gardens, and their adjuncts'. Such adjuncts include 'nursery maids, and townmade children, with parenthetical legs' (*SB* 369). Though these observations, taken from the first paragraph, are not the passage to which I will come in a moment, it is worth pausing over them. The subject's life is defined in part by where he lives, location as significant in a small way as his public persona. At the same time, however, the situation opens to the reader a brief image of one facet of town life. The extent to which London informs one's being extends therefore beyond Noakes to include and define even the most marginal and anonymous of characters perceived at a distance, but comprehended as of the city. Moreover, such detail is presented prior to, if not independent of, any more considered explication of Percy Noakes's character or interests.

The optical recording device called Boz places Noakes in, and yet separate from, the city, the law student being seen initially as others of his world see him and positioned in his world, one distinct from that outside his window. The extensive view from the chambers is implicitly Noakes's and it is through the frame of the window, with its 'extensive' view, that everyday London and London's others first become visible. Beneath the surface of the text's seemingly disinterested representation, social worlds are suggested, vision being what links them, the view from Gray's Inn Square being one that is elevated (Percy's chambers are on the fourth floor), enclosed, set off from a world of the streets, into which Percy Noakes must go. The first sight, that extensive view, is thus offered as a momentarily stable image, the frame of which has to be crossed, with Percy Noakes's descent into 'everyday life and everyday people', as Dickens's title has it. London has, in a fashion, already arrived, however, for the children are 'townmade', the portmanteau term redolent of the singularity of production. Percy may not be observant, but the reader is invited to look, as if on a painting. The 'flaunting' nursery maids and the 'townmade' children, 'with parenthetical legs', arrive to the eye in postures, the window of the fourth floor chambers granting 'to the gaze the ability to . . . cross the distance'. It is not, as Jean-Luc Marion observes of the work of painting but in a remark that is strikingly pertinent to reading Dickens and Dickens's London, 'so much that we learn to see the painting [or the view of London from the window] as that the painting [or scene], by having given itself, teaches us to see it' (Marion 2004, 42). The humour by which the moment is translated and made visible, revealed in the brief gaze, calls us to consider and reflect on the conditions by which our perception is drawn.

In this, the detail of the initial sentence of the first paragraph, London's significance is foregrounded in telegraphic fashion. It forms as well as informs, it serves to provide place in relation to person, and serves in establishing various aspects of identity, both individual and, in passing, collective. But it is Noakes who bears the burden of the narrative, charged by friends and acquaintances with the organisation of the excursion on the Thames to which the title alludes. After much frantic activity and anxiety for Noakes in the arrangements, the morning of the intended excursion arrives; at five o'clock (*SB* 376) he rises and sets off, intending 'he would walk leisurely to Strand Lane, and have a boat to the Custom House' (*SB* 376). To recall an earlier citation, the passage is concerned not merely with what appears. It is also taken with the manner of appearing, the mode by which the phenomena of the scene are given. In turn, this 'involvement' of perception *in* the event and its internal 'emotional' and 'spatial' relations is translated into the writing of the scene. The sweep is placed to one side, his eye is 'longing'; a strange contrast – in fact, a complex matrix of interrelations of different orders – is drawn between and from 'wan looks', 'gaudy finery', 'forced merriment' and 'gay sunlight'. The time is measured indirectly but precisely, this being at the hour, as Dickens might say, when both policemen and milkwomen move through the streets but servants, if awake, are not yet at work, either inside or outside the houses of their employers.

Who sees the street-breakfast? For whom is this scene presented? Whose perspective or perception is this? The streets may well look 'lonely and deserted' in this 'picture of desolation', but if this is such a picture, if London in the early morning has about it in its manner of appearing or giving itself a desolate, even eschatological aura (we read, after all, that the overcrowding of the previous night was *as if for the last time*), then this is hardly the world of Mr Percy Noakes, whose walk is brisk, and whose journey, as it is described from Gray's Inn Square, via Temple Bar to Strand Lane, terminating at what is now Victoria Embankment, is of only a mile approximately.[13] The street-breakfast is an anomaly in 'The Steam Excursion'. It is a fortuitous moment of experience and perception, something briefly becoming visible before disappearing again, save for whatever might remain in memory of the moment. That it *does* remain in memory and returns as re-presentation is given witness by the fact of its appearing, unbidden, in this otherwise humorous sketch. It is a sketch within a sketch. An extract of just under 250 words in a short story of roughly 8,000, it can hardly be said to be taken as significant on a first reading. It resides at a margin, as it were. Peripheral to the narrative as a whole, and even more marginal to the life and world of Mr Percy Noakes, the moment and its perception remain, confronting us, and offering to liberate our 'gaze from objectivity' (Marion 2004, 42) through its appeal to conscience of one's own subjectivity in relation and in proximity to our invisible others, which the space of the city causes to occur.

Certainly, the passage in which the breakfast is presented gives no hint that Noakes is the one observing. Neither does it appear in any appreciable manner to impose itself on his consciousness. He exists outside this narrative event – and it is an event in that it arrives to disturb narrative trajectory and the light, comic tone in which the story is generally conveyed. Of course, the walk is quite specifically figured, and in any form of fiction aspiring to realist representation the burden on the narrative is to move its characters from place to place, and to offer such information as conveys the appropriate sense of place – hence the naming in 'The Steam Excursion' of Gray's Inn Square, Portland Street, Temple Bar and so forth. On the outside of the inside, we might say, the street-breakfast breaks into, without becoming accommodated by, the life and places of Noakes and, by extension, his associates and friends, figures not too unlike some of the readers who purchased the *Monthly Magazine*, perhaps, or those who bought *Sketches by Boz*.

Yet if the breakfast occupies or marks a boundary that is not of the narrative centre, it is near to the structural centre of the story. Its time is liminal, between night and day, between pleasure and work, between

sleep and wakefulness. Its location, on a corner of a bystreet, is something of a periphery also. There is something makeshift, provisional, in
the establishment of the 'itinerant coffee-house', in which even the food
bears a passing resemblance to the plank employed as seating. Much, if
not everything, about the scene has an edge, is on or of the edge, and
in its being so assumes a phenomenal weight out of proportion to its
brevity or narrative marginality. Such 'edginess' is in the discomfiting
resonances of particular terms and the rhetoric to which they belong.
The 'ladies' are not *ladies*; or rather, they belong to an unspeakable
demi-monde rather than being of another that is socially acceptable, as
the quotation marks observe silently. To go back to particular observations already cited, looks are 'wan', clothing 'gaudy'. Stepping back a
little from the detail, it is observed that the principal group of this scene
of London life, those gathered at the coffee stand, is kept under surveillance, not only by a hungry sweep but also by a policeman. There is also
that merest hint of the foreign in the presence of an 'Irish' workman, the
situation mapping the suggestion of the illicit, desire, excess, debauchery
and potential threat, all of which is contained to a degree by the gaze of
the law.

Boz sees what Percy Noakes does not, and shows the reader what he
sees, in a manner that invites us to pause, in order to receive the event
with its full weight. The street-breakfast as image offers to the subject's
gaze phenomena that are products, projections, effects and conditions
of London; all are 'townmade' in effect, and the reader is held so as to
receive what is offered, that which 'phenomenology holds for the phenomenon par excellence – that it shows itself on its own terms' (Marion
2004, 43). Hence, the dissonance in tone in the breakfast scene, which
cannot account for the eventual outcome of the steam excursion, a comic
disaster in which nothing turns out as anticipated. This brief scene, seen
as it were from some angle of social parallax, though positioned mar-
ginally in the story as a whole, 'does not live in a peripheral section
of the phenomenal universe, rendered secondary by some function of
imitation; it appears . . . out of the confrontation [between phenomena]
between the unseen and the visible' (Marion 2004, 43). There is in the
figuring of the breakfast another purpose, a sense of lives not quite able
to rise to optimism or hope, not capable of becoming comic in their
misadventures. The breakfast belongs to a different world to that of the
excursion, even as, we get the sense, Mr Percy Noakes, though a '"devilish good fellow"', is not at that stage of dissolution that is implied in the
two young men, of 'uproarious mirth', 'disordered dress' or 'boisterous
hilarity' – not yet, at any rate. Perhaps what impinges most is a brief
awareness, in the mode of appearing, of class tensions, emergent in the

sense of coming to awareness as the difference in both phenomena and modes of appearance and re-presentation rather than being merely a novel condition.

This is what is traced in the street-breakfast, amongst other things, in that moment's manner of appearing. The event gives us to apprehend, as if from the corner of the eye, at the corner of a street leading off a main London thoroughfare, other Londons, somewhat less salubrious than the London of law students, their acquaintances who live 'in Portland Street, Oxford Street', who move in similar 'orbits' (*SB* 373), and who can afford to engage in pleasure trips. And in this, this otherwise seemingly anomalous narrative and scenic interjection (bordering as it does on the principal world, the principal action) contributes to a material historicity in its making the reading subject conscious of the modal or tonal difference, so as 'to become aware of the appearing'; which manifestation calls to us, demanding that we 'analyze it in and for itself'; Henry 2008, 2). Such a momentary manifestation invites the reader to pause, not walk briskly by, and to 'think reality' in such a way that certain otherwise invisible spheres of reality, in becoming 'the object[s] of a new analysis' in order to extend not only the 'task of understanding reality' in historically and materially given ways, but also, in this process, to arrive at a 'self-understanding of this understanding' (Henry 2008, 6), to place oneself in relation to historicity, to the material conditions of one's identity in a manner not available to Mr Percy Noakes, who, as Dickens concludes in a timeless present tense at the close of 'The Steam Excursion', is 'as light-hearted and careless as ever' (*SB* 387). We have been offered the occasion to learn how to see, to have our gaze delivered 'from the objective restraints of an object' (Marion 2004, 43), even if Mr Percy Noakes has failed to rise to the occasion, and so remains blind, out of the flow of time, and the material conditions of history.

Chambers • Holborn, Staple Inn, Furnival's Inn

Staple Inn

The Mystery of Edwin Drood

Behind the most ancient part of Holborn, London, where certain gabled houses some centuries of age still stand looking on the public way, as if disconsolately looking for the Old Bourne that has long run dry, is a little nook composed of two irregular quadrangles, called Staple Inn. It is one of those nooks, the turning into which out of the clashing street, imparts to the relieved pedestrian the sensation of having put cotton in his ears, and velvet soles on his boots. It is one of those nooks where a few smoky sparrows twitter in smoky trees, as though they called to one another, 'Let us play at country,' and where a few feet of garden-mould and a few yards of gravel enable them to do that refreshing violence to their tiny understandings. Moreover, it is one of those nooks which are legal nooks; and it contains a little Hall, with a little lantern in its roof: to what obstructive purposes devoted, and at whose expense, this history knoweth not . . . in those days no neighbouring architecture of lofty proportions had arisen to overshadow Staple Inn. The westering sun bestowed bright glances on it, and the south-west wind blew into it unimpeded.

Neither wind nor sun, however, favoured Staple Inn one December afternoon towards six o'clock, when it was filled with fog, and candles shed murky and blurred rays through the windows of all its then-occupied sets of chambers; notably from a set of chambers in a corner house in the little inner quadrangle, presenting in black and white over its ugly portal the mysterious inscription:

$$P$$
$$J \qquad T$$
$$1747$$

In which set of chambers, never having troubled his head about the inscription, unless to bethink himself at odd times on glancing up at it, that haply it might mean Perhaps John Thomas, or Perhaps Joe Tyler, sat Mr. Grewgious writing by his fire. [. . .]

There was no luxury in his room. Even its comforts were limited to its being dry and warm, and having a snug though faded fireside. What may be called its private life was confined to the hearth, and an easy chair, and an old-fashioned occasional round table that was brought out upon the rug after business hours, from a corner where it elsewise remained turned up like a shining mahogany shield . . . Three hundred days in the year, at least, he crossed over to the hotel in Furnival's Inn for his dinner, and after dinner crossed back again, to make the most of these simplicities until it should become broad business day once more, with P. J. T., date seventeen-forty-seven. (*MED* 133–5)

In Dickens's final, unfinished, novel, *The Mystery of Edwin Drood*, we find ourselves once more around the Inns of Court, in Staple Inn, to be precise, with a brief excursion to Furnival's Inn outside business hours. Staple Inn is situated just south, south-east of the corner of Gray's Inn Road and High Holborn. Not quite in the present, we are in a recent past, as can be discerned from the absence of more modern 'neighbouring architecture of lofty proportions [that] had arisen to overshadow' the Inn. Elsewhere, throughout this extract, and as on a number of occasions, person (Mr Grewgious) and place (his set of chambers) exist in each other. There is no separate identity; together, person and place present a communal fiction. One does not simply reflect the other. Each is, in a reciprocal fashion, a mediation or version of the other, the boundaries between the two if not erased, then to be of no particular importance. Mr Grewgious *is* his work; his workplace that which defines everything about him. Neither room nor lawyer has a 'private life', this being one more convenient fiction supplementing both. Mr Grewgious is as much a 'fixture' or 'feature' of the Inn, as the Inn, and the set of chambers in question in particular, give outward frame to his existence and identity. Grewgious is merely a function, an agent of place, and this is woven into the fabric of this image of the law, as much as is that 'mysterious inscription'.

The inscription is both a siglum and a paraph of sorts. Its significance might be much or little, the initials of a builder or architect being the most likely explanation, not that Mr Grewgious is concerned. A 'real' feature of Staple Inn, its presence in the fictive narrative illustrates briefly how reality and the imagined world bleed into one another in the London of Dickens's texts; it also indicates how a feature is never simply there for its own sake, but instead belongs to a wider phenomenal register aimed at and reflecting that subjective consciousness of an assumed narrator or walker. That the initials are dated indicates how parts of this passage are countersigned, marked by the signs of contretemps. Time goes against the appearance in the present of any object, so that the objective is undone from within, appearance giving way to the essential, temporally marked reality that is there to be read, and which is decrypted in part for the reader, by an act of reading become writing on the part of the narrator. Holborn is, for example, the absent old bourne, a chimera of the past, the narrative present being a palimpsest of sorts, the one borne inside the other at a semantic level, wherein that which is the older remnant remains partially to view in meaning if not in material condition. Already not of its time but signalling two pasts, recent and more remote, the architecture of the latter having only partially disappeared, the topography transformed, and the structures of the former marking themselves in negative representation through not yet having been erect, this particular presentation of a London location is rent by, even as it is delineated through anachrony. The temporality of the image is multiple, a place of contest between the remnants of one time, the gabled houses, and the perceived presence of another, the 'clashing street'. Those gabled dwellings are also out of time; they impart the impression of appearing to look for what is no longer there, an ancient stream, while that sensate awareness of anachrony imparts itself in the narrative at a lexical level, in quaint terms and archaisms, such as 'bourne' but also 'nook' and 'this history knoweth not'. Between times and out of time, then, there is an intermedial heterovocality that amplifies the echoic dimension of the site.

This distinction between objective and phenomenal appearance, the difference that articulates the distinction and, in that, the 'discernibilization' (to recall the Deleuzian notion), making available the double readings and the divergence they enable assign to the image a subject who reads not only spatially but temporally also. The urban subject – and this is a sign of his modernity – reads in a given site the traces of those other times, and thus unfolds the present image, in the perception of the difference of image. To call this psychogeography would be to engage in an anachronistic – or, some might say, 'postmodern' – reading oneself. Yet such a gesture would not be wholly without precedent, not least in thinking through the genealogy of acts of modern reading / writing the city, in which the surface of what is seen is traced and subsequently re-membered. There is in the very manner of this narrative from the late Dickens, the echo, if not the memory, of reading belonging to his younger, posthumous self, that younger, other writer, who had worked for the *True Sun*. While employed there briefly in 1832 as a parliamentary reporter, he encountered his elder contemporary, the essayist and radical Leigh Hunt, who the following year was, like Dickens, to begin writing sketches of metropolitan life.[14] Hunt defined his essays as engaging in 'townosophy'. In visiting various districts of the metropolis, Hunt's peripatetic narrator would, in observing place, open from within the reflection on the present location its associations, its history, expounding on the traces of the past that remained.

Through such psychogeographical or townosophic reflective medi(t)ation, the temporal current of the present is interrupted, suspended even. With this, the emergent temporal complexity of patterning discerned in the spatial and visual sketch of place admits of a work irreducible to aesthetic effect alone. Perception in its marked singularity – this is a vision for one person only – breaks the objective and mimetic frame of reference. The appreciation of temporality as a key to the perception of the site as a locus of memory – materiality being the condition that, in its being built, in given structural form and presence, allows for the taking place of inscription – allows for similarity and difference, convergence and doubling, singularity and iterability between times and between person and place to make themselves felt. The real gives way to or enables, puts in play, access to transcendental schema that connect apprehension of conceptual forms to the phenomenal appearance of material conditions and the objects that 'make' the world available to the subject. The 'townosophic' willingness to open the reading of place to that which informs it in spectral fashion belongs to a greater 'willingness to imagine supplementary or alternative versions' of the novels, hints of which are to be found throughout the novels, as Robert

Douglas-Fairhurst notes (2011, 13). Here is a writer, glimpsed inside the phantom narrator, who, later was to become known as someone with an interest in 'locating the dead' (Douglas-Fairhurst 2011, 158) and 'not content simply to reflect the world' (2011, 159), described himself jokingly as a 'resurrectionist, in search of a subject' (Hotten 1870, 36–7; Douglas-Fairhurst 2011, 158–9).

There is a transcendence or 'transcendentalism' at work here because in perception judgement comes to take place. The illusion of the objective world in its materiality is transcended, if by transcendentalism we can suggest a perceptual translation. Transcendence thus refers not to a final, stable meaning, an abstract truth pertaining to what one sees, but a judgement grounded in the authenticity of the perception. Judgement or discernment makes possible the application of 'concepts of understanding' (Kant 1997, 267) to phenomena, to the appearances that are otherwise taken either as merely empirical or belonging to a deliberately controlled aesthetic pertaining to some mistaken notion of 'authorial intention'. To see what takes place as *just* aesthetic would be to suggest a controlling consciousness at a remove from that which appears. Yet it is this proximity, this involvement that always places the subject in a relation to the world, revealing subjectivity as being inextricably mediated by and mediating place and world. There becomes revealed in the image of place or building a subjective 'always already' of perception and experience. In this process all 'empirical intuitions can be subsumed' (Kant 2007, 326). Thus, the text of Dickens in its modes of representation and re-presentation, through its rhetorical engagement of hypotyposis, 'builds' or performs an image, the phantasmal equivalent of a photograph, sketch or painting that also signals the consciousness that performs the image, with such intensity that the place appears before me, as if it were there, and as if I were there.

That this takes place may be understood if we take into account the significance of representational and tropic iterability in the various images that are constructed, particularly as they concern the representation of London, its locations, neighbourhoods, places, streets, buildings and so forth. There are recurring structures that establish patterns of understanding in relation to corporeal experience, linguistic rendering, and the determination of subjectivity in relation to place as these are reciprocally informed through the historicity of event and experience. If this remains a problem for some, we should remind ourselves of that displacement from within the present by the traces of anachronic time, temporal signatures, if you will, of the other of place. For, as Kant argues and the subject in the text of Dickens perceives, time does not 'subsist for itself or attach to things as an objective determination'. It is always part of the 'subjective conditions of . . . intuition', and is, therefore, 'nothing other than the form of inner sense' (Kant 1997, 180); not, though, merely an inner sense of self, as Kant would have it, but instead an inner sense, a phenomenal apprehension of that which is temporal in the appearance to someone of place, and the subject's relation to that.

Coming back to the rhetorical figure of 'hypotyposis' will, hopefully, allow us to explain the possible connection between the image in Dickens and the philosophical reflection on the part of Kant. From the Greek, meaning to sketch (*hypotypoein*), hypotyposis announces the verbal / visual exchange. Though a rhetorical term referring conventionally to a vivid depiction of scenes or events (*Hypotyposes by Boz*), or a lively sketch, employed to provide the appearance of reality, Kant defines hypotyposis in the following manner, as a 'rendering in terms of sense', which, he continues to observe (at least implicitly), is already mediated inasmuch as any act of hypotyposis is always a presentation rather than being merely a mark, which serves solely to designate (2007, 179). Between rhetoric and a first phenomenology, then: Dickensian hypotyposis, moving beyond the mimetic representation in order to register on the subject the experience and proximity of a perception, given or rendered in such a manner that re-presentation takes on the work of a perceptual analogy once more, creating me as its subject in constructing and projecting for me the image as if it were before me. The image is thus always the manifestation, the apparition rather than the embodiment, of a complex idea in the re-presentation to the reading subject, another subject's consciousness is implied, over which the reading subject's consciousness – mine, for the sake of argument – comes to be layered, as a palimpsest of the other. In this, the otherwise 'invisible, only intuitable . . . true, intuitiable, *ur*-phenomenal nature would become visible after the fashion of a likeness . . . *only* in art' (Benjamin 1996, 180).[15] Presentation and re-presentation, that which is presented for some consciousness, is no longer the figuring of that which is identical with content, but instead a correlate in which perception uncovers that which in the world is never directly available to the subject. In the present passage, this is achieved through that sketch that is composed through the relation between person and place, and the manner of temporal mapping that informs the given locale.

Those aspects of multi- and intra-temporality that inform image and the manner of perception and re-presentation of Staple Inn are persistent in the text of Dickens, whether overtly fictional, belonging to essays more 'factual' or occasional in their observation, or coming to find themselves in those occasional pieces that occupy a liminal narrative mode,

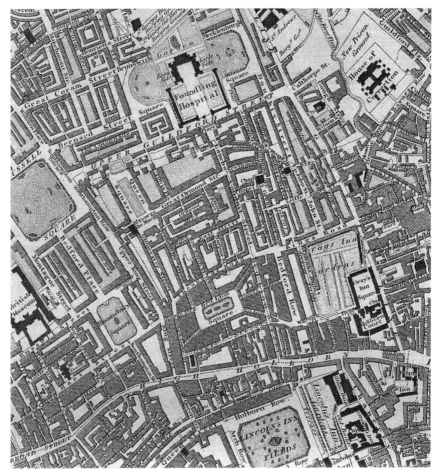

Staple Inn, Coram's Fields, Lincoln's Inn Fields, Gray's Inn

neither wholly 'fictional' nor 'documentary' in any conventional sense (but then what is, in Dickens's writing?); blurring, if not erasing the boundaries of both. It is in such a hybrid, and in some ways fundamentally, urban form, a form appropriate to the modern urban condition, that 'narrators' such as Boz, Master Humphrey or the Uncommercial Traveller persist.[16] As is already implied, this is not to suggest the narrative 'voices' of characters such as David Copperfield, Philip Pirrip or Ada Summerson are not equally subjects projected from the response to the city, or the need for a subjectivity appropriate to such hybridity of mode. It is, though, to read the phantasmic figures of Boz and his relatives as foregrounding more immediately that confusion and dissolution of genres than their counterparts who are anchored by the constraints of a narrative that purports to be wholly fictional, in some conventional understanding. Master Humphrey, Boz and the Uncommercial Traveller are, to adopt Leigh Hunt's nomination, 'Townsmen'; not wholly anonymous like Hunt's imagined figure, they remain related none the less through that shadowy half-presence they maintain, which allows them to pass, mostly unobserved, through the streets of the capital, and to move with all the leisure of a *flâneur*.

The walker's reading of the city is a motion that rewrites, re-presents the image as if before him once again. In his reading / writing London, there is, through the agency of memory and pen, an 'eye' that does more than simply observe; it records. In doing so, it plays back the experience, presenting a 'performance' of the city, its architectonics and architectures, its mapping and its memories. At the heart of such textual production is memory, and the impression left on that. As such, the idea of the sketch does not pretend to empirical observation detached from personal response; indeed, it is the transformation of the objective into so many perceptions that makes the immediacy of another's experience and perception at once comprehensible, capable of transmission and comprehension, and yet also apprehensible as remaining the experience of an other. At the same time, there is in this singular account a transcendent sense of institutional anachrony. Locus thus is always double, haunted by what it was, which few remember, certainly not the lawyer who inhabits the place, and yet which leaves its mark in the present, as the anonymous narrator observes. Such doubling is not merely figural; it assumes a spectral quality, however slightly; for through the image of Staple Inn, with its lost stream, its pathetic invocation of the pastoral, and its mute retirement from the 'clashing street', an other world gives itself as a passing apparition to that anonymous pedestrian, who is so scarcely there, so silently in motion, as to have almost passed unremarked.

Dismal • Little Britain, Smithfield, Saint Paul's Cathedral

Great Expectations

Mr Jaggers's room was lighted by a skylight only, and was a most dismal place; the skylight, eccentrically patched like a broken head, and the distorted adjoining houses looking as if they had twisted themselves to peep down at me through it. There were not so many papers about, as I should have expected to see; and there were some rusty old objects about, that I should not have expected to see—such as an old rusty pistol, a sword in a scabbard, several strange-looking boxes and packages, and two dreadful casts on a shelf, of faces peculiarly swollen, and twitchy about the nose. Mr Jaggers's own high-backed chair was of deadly black horsehair, with rows of brass nails round it, like a coffin; and I fancied I could see how he leaned back in it, and bit his forefinger at the clients. The room was but small, and the clients seemed to have had a habit of backing up against the wall: the wall, especially opposite to Mr Jaggers's chair, being greasy with shoulders . . .

I sat down in the cliental chair placed over against Mr Jaggers's chair, and became fascinated by the dismal atmosphere of the place. I called to mind that the clerk had the same air of knowing something to everybody else's disadvantage, as his master had. I wondered whether the two swollen faces were of Mr Jaggers's family, and, if he were so unfortunate as to have had a pair of ill-looking relations, why he stuck them on that dusty perch for the blacks and flies to settle on, instead of giving them a place at home. Of course I had no experience of a London summer day, and my spirits may have been oppressed by the hot exhausted air, and by the dust and grit that lay thick on everything. But I sat wondering and waiting in Mr Jaggers's close room, until I really could not bear the two casts on the shelf above Mr Jaggers's chair, and got up and went out.

. . . I came into Smithfield; and the shameful place, being all asmear with filth and fat and blood and foam, seemed to stick to me. So I rubbed it off with all possible speed by turning into a street where I saw the great black dome of Saint Paul's bulging at me from behind a grim stone building which a bystander said was Newgate Prison. (*GE* 164–5)

Pip's imagination, which appears with his coming into being for the reader, and which manifests itself with '[m]y first and most vivid impression of the identity of things, [which] seems to me to have been gained on a memorable raw afternoon towards evening' (*GE* 3), is given great exercise when confronted by the office of Mr Jaggers. However, while this is Pip's somewhat singular impression of the lawyer's office, and fully in keeping with the grotesque, if not Gothic, turn of representation, where imagination overleaps mimetic fidelity, it begs the question as to what extent the imagination is solely Pip's. On the one hand, imminent and insistent are the traces of those literary fictions read by Pip, those which, in effect, serve in the early constitution of his subjectivity. On the other hand, there are the signs here of the city: there is, in the manifestation of London for the subject in the early nineteenth century, a monstrous power determining the modalities of representation by which in afterthought the urban spaces, exteriors and interiors are re-presented. There is recognisable a narrative motion, taken up in and put into play by the various tropes and images, which signifies the discourse of the city impressing itself on the subject, with a degree of force, not to say imminent violence, which is not a little remarkable.

The room is lit from above; the lawyer's chambers present themselves through that single means of illumination, the skylight. We are inside the skull of Jaggers, as it were, the window 'patched like a broken head', and a head, moreover that finds its corollary in those death masks, the two 'dreadful casts' of 'swollen faces'. This is a dismal place, with a dismal atmosphere. All is dismal, dreadful, distorted, dusty, deadly, this last quality perceived in the colour of the horsehair covering of Jaggers's high-backed chair. Even the tacks holding the horsehair cover in place are coffin-like. In the 'blacks and flies', and the deposits of grease left upon the chair from years of habitual use, the interior suggests the exterior, that hitherto unexperienced 'London summer day', with its exhausted air, its dust and grit, the smear of filth and fat and blood and foam, all tending towards the dome of St Paul's – which is great and black – that bulges from behind the grim stone of Newgate Prison.

More than merely suggesting, the interior bleeds into its surrounding streets and buildings, even as, reciprocally, they suffuse Jaggers's office. There is no absolute exterior or interior here, only the phenomena of the hideous city, which leave their marks on the mind of the subject as much as they appear to do, in the reader's eye, on furnishings and walls. That bulging dome of the cathedral completes the impression of distortion, intimated first by the appearance of the 'distorted adjoining houses' glimpsed through the skylight, and subsequently in the distortion of the death masks. This particular London, which exceeds Pip's imagination, presenting him with a Gothic vision in excess of anything he has previously imagined, is a charnel house, the locus of atrocities and the site of slaughter, whether in the name of sustenance or justice; it is also a place of decay and oppression, one where engines of destruction in the form of anachronistic weapons present themselves as much as the casts as uncanny *memento mori*.

That extension of the image, from room to the outside world, but first illuminated from without, with its relation to the mind of the subject and the singularity of the force of impression, invites us to question both the relation between the text and its images, and the source of the referents, whether they are 'real' or imagined, and so forth. This is not to say that phenomena are illusory, but that the power by which they become transformed, or with which they are informed, and so deformed, suggests not only this intimate text / image relation but also the inaccessibility of any simple object before the image. At work is an ekphrastic modality, which serves through the intimation of a Gothic or pre-modern register for the pictorial world, to offer up a distortion of the modern that *is* modern in that very distortedness and its phenomenal effects. In this image, the world of exhaustion and deformation are all there is. Language strives to figure the visual image as graphically as possible, generating or projecting an iconotext through its hybrid modalities. The image, taking as its inaugural departure point the illumination from without, and which is followed shortly thereafter by Pip's half-comprehending mental 'enlightenment' (he does not fully realise what he sees, even though he apprehends all too clearly the resonance of this world through its alignment with his memory of earlier perceptions and interpretations), functions as both mediation of and opening on to a 'shameful' city, a city that remains *there* but which remains at the same moment invisible, unless the subject cannot avoid being confronted with it. The 'narrative functions of the image in the text may' be apprehended, therefore, 'along the lines of a supplement', whereby that which composes the image, the various mementos of the city's oppressive energies – in which atmospheric conditions serve as a supplement to human activities – establish a sequence of visual spaces that import 'their orientations and capacities for disruption'. In this manner, room and street, furnishing and architecture, constitute a 'contending site', the image(s) maintaining 'an epistemology and phenomenology' (Louvel 2011, 7) of confinement, unease, claustrophobia, destruction and death: in short, this *other* London.

Pip is *there* doubly, remembering, re-presenting, and in the event, before the very experience with an apparent immediacy, a proximity, which mediates the sensory apprehension and revenance of the image for the reader. The subject, more than merely being present, becomes the place wherein a dialogue between text and image are given, taking place, and so becoming available after the event. Simply seeing what is there is insufficient. It is necessary that the subject read what is there, reading the image and so writing the text, translating from the materiality of the world into the materiality of the text, as that first, initially pre-phenomenal materiality gives itself to the subject as translatable phenomena. The world is thus seen, read and known, through a subjective schematisation of experience 'of the legible and the visible in a chiasmic mode' figured in the 'common ground' (Louvel 2011, 39) that is subjectivity. The subject is, we might say, revealed as the site of a deconstructive phenomenology, whereby the authenticity and historicity of place may come to be figured as the supplement of experience, and so made available in iterable revenance, as if the experience were, phantasmally, my own. That we are meant to see the larger world in the smaller, to take Jaggers's room as visual figure for that larger world of death-dealing London cannot be in doubt, if we remember that the particular location is 'Little Britain', the neighbourhood and street in the City, which runs from St Martin's Le Grand to Smithfield. Pip's vision is thus one of the unseen everyday, the hidden within the visible; there is, in this, the formulation of what Markus Poetzsch has called 'visionary dreariness' (2006), an inheritance of Romantic apprehension at the level of the quotidian.

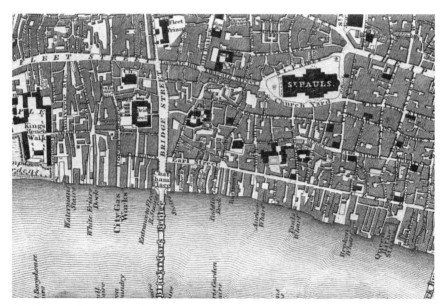

Blackfriars, Fleet Street, Fleet Prison, St Paul's Cathedral

Exteriors • Golden Square, Portland Place, Bryanstone Square

Nicholas Nickleby / Dombey and Son

Although a few members of the graver professions live about Golden Square, it is not exactly in anybody's way to or from anywhere. It is one of the squares that have been; a quarter of the town that has gone down in the world, and taken to letting lodgings. Many of its first and second floors are let, furnished, to single gentlemen; and it takes boarders besides. It is a great resort of foreigners. The dark-complexioned men who wear large rings, and heavy watch-guards, and bushy whiskers, and who congregate under the Opera Colonnade, and about the box-office in the season, between four and five in the afternoon, when they give away the orders,—all live in Golden Square, or within a street of it. Two or three violins and a wind instrument from the Opera band reside within its precincts. Its boarding-houses are musical, and the notes of pianos and harps float in the evening time round the head of the mournful statue, the guardian genius of a little wilderness of shrubs, in the centre of the square. On a summer's night, windows are thrown open, and groups of swarthy moustached men are seen by the passer-by, lounging at the casements, and smoking fearfully. Sounds of gruff voices practising vocal music invade the evening's silence; and the fumes of choice tobacco scent the air. There, snuff and cigars, and German pipes and flutes, and violins and violoncellos, divide the supremacy between them. It is the region of song and smoke. Street bands are on their mettle in Golden Square; and itinerant glee-singers quaver involuntarily as they raise their voices within its boundaries. (*NN* 65)

In that quarter of London in which Golden Square is situated, there is a bygone, faded, tumbledown street, with two irregular rows of tall meagre houses, which seem to have stared each other out of countenance years ago. The very chimneys appear to have grown dismal and melancholy, from having had nothing better to look at than the chimneys over the way. Their tops are battered, and broken, and blackened with smoke; and here and there some taller stack than the rest, inclining heavily to one side, and toppling over the roof, seems to meditate taking revenge for half a century's neglect, by crushing the inhabitants of the garrets beneath.

The fowls who peck about the kennels, jerking their bodies hither and thither with a gait which none but town fowls are ever seen to adopt, and which any country cock or hen would be puzzled to understand, are perfectly in keeping with the crazy habitations of their owners. Dingy, ill-plumed, drowsy flutterers, sent, like many of the neighbouring children, to get a livelihood in the streets, they hop from stone to stone in forlorn search of some hidden eatable in the mud, and can scarcely raise a crow among them . . .

To judge from the size of the houses, they have been at one time tenanted by persons of better condition than their present occupants, but they are now let off by the week in floors or rooms, and every door has almost as many plates or bell-handles as there are apartments within. The windows are for the same reason sufficiently diversified in appearance, being ornamented with every variety of common blind and curtain that can easily be imagined, while every doorway is blocked up and rendered nearly impassable by a motley collection of children and porter pots of all sizes, from the baby in arms and the half-pint pot, to the full-grown girl and half-gallon can.

In the parlour of one of these houses, which was perhaps a thought dirtier than any of its neighbours; which exhibited more bell-handles, children and porter pots, and caught in all its freshness the first gust of the thick black smoke that poured forth night and day from a large brewery hard by, hung a bill announcing that there was yet one room to let within its walls, although on what storey the vacant room would be—regard being had to the outward tokens of many lodgers which the whole front displayed, from the mangle in the kitchen window to the flower-pots on the parapet—it would have been beyond the power of a calculating boy to discover.

The common stairs of this mansion were bare and carpetless; but a curious visitor who had to climb his way to the top, might have observed that there were not wanting indications of the progressive poverty of the inmates, although their rooms were shut. Thus the first-floor lodgers, being flush of furniture, kept an old mahogany table—real mahogany—on the landing place outside, which was only taken in when occasion required. On the second storey the spare furniture dwindled down to a couple of old deal chairs, of which one, belonging to the back room, was shorn of a leg and bottomless. The storey above boasted no greater excess than a worm-eaten wash-tub: and the garret landing-place displayed no costlier articles than two crippled pitchers, and some broken blacking-bottles. (*NN* 227–8)

Mr Dombey's house was a large one, on the shady side of a tall, dark, dreadfully genteel street in the region between Portland Place and Bryanstone Square. It was a corner house, with great wide areas containing cellars frowned upon by barred windows, and leered at by crooked-eyed doors leading to dustbins. It was a house of dismal state, with a circular back to it, containing a whole suite of drawing-rooms looking upon a gravelled yard, where two gaunt trees, with blackened trunks and branches, rattled rather than rustled, their leaves were so smoked-dried. The summer sun was never on the street, but in the morning about breakfast-time, when it came with the water-carts and the old clothes men, and the people with geraniums, and the umbrella-mender, and the man who trilled the little bell of the Dutch clock as he went along. It was soon gone again to return no more that day; and the bands of music and the straggling Punch's shows going after it, left

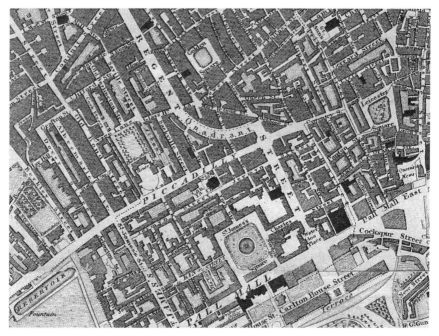

Golden Square, Gerrard Street, Soho

it a prey to the most dismal of organs, and white mice; with now and then a porcupine, to vary the entertainments; until the butlers whose families were dining out, began to stand at the house-doors in the twilight, and the lamp-lighter made his nightly failure in attempting to brighten up the street with gas. (DS 74–5)

Faded Gentility • Camden Town

David Copperfield

It may have been ... for no better reason than because there was a certain similarity in the sound of the words skittles and Traddles, that it came into my head, next day, to go and look after Traddles. The time he had mentioned was more than out, and he lived in a little street, near the Veterinary College at Camden Town, which was principally tenanted, as one of our clerks who lived in that direction informed me, by gentlemen students, who bought live donkeys, and made experiments on those quadrupeds in their private apartments. Having obtained from this clerk a direction to the academic grove in question, I set out, the same afternoon, to visit my old schoolfellow.

I found that the street was not as desirable a one as I could have wished it to be, for the sake of Traddles. The inhabitants appeared to have a propensity to throw any little trifles they were not in want of, into the road: which not only made it rank and sloppy, but untidy too, on account of the cabbage-leaves. The refuse was not wholly vegetable either, for I myself saw a shoe, a doubled-up saucepan, a black bonnet, and an umbrella, in various stages of decomposition, as I was looking out for the number I wanted.

The general air of the place reminded me forcibly of the days when I lived with Mr and Mrs Micawber. An indescribable character of faded gentility that attached to the house I sought, and made it unlike all the other houses in the street—though they were all built on one monotonous pattern, and looked like the early copies of a blundering boy who was learning to make houses, and had not yet got out of his cramped brick-and-mortar pothooks—reminded me still more of Mr and Mrs Micawber. [. . .]

When I got to the top of the stairs—the house was only one story high above the ground-floor—Traddles was on the landing to meet me. He . . . gave me welcome . . . to his little room. It was in the front of the house, and extremely neat, though sparely furnished. It was his only room, I saw; for there was a sofa-bedstead in it, and his blacking-brushes and blacking were among his books—on the top shelf, behind the dictionary. His table was covered with papers, and he was hard at work in an old coat. I looked at nothing, that I know of, but I saw everything, even to the prospect of a church upon his china inkstand, as I sat down—and this, too, was a faculty confirmed in me in the old Micawber times. Various ingenious arrangements he had made, for the disguise of his chest of drawers, and the accommodation of his boots, his shaving-glass, and so forth, particularly impressed themselves upon me, as evidences of the same Traddles who used to make models of elephants' dens in writing-paper to put flies in; and to comfort himself, under ill usage, with the memorable works of art I have so often mentioned. (*DC* 372–3, 374)

Here, typically for David Copperfield, place and memory are associated, in this case the particular *lieux de mémoire* having the power to recall not experience of Camden side-streets themselves, but other times and places for David. Place provokes memory but not of itself; rather the subject connects with his other selves, and in this manner to the memory of others, and other perceptions, by associative analogy; the phenomena of the scene engender the modality of re-presentation. This is so whether Copperfield observes the conditions of the streets surrounding the Veterinary College, or, somewhat differently, the condition of Traddles's room. This is, itself, a singular location in a singular building, all the more worthy of remark apparently, and so worthy of our attention, precisely because its singularity stands out despite the building resembling every other house in the terrace. Typical, again, of a Copperfield narration is the hybrid determination of place through the mix of the ordinary and the exotic – or, perhaps more precisely, the filtering of the quotidian through an exotic prism of the imaginary, whereby an aesthetic apprehension serves in exceeding representation in order to draw attention to detail and, simultaneously, to make strange the unremarkable, bringing out the visible from the invisible. This quality of exoticism is extended further in the narrator's registration of the uses to which items are put, or otherwise made different from themselves and their proper uses, by Traddles in his room. The exoticism of phenomena resides, therefore, in their exhaustion, their inutility, their confusion and disorder, or else in their being put to uses for which they were not intended. In this, Traddles and the neighbourhood belong to one another. As there are various 'little trifles' – as David calls them; whether with an affected nicety or irony it is hard to tell – of the vegetable and inorganic kind thrown into the street, so Traddles's papers cover the table, his blacking and brushes wedged behind the dictionary; his chest of drawers is 'disguised', and his other personal items stowed in such a way as to call up for David the memory of a younger Traddles. Objects in themselves are nothing, but, associated with another, they are keys to remembrance, as well as the personality of another, who haunts the present older self in the maintenance of habit.

All this is seen without looking: 'I looked at nothing, that I know of, but I saw everything.' In Copperfield's admission there is sketched a connection between unconscious awareness and visionary perception, which by-passes both the material world and the present, the details to return only in memory. Reality acts as the prompt for the element of unreality to surface in the image of what is there and the vision of what is not, strictly speaking. What is seen can only be seen authentically in a belated manner, in the mode of a reverie, 'in the dreams of memory' that affect, Gaston Bachelard notes, 'the dreamer when he is faced with the most concrete things' (Bachelard 1994, 59), beginning with the experience and perception of the street in Camden Town. Though the places Copperfield has occasion to visit are not his, not concrete locations belonging to his experience or memory, yet there is that in them which assumes, or gives to Copperfield, a sequence of phantasmal images conjured from memories of childhood. This is all the more marked because the narrator has already acknowledged lack of knowledge about Camden in passing, having asked 'one of our clerks' for directions. Though the doxa concerning medical students' experiments on donkeys might be taken as a sign of what is to come for the reader, yet it is only fully in the face-to-face encounter with the trifles of the street and, subsequently, the confined disarray of Traddles's quarters, that the subject's act of re-presentation comes into being. It is perhaps in the chance aural association of 'skittles' and 'Traddles' that the seed of the unreal might be said to have begun to germinate, preparing Copperfield, despite his topographical unfamiliarity, to enter so unexpectedly into the instant visionary revenance, where 'imagination, memory and perception exchange functions'. In this way, the image – a sonic image given a particular form in that moment of linguistic condensation – 'is created through co-operation between the real and unreal' (Bachelard 1994, 59), the imminent become manifest through the encounter between subject and place, however unfamiliar with the concrete reality of Camden David might be. The past thus returns, 'situated elsewhere', 'time and place impregnated with a sense of unreality . . . Thus, on the threshold of our space, before the era of our own time, we hove between awareness of being and loss of being.' And, Bachelard observes, 'the entire reality of memory becomes spectral' (Bachelard 1994, 58).

That which is observed in its oddity, its inutility, misuse or incongruity causes to reveal, through its perceived strangeness and the estrangement it unveils from within itself, the ability to give the younger self to the older subject, as the younger subject calls to his older, unaware *doppelgänger*, from within the uncanny singularity of the object and its phenomenal oscillation. One's being comes to be given, to return as the ghost of being, in the estrangement of the image and in that – again singular – juxtaposition of images. Singularity has arisen through conjunction, material forms in perceived relation mimicking, and perhaps echoing, or perhaps supplementing, that earlier chance association and condensation of the motifs 'skittles' and 'Traddles'. Singularity in this instance – first, the subjective association between words, through sonorous approximation and, subsequently, the emergence of Traddles's house as singular despite its being exactly the same as all the other houses in the street – presents itself precisely in what is taking place in David, through the complex interplay and tensions between past and present, perception and re-presentation, image and memory.

What I have called 'conflation' and 'condensation' here is also, strangely, a motion of displacement, that which Freud had termed *Verschiebung*, and which is only poorly served in the English term 'displacement', the one suggesting the other through that 'certain similarity in the sound', but also there being marked the movement, the shift or motion, the displacement by which this extract appears motivated, and which in turn informs David's perceptions of Camden and the subsequent emergence of the occluded relation between self and place. David, a stranger to this neighbourhood of north London, is displaced from within himself, a shift occurring within him, as memory, image and perception are, themselves, the subjects and vehicles of phenomenal dislocation. What the reader witnesses taking place in David's subjective experience of Camden, therefore, is what Bachelard terms a 'decisive psychic action' in the 'dynamic imagination' (Bachelard 1994, 198). However, that action, whereby condensation and displacement determine the instant of visionary revenance, does not 'save' the subject from the painful memory. Instead, the self in the present and the present place are displaced by the return of what Copperfield calls here 'the old Micawber times', which times return through that portal in reality opened by both the play between game (skittles) and name (Traddles), and those phenomena in the street (shoes, cabbage leaves, saucepans, bonnets, decaying umbrellas), which, if they do not change names exactly, are metonymic[17] to the extent that they change from being functional realities to become unreal and incapable of functioning. Out of the immensity unfolded through the action of place upon Copperfield through the subject's perception of Camden Town, an unexpected intimacy, a proximity that is emotional and psychic rather than simply material or topographical, reveals itself, between subject and place. Unreal London can arrive, without warning, with a greater force and the ability to touch one uncannily, even at those moments when this is little to be expected. The small, the inconsequential and the random, are not always what they appear in reality.

Gothic • Seven Dials, Walworth, Covent Garden, India House, Aldgate Pump, Whitechapel Church, Commercial Road, Wapping Old Stairs, St George's in the East, Snow Hill, Newgate

Sketches by Boz / The Uncommercial Traveller / Nicholas Nickleby

But what involutions can compare with those of Seven Dials? Where is there such another maze of streets, courts, lanes, and alleys? Where such a pure mixture of Englishmen and Irishmen, as in this complicated part of London? . . .

The stranger who finds himself in 'The Dials' for the first time, and stands Belzoni like, at the entrance of seven obscure passages, uncertain which to take, will see enough around him to keep his curiosity and attention awake for no inconsiderable time. From the irregular square into which he has plunged, the streets and courts dart in all directions, until they are lost in the unwholesome vapour which hangs over the house tops, and renders the dirty perspective uncertain and confined . . .

The peculiar character of these streets, and the close resemblance each one bears to its neighbour, by no means tends to decrease the bewilderment in which the unexperienced wayfarer through 'the Dials' finds himself involved. He traverses streets of dirty, straggling houses, with now and then an unexpected court composed of buildings as ill proportioned and deformed as the half naked children that wallow in the kennels. Here and there, a little dark chandler's shop, with a cracked bell hung up behind the door . . . some handsome lofty building, which usurps the place of a low dingy public house; long rows of brown and patched windows . . . shops for the purchase of rags, bones, old iron, and kitchen stuff . . . Brokers' shops . . . interspersed with announcements of day-schools, penny theatres, petition writers, mangles, and music for balls or routs, complete the 'still life' of the subject; and dirty men, filthy women, squalid children, fluttering shuttlecocks, noisy battledores, reeking pipes, bad fruit, more than doubtful oysters, attenuated cats, depressed dogs, and anatomical fowls, are its cheerful accompaniments. (*SB* 70–4)

The back part of Walworth, at its greatest distance from town, is a straggling miserable place enough, even in these days; but, five-and-thirty years ago, the greater portion of it was little better than a dreary waste, inhabited by a few scattered people of questionable character, whose poverty prevented their living in any better neighbourhood, or whose pursuits or mode of life rendered its solitude desirable. Very many of the houses which have since sprung up on all sides, . . . were of the rudest and most miserable description.

The appearance of the place . . . was not calculated to raise the spirits . . . or to dispel any feeling of anxiety or depression . . . [the] way lay across a marshy common, through irregular lanes, with here and there a ruinous and dismantled cottage fast falling to pieces with decay and neglect. A stunted tree, or pool of stagnant water, roused into a sluggish action by the heavy rain of the preceding night, skirted the path occasionally; and, now and then, a miserable patch of garden ground, with a few old boards knocked together for a summer house, and old palings imperfectly mended with stakes pilfered from the neighbouring hedges bore testimony, at once to the poverty of the inhabitants, and the little scruple they entertained in appropriating the property of other people to their own use . . . scarcely anything was stirring around; and so much of the prospect as could be faintly traced through the cold damp mist which hung heavily over it, presented a lonely and dreary appearance perfectly in keeping with the objects we have described. (*SB* 363–4)

My day's no-business beckoning me to the East-end of London, I had turned my face to that point of the metropolitan compass on leaving Covent-garden, and had got past the India House, thinking in my idle manner of Tippoo-Sahib and Charles Lamb, and had got past my little wooden mid-shipman, after affectionately patting him on one leg of his knee-shorts for old acquaintance' sake, and had got past Aldgate Pump, and had got past the Saracen's Head (with an ignominious rash of posting bills disfiguring his swarthy countenance), and had strolled up the empty yard of his ancient neighbour the Black or Blue Boar, or Bull, who departed this life I don't know when, and whose coaches are all gone I don't know where; and I had come out again into the age of railways, and I had got past Whitechapel Church, and was—rather inappropriately for an Uncommercial Traveller— in the Commercial Road. Pleasantly wallowing in the abundant mud of that thoroughfare, and greatly enjoying the huge piles of building belonging to the sugar refiners, the little masts and vanes in small back gardens in back streets, the neighbouring canals and docks, the India vans lumbering along their stone tramway, and the pawnbrokers' shops where hard-up Mates had pawned so many sextants and quadrants, that I should have bought a few cheap if I had the least notion how to use them, I at last began to file off to the right, towards Wapping.

   Not that I intended to take boat at Wapping Old Stairs, or that I was going to look at the locality, because I believe (for I don't) in the constancy of the young woman who told her sea-going lover, to such a beautiful old tune, that she had ever continued the same, since she gave him the 'baccer-box marked with his name; I am afraid he usually got the worst of those transactions, and was frightfully taken in. No, I was going to Wapping, because an Eastern police magistrate had said, through the morning papers, that there was no classification at the Wapping workhouse for women, and that it was a dis-grace and a shame, and divers other hard names, and because I wished to see how the fact really stood. For, that Eastern police magistrates are not always the wisest men of the East, may be inferred from their course of procedure respecting the fancy-dressing and pantomime-posturing at St. George's in that quarter: which is usually, to discuss the matter at issue, in a state of mind

betokening the weakest perplexity, with all parties concerned and uncon-
cerned, and, for a final expedient, to consult the complainant as to what he
thinks ought to be done with the defendant, and take the defendant's opinion
as to what he would recommend to be done with himself.

Long before I reached Wapping, I gave myself up as having lost my way,
and, abandoning myself to the narrow streets in a Turkish frame of mind,
relied on predestination to bring me somehow or other to the place I wanted
if I were ever to get there. When I had ceased for an hour or so to take any
trouble about the matter, I found myself on a swing-bridge looking down
at some dark locks in some dirty water. Over against me, stood a creature
remotely in the likeness of a young man, with a puffed sallow face, and a
figure all dirty and shiny and slimy, who may have been the youngest son of
his filthy old father, Thames, or the drowned man about whom there was a
placard on the granite post like a large thimble, that stood between us.

I asked this apparition what it called the place? Unto which, it replied, with
a ghastly grin and a sound like gurgling water in its throat:

'Mr. Baker's trap.' (*UT* Ch. III)

at the very core of London, at the heart of its business and animation, in the
midst of a whirl of noise and motion: stemming as it were the giant currents
of life that flow ceaselessly on from different quarters . . . stands Newgate;
and in that crowded street on which it frowns so darkly . . . scores of human
beings, amidst a roar of sounds to which even the tumult of a great city is as
nothing, four, six, or eight strong men at a time, have been hurried violently
and swiftly from the world, when the scene has been rendered frightful with
excess of human life . . . (*NN*, 89)

Along a narrow passage, up a dark stair, through a crazy door, into a room
not very light, not very large, not in the least splendid; with queer corners,
and quaint carvings, and massive chimney-pieces; with tall cupboards with
prim doors, and squat counters with deep dumpy drawers; with packages,
out of whose ends flash all the colours of the rainbow—where all is as quiet
as a playhouse at daybreak, or a church at midnight—where, in truth, there
is nobody to make a noise, except one well dressed man, one attendant porter
(neither of whom seem to be doing anything in particular), and one remark-
ably fine male cat, admiring, before the fire, the ends of his silky paws—where
the door, as we enter, shuts with a deep, dull, muffled sound, that is more
startling than a noise—where there is less bustle than at a Quakers' meeting,
and less business going on than in a Government office—the well-dressed
man threads the mazes of the piles, and desks, and cupboards and counters,
with a slow step, to greet us, and to assure us, in reply to our apology, that we
have *not* made any mistake whatever, and that we are in the silk warehouse
which we seek . . . (*SJ* 295)

'Self-consciousness is only *something*, it only has *reality*, insofar as it
estranges itself,' observes Hegel (1977, 363–4). What estrangement
might be is another matter; but it is at least remarked through a certain
self-consciousness, an awareness or self-perception in relation to the

experience of place. Such estrangement might come in the form of terror, boredom, ennui, anxiety, resignation, melancholy or some more inchoate sensibility. Whatever the determining modality or motif, the tenor or hue, so to speak, estrangement is only possible in relation to an other, in a relation that is a response, and this comes about only in the face of a phenomenal encounter, by which I am suddenly called from my forgetfulness of myself, to become the I who responds: 'nothing manages to give itself as a phenomenon if a response does not give itself over to it as an originary claim' (Marion 1998, 198). I give myself to myself as subject of some experience, event, place and perception focused in this intimate interchange. 'The claim calls me' (Marion 1998, 198).

In a number of ways Dickensian subjectivity is always estranged by London, called by it, called into the estranged existence of a response that always has a particular modality of perception, presentation and re-presentation; the urban subject in the text of Dickens comes into being through the estrangement that is attendant on the encounter with urban modernity, through a response to what the city gives, which response finds itself formed through the presentation of image as memory and re-representation of perception, experience and event. Consciousness arrives as a self-consciousness of one's place and time through the estrangement that the encounter with London causes. London gives to the subject an awareness, a self-consciousness, of being in a given place, at a given moment. The motif of the self is thus generated in giving form to the belated recollection of the earlier perception. A Dickensian urban and, as I am arguing, modern subjectivity is produced, moreover, even as this is filtered through tropes that are often recognisably Gothic; in order to 'invent' the modern urban self in the face of the material conditions of the city, the constitution of the subject in relation to the urban location is formed through recourse to the language, the tropes, of Gothic narrative. There is a necessary recourse to the literary in order to give language to an experience of the modern for which there is, at the moment of that first encounter with the urban, no accessible originary register.[18]

The subject, irreducible to any given character, is that which presents itself, is given, perceived or implied *as* or *through* the narrator or narrator-effect, and imagined as the place on to which the city is projected and from which a text is written or, seemingly, spoken. Subjectivity is no longer 'in itself', but is presented; it 'refers to and presupposes sensibility [oriented by, and towards, the encounter with a particular aspect of London], while this givenness presupposes an original body that is always the ultimate givenness' (Henry 2008, 110). Self and locus – manifested through the phantasm of the 'narrator' – are always insuperable in this relation. Analogue to London, or to that singular urban locus in which the subject is found, and finds himself (or herself), subjectivity reads / writes that which calls for attestation and which inscribes itself on to the subject. Otherwise a pure nothingness, subjectivity must be the trace of a materiality and historicity before 'it' is anything. Responding to, and with respect to the other – *respect* [-*spectare*; *specere*] announces an authentic envisioning, regardless of whatever anachronies, paradoxes or contradictions might appear to inform the image, the memory, the re-representation, which extends beyond, or unfolds from within, in excess of mere empirical sight –[19]; responding that is to say, to the phenomena of the city as these come to be given at a particular moment, the 'narrator' is thus given in that time, and for that time only, save for its becoming iterable in being read by another. The more subjectivity attends to detail, the more that detail applies to the subject, but only on the condition that one recognises, not a local attentiveness on the part of someone – this would be to make of the spectral condition of narration an object in the form of a body, the 'narrator'[20]; rather, a pure attentiveness, an authentic attestation comes to be given, with the possibility of that attestation and vision being reiterated *for* the good reader. Such a chance is enabled, in the present examples, by those motifs of the Gothic, which have the force to appeal to radically different sensibilities, at different times.

From a critical apprehension of subjectivity given form in narration, we will more clearly be able to understand consciousness as a phe-nomenon bearing witness, but also shaped in its response, to London. As I have suggested elsewhere, there are certain examples where the 'Dickensian narrator' is, if not pure appearance, then neither fully 'fleshed' nor realised. There is no body or embodiment save for a phan-tasmal concatenation of the traces of phenomena. This shadowy figure is maintained through the incarnation of the city given voice, a coming, a givenness, that takes place between, in the 'inter-space [*l'entre-deux*]' (Nancy 2008, 64/5) constituted through place and consciousness, *as* the authenticity of historicised attestation. Dickensian urban subjectivity is both a phenomenon of the city and a screen on to which the material-ity of the early nineteenth-century metropolis is projected. The subject as 'form' – a form given shape through narration in response and as witness to the city – '*consists in this, that a now becomes constituted by means of an impression*', and furthermore, that impression is con-stituted through 'a trail of retentions and a horizon of protentions . . . [as this] abiding form supports the consciousness of constant change' (Husserl 1995, 118). The successive *now* of any narrating, narrated re-presentation of the city is, therefore, always the impression left by the material historicity of place, which must subsequently be given form through available language. But it is formulated on several occasions, in the singular example of the text of Dickens through the retention of the Gothic trope, as fictive memory appropriate to the re-presentation of the city, and as that fictive modality that serves to inform in the face of the otherwise inexpressible. It is thus the anachronistic contest between Gothic and modern, which presents London and a subjectivity appropriate to it in the nineteenth century.

Equally, the 'Gothic' is not just the 'intertextual' aesthetic modality through which subject–place relation is made normative – if anything, 'Gothic' is domesticated, in part. Importantly, 'Gothic' in the passages in question and elsewhere in the text of Dickens is translated into a modality of gaze, rendering the incommensurable into a visual impression, for what Liliane Louvel describes as the art of memory (2008, 2). Here, then, experiment with form results from walking the streets, and with that the transformation of both memory into re-presentation, in order that the experience of the subject be made transmissible to another reception, another perception, and the experimentation with traditional form in the face of the monstrous novelty and modernity of the city; *literary* language undergoes an invention that maintains its transference while the urban impression finds appropriate, and therefore authentic, production through what Roger Fry, apropos Vanessa Bell, described as the 'plastic sense' working 'its way in words', giving itself to be *seen*.

Apropos the subject of urban Gothic and, especially, the representation of London, four or five questions arise immediately as co-ordinates for this otherwise impossible topography: *Who* is the subject in Dickens? *What* is the subject in Dickens? What does the text of Dickens give us to see, producing both for and in us a mode, if not of connection, then perhaps communication between the *who* and the *what*, albeit of a fragmentary and discontinuous kind? Fourth question: in what ways does the *what* address the *who*, producing in the process and manner of address a subject who not only bears witness to the city but, in effect and apprehension, becomes written by the urban, as the city's subject? Certain answers suggest themselves in part, and can be found in the sketch of 'Seven Dials', to which I will turn shortly.

Before that, however, it is necessary to give consciousness to character briefly, if only so as to illustrate the principles of subjectivity more broadly and, it is hoped, more immediately. Although, at the risk of repeating myself, character is not my focus, to grasp from the outset how we might begin to respond to the questions I have raised it is helpful to pause over an example of the proximity in formation between a particular character's self-consciousness and early phenomenological definitions of reflective being, as an initial stage in the present investigation. Kevin McLaughlin provides such a model (1993, 875–90). He offers the comparison between Esther Summerson and Hegel's theorisation of what the philosopher calls 'self-estranged spirit'. McLaughlin is particularly interested in that initial moment when, following her recovery from smallpox, Esther observes herself in a mirror, commenting on how strange she looks to herself (*BH* 572). Having first drawn back a muslin veil that covers the mirror, in a miniature domestic imitation of all such Gothic scenes where a curtain or tapestry is drawn aside, a door opened, the threshold interrupted and ruptured to reveal the monstrous other, Esther remarks on her reflection, not herself; privileging the givenness of the phenomenal other rather than seeing it as Being, she refers to the reflection as 'it', an inhuman displacement of herself in a moment of stark reduction, which, neutrally she marks, looks back 'placidly' at her (*BH* 572). The placidity is that of the death mask, echoing and intensifying the work of the ungendered pronoun; alike and yet not like, lacking all animation, the face of the other returns in this intimate moment, before, in that instant of self-conscious estrangement, Esther perceives the strangeness of the face. We may interpret the scene as shocking, folding ourselves into the Gothic. For Esther, however, there is no such colouration of the impression. For McLaughlin, here is that phenomenological revelation of subjectivity in its haunted relation to itself addressed by Hegel in the comment with which I began. Such 'estrangement' is not overdetermined by the modality of perception it adopts; it is just consciousness giving itself to the subject in a manner that cannot be conveyed wholly to another, and of which, therefore, one must form an impression, seeing with an intuitive sense, with respect to the other. It is in recognition of this that Lizzie Hexam responds to Charley, when he asks that she show him the pictures she witnesses in the burning coals, '"Ah! It wants my eyes, Charley"' (*OMF* 37). Charley has the good sense at least to ask Lizzie to narrate the vision, apprehending the distinction between the impossibility of showing and the possibility of telling. Vision remains singular, estranged; telling has to bear the burden of witness and attestation, therefore.

While more might be said concerning Hegel's theorisation of the subject, let us leave Esther looking at her other self and continue with a remark on the limit of McLaughlin's reading. Whilst McLaughlin is right to make the comparison, reading Esther's estranged self-reading as a conscious displacement effected in the subject through the encounter with the self as other, what this does not account for is the source of such all such subjectivity in Dickens. Subjectivity always begins as estranged, subject to its own knowledge as singular participant *and* observer, through the encounter with and experience of the event of the city, of what takes place and comes to pass. There is no subjectivity for

Dickens without the earliest experiences and representations of London. The text of the city gives voice and impression, word and vision, to a strikingly modern consciousness, a consciousness necessarily estranged in the condition of its nascent modernity. London shapes – or deforms – subjectivity. And this subject is both modern *and* Gothic: modern because of the phenomenological register and reinscription of subjectivity as mediating identity and medium for the other; and Gothic because subjectivity, in being displaced, doubled, deferred from any pure presence, finds itself, is taken by surprise by its other self, as *always already* perceived, and perceives itself as being a haunted structure within which the flight and flux of becoming is rendered momentarily available.

Consider the commentary on Seven Dials, first published in *Bell's Life in London*, 27 September 1837. 'Where', inquires our narrator, 'is there such another maze of streets, courts, lanes and alleys . . . as in this complicated part of London?' Here is a place, unlike any other – except that, in Dickens, every singular site is just like every other singular site in its difference – comprising 'obscure passages' and an 'irregular square'. The 'peculiar character' is in the perception of their close resemblance to one another. Every street is different but every street looks the same as every other. Thus, the impression of the 'stranger' or 'unexperienced wayfarer',[21] who 'finds himself involved', his bewilderment 'increased' at every turn. Now and then, here and there: the impression, the image, intuition and vision, are all sudden surges, iterable confrontations and the repetition spatially and temporally of the same estrangement, the immersion in the labyrinthine, as the very condition of perception. This 'stranger', it is imagined, who has 'plunged' into this square, will perceive himself as lost, disorientated, as the streets and courts 'dart in all directions until they are lost in the unwholesome vapour which hangs over the house tops, and renders the dirty perspective uncertain and confined'. Something fascinating and complex is in motion here, as a result of plunging into 'these streets' with their 'peculiar character'.

From the questions defying certainty with which the image begins, and which themselves have sprung not from reality but narrative recollection, the reader is immediately plunged into the experience, perception and impression of the 'stranger'. There is in the stranger's vision a curious moment of abyssal uncertainty. For the image, in being circumscribed visually by a miasma hanging on the roofs, at once 'renders the perspective uncertain and confined'. Uncertain *and* confined? At once, the perception is of an abyss and a cell, of indistinguishable endlessness *and* enclosure. What the stranger experiences, the narrator re-presents, as if the discourse of the latter were simply the transcribed sensate apprehension of the other. Though no double is encountered, yet there takes place what can be called a *doppelgänger-effect*. An uncanny phenomenon, and perhaps the locus where Gothic and modern intersect through the agency of the urban, doubling, displacing and refiguring subjects is a not infrequent device in the text of Dickens. Here, though, the narrator and the stranger are, in effect, if not one and the same, then overlaid one on the other, each a partial palimpsest of the other; each is the displaced, estranged and doubled figure of the other: the one invisible, paused, observing in detail that which would keep one's 'curiosity and attention awake for no inconsiderable time', the other unable to orientate himself. Already doubled, the narrator's selfhood has no greater vantage point than that of the stranger, his other, and so is demoted from transcendental primacy. In this, the reader apprehends narratorial subjectivity as 'the condition of the experience of the other' (Henry 2008, 110). And as the stranger is lost, so too are the streets, becoming invisible at a certain distance, from flagstones to rooftops. Elements in the scene appear momentarily, pausing before that plunge, that disappearance and anonymity. All we witness, our narrating subject assures us, 'would fill any mind but a regular Londoner's with astonishment' (*SB* 72), a phrase implicitly placing the 'regularity' of the Londoner against the irregularity of topography, architecture, map and the city in general. That mind, the stranger's, we already know and will continue to find out, is confronted by confusion, complication, excess, indecipherability and, as we have observed, 'bewilderment'. No further familiarity with the streets or their character will 'decrease the bewilderment in which the unexperienced wayfarer . . . finds himself involved'. There is here, to stress the point, a serial iterability, a duplication and a return of the same in which self gives way to perception, and the stranger is reduced to the condition of a thing, uncannily alive *and* dead, through a perceptual experience that is scarcely delimitable.

Not yet obviously Gothic in its figural work, save perhaps for the intuition of the labyrinth, the experience of which maintains just below the surface the immanent though inchoate (as yet) anxiety of loss of self, the passage none the less invents a mode of representation and re-representation, experience and perception, which, in the modernity of its subjective partiality and loss, bespeaks in an original manner that constellation of sensations and apprehension attributed to the Gothic subject. In the figure of the labyrinth, the Gothic might be said to appear to the extent that the subject desires the familiarity of an aesthetic form, with all the stability which that promises, in order to keep at bay the truly vertiginous, disorienting and threatening demands of the labyrinth on the self. Gothic form, Gothic trope, Gothic narrative: all are submerged into Gothic sensibility, a constellated sensibility of perceptual engulfment in the face of phenomenal overflow or excess that is, it might be said, as atavistic as it might be said to be Freudian or Heideggerian in its modernity. (Again, the proper name functions much as the idea of the Gothic, in order to determine ontologically, and so keep at bay the unspeakable threat to the subject.) Confusion, loss, doubling and iterable fragmentation, disorientation, anxiety and one's suddenly perceiving oneself as being caught up in something beyond one's knowledge, all elements of Gothic sensibility if not narration, are figured here *just as* the identity of one London district *and*, simultaneously, the event of perception for narrator and stranger alike.

Such experience is implied as that which the contours of that district are capable of projecting on to, thereby determining the subject. This district only serves to heighten, furthermore, the subject's anonymity in the experience in which, if we recall the phrase, 'he finds himself involved.' Subjectivity is illuminated only through being estranged and becoming conscious of itself, as estranged and as an other, always on the threshold of abjection. If, as Maurice Natanson claims, '[e]ssentially, the way in which I know the Other is through the largely tacit construction of a miniature ideal type' (Natanson 1979, 535), then in 'Seven Dials', the only way I know the other is to see him iterated and divided between the stranger and the analogous apperception of the narrating subject, and to perceive myself in both of those. In this there is the uncanny experience of perceiving simultaneously relation and the unfamiliar, the *doppelgänger* in the self's relation to another like itself. Concomitantly, the transcendental privilege my Ego affords me is diminished, if not lost, also. Not having the certainty of stability, subjectivity is given in moments of suspension before an image or in instances of intensified self-conscious reflection. This is extended from the human to the non-human, from the animate to the inanimate, architecture the analogue for the human, in those 'buildings as ill proportioned and deformed as the half naked children'. Is it that the buildings are anthropomorphised or the children dehumanised? The undecidability of the image might be said to invoke the uncanny, and this all the more so, not because this is a scene of remote horror, but instead an intimate encounter with, and memory of that which appalls in being the extreme of the urban condition for many, brought into the vision of the subject.

As buildings and streets reiterate themselves, so too is there a resemblance between one character and his neighbour. That being so, my loss of self, and that concomitant estrangement of relation, comes in seeing how, like those figures of the other, visible and invisible, I am unable to extricate myself from this labyrinthine and threatening location, in which *I find myself involved*. All I am left with, finally, is to stand before

a '"still life"', the image suspending all motion; I confront genre painting, scenes of everyday life – familiar through the images of London
produced by Hogarth – transposed or translated into another genre, in
which all that remains for the subjective eye to observe is a list of the
objects represented therein. To call this a still life, as Boz does, is to
acknowledge formal arrangement over the natural, but to maintain the
neutral observation of phenomena as the basis for formal experiment. It
is also to admit to a shift in register occasioned by the modernity of the
urban, and the concomitant need for subjective perception to invent the
appropriate mode of re-presentation. Additionally, there is a closing up
at work in this. Suspension of all movement, save for the eye across the
'canvas' from Brokers' shops, to filthy women, to anatomical fowls and
attenuated cats, suggests the seeming arbitrariness of organisation whilst
also bringing the reader as close as possible to the image, in a collapse of
subject positions, so that *I* – like the stranger, the wayfarer, Boz – *find
myself involved*.

I employ this phrase again, because it signals the perceptual experience of reading / writing London in the wake of the event that determines one's selfhood *in* and in relation to place. To pursue the strong
reading, the modern urban subject, subjectivity in London, *finds itself*,
and finds itself moreover, coming to itself in that reflexive arrival of
consciousness as if by surprise, or as if encountering one's double in the
other, *involved*. Involvement is predicated on one's being in the midst
of becoming surrounded by or enveloped within the agency of material
and phenomenal forces; for the subject of London's streets, this enfolding is always double, for there is always the implication and impression,
and so the experience and perception on the one hand of the materiality
of the built environment, rising on all sides, obscuring vision even as it
occludes one, in principle, from the vision of another, while also, on the
other hand, the imposition on one's perception of the traces of the material, through the phenomenological reception. If one aspect of London's
modernity is its constant becoming, its being remade, remodelled, transformed, then the urban subject's modernity emerges as a becoming also,
significantly registered as a becoming-involved.

The written 'passages' of 'Seven Dials' act on the reading subject in
a manner analogous to the effect of the architectural and topographical
passages encountered by the stranger and the narrator-effect, that phantasm called Boz. There and not there, this figure re-presents in detail all
there is before the stranger, while admitting to the limits of representational power, and confessing furthermore that the city is ultimately
unknowable, impenetrable in its mysteries, and therefore undecidable.
The presumed universality of narrative realism, in its attention to detail,

collapses back into the partiality and interpretive provisionality of phenomenological perception. The passage thus closes in its play around
'still life', as the expression of a perceptual experience of a modernity,
which has become another *now*, and which, therefore, is also *my* experience. The 'pictorial genre, *topos* or technique', as Louvel puts it (2008,
9), highlights a moment in the literary when the aporetic experience of
the modern needs to be overcome, and this with a fall into an attestation
that is markedly subjective. This recursion is not, however, a failure but
a reduction, which, in freeing the elements of composition from their
being enchained in mimetic service, makes their fragmentary and iterable signs appear to *my* consciousness as the signs of historicity, thereby
exceeding the merely historical and the merely factual. Thus freed, communication of perceptual experience becomes, in Husserl's term 'virtual
. . . sensibly experienceable . . . Accordingly, then, the writing-down
effects a transformation of the original mode of being of the meaning
structure' (Husserl 1989, 164). This writing down, the reading / writing
by which initial perception becomes the transposition of memory, produces the illusion of the *acheiropoietic* image, a vision of what is merely
there, not crafted by a human hand and yet, also, the projection filtered
by subjective sensibility. The subject responds rather than creates; or, it
should be observed, the subject 'invents', finding rather than fashioning
anew, but giving as the response, the re-presentation of perceptual experience, the apparent novelty of what is found, so as to convey the experience of a first time. When I read it is as if that first time were my time.

Therefore, if, as Peter de Bolla argues, 'every age has its own concept
of selfhood, and every succeeding "age" may or may not choose to
interpret this concept in its own fashion, and very often in its own self-
image' (1989, 5), the 'age' of London's subject imposes a daunting task
on its readers in the formation of a consciousness capable of bearing
witness to the city, while also illuminating the process in all its historial,
phenomenal tenor. The singularity of the event, though never repeat-
able in its experience as such, is none the less open to transmission and
translation in the ways already considered. The frequent use of present
tense throughout the *Sketches* and later essays effects the transport
and phenomenal iterability between discrete moments or locations in
a more immediately accessible fashion, through the illusion of the 'as-
if-for-a-first-time'. Such a phantasmal experience is defined by Husserl
as *Erstmaligkeit*, a 'first-timeliness' 'as pertaining to a transcendental
history' which opens, in Derrida's reading of Husserl, a 'profoundly
reconceived, newly understood, "historical ground"' (Kates 2008, 139)
produced through the mediation and the material of language itself.[22]
Dickens's narrator-effect is thus the medium, not only between distinct

modes of being, the estranged being of the stranger and my estranged mode as reader, but also between modern consciousness and Gothic as an other sensibly experiential virtual reality producing not dissimilar experiences.

In this mediumistic transformation, the re-presentation of the perceptual experience of the city partakes of the less obvious and more playful aspects of Gothic discourse. If the Gothic consists in part of elements of carnivalesque, as Robert Miles asserts, along with 'contending discourses', having 'as their foci issues of . . . origin, the sublime, . . . vision, [and] reverie' (Miles 1993, 6), then these are arguably the very discourses from which London gives itself to be re-presented and through which modalities the subject presents itself. A performative writing, urban figuration in the text of Dickens does not merely show; it acts out, even as it induces, or seeks to induce the experience for the reader's perception. It is not that Dickens's urban writing is necessarily or overtly Gothic, therefore. What can be argued, instead, is that reading / writing London has on occasions recourse to a Gothic 'turn', as I have already intimated, in order to explain the inexplicable, to give expression to that for which there is no language and so move beyond the initial reduction to the play of the trace towards the promise of a stable ontology.

Gothic considered as a tropological field, as a source of motifs by which to translate the effect of the visual, informs the determination of re-presentation in the face of what would otherwise remain unpassable, inexpressible. In that a given London is read and written in a manner analogous with and drawing from the textual effects, tropes and forms of Gothic, the writing of the city, being expressed through a language that maps a problematised consciousness, reveals a 'deeper wound' or 'fracture, an imbalance, a "gap" in the social self which w[ill] not go away' (Punter 1987, 26). Thus, on particular occasions, the acts of reading / writing London come to be shaped, given a certain recognisable aesthetic form, as an encrypted, tropic Gothic, rather than one composed of the more obvious surface *grand guignol* effects, and mundane narratives of monstrosity. Dirty men, filthy women and deformed children are all far more monstrous for the modern subject, in principle and when intimately encountered, living invisibly at the centre of the modern world, than the idea of the undead. (It might even be suggested that to call such an image a 'still life' is to figure uncannily a world of undead creatures, captured in the moment of the vision.) If Gothic is a means of stabilising the image, thereby seeking to produce the appropriate response in the subject through the use of an aesthetic register or modality that gives to the image of the modern urban condition an authenticity, it also illustrates how the residuum of Gothic comes to inform the process of reading and writing London's – perhaps anachronistic – modernity in order that the subject can bear witness rather than remain silent in the face of that modernity.

The representation of Walworth in 'The Black Veil' is instructive here, the second extract above being the passage in question. The re-presentation of a south London suburb moves between objective or documentary representation and subjective re-presentation that develops its mode of apprehension through access to the effect of place on perception. Clearly not a material Gothic setting, the register here is such that, with the 'appearance' of dismal gloominess that lowers the spirits even as it is imbued with the power implicitly to induce anxiety, a Gothic of the senses takes effect. Particular objects or phenomena – the ruined cottage, the stunted tree, the suggestion of danger and isolation, the mist and residue of rain – in their abject or ruinous condition maintain or intensify the effect on the one who bears witness, even as they appear, collectively, as a suburban, domestic transformation of the conventions of Gothic landscape. The connection between the empirical and the subjective is carefully traced, as is the mediation between the material and its appearance for the viewing – and reading – subject. Though confronted with a 'real' landscape, the urban subject is placed under the sign of the Gothic in his perception, this being transmitted to, and so reduplicated in, the reader, as empirical location is subsumed within phantasmic reception of overdetermined phenomena. A counter-signature to the picturesque is thereby produced, through the 'givenness of the impression, whose essence is the pure fact of being impressed as such, is stripped of its role in givenness, in favour of an originary consciousness' (Henry 2008, 25) that is perfectly in keeping, 'with the objects we have described'. Such Gothic effects thus place the reading subject in the midst of a complex problem of perception and orientation.

Here, one is forced to respond, not to documentary verisimilitude, but rather to what Robert Miles calls 'Gothic's discursive practices', rendering problematic 'what it is possible to say with clarity and the slippery nature of language itself; between the territory of social experience narrative allows [the writer] to map out, and the uncharted character of' phenomenological apprehension that is not, itself, 'immediately intelligible' to Dickens as such (1993, 143). Hence the struggle, the 'apposition' of dialogic, as Miles calls it, between journalistic observation and the discursive matrix of Gothic, 'to make their articulations discernible' (Miles 1993, 144). And, as another commentator on Gothic, Robert Mighall, observes of W. M. Reynolds's *The Mysteries of London*, 'a closely-knit collection of courts and alleys is one thing – an observable topographical phenomenon that can be charted . . . [However,] to label even the most architectural complex "labyrinthine"' (1999, 33) not only imports 'effects from the earlier [Gothic] literary tradition' (31), it also 'reveals less about its actual condition than [it does] the concerns of the perceiver and these are . . . historically determined' (33). Hence, the aesthetic residuum in the service of presenting the modernity of London in its effects on, and involvement of, a concomitant or analogous modern subjectivity in relation to place and what takes place, whose attestation and the linguistic modality of such map the inextricable intimacy of subject and city.

Such intimacy, such proximity, enfoldedness, immanence and relation reveal urban modernity in presenting the perception of 'life on the boundary of all that is where this whole remains insistent because something quite other than individual entities, interests, and realities within it inevitably emerges here' (Patocka 1996, 39) – the historically and materially determined concerns and perceptions of the perceiving subject, for which 'Gothic' is merely the intervening medium of access. Gothic is exploited in order to make the reader feel, and so see, a 'glimpse of authentic life . . . the *world* opens itself . . . it is no longer merely an involuntary background' (Patocka 1996, 39). What we in turn receive are the signs of an always-immanent phenomenological and transcendent structure and mode of perception. In this, an 'irreducible historicity is recognized', therefore, in that this mode of perception arrives through the dialogic struggle 'only *after* the fact of the event' (Derrida 1989, 49) – which event is double: on the one hand, constituted through the writing subject's encounter with the city; on the other hand, produced through the demand to transform the materiality of history and experience into the materiality of the letter, whereby the irreducible historicity might be transmitted. London thus gives to the text of Dickens, and therefore those of us who read the city after that initial experience of the modern urban subject, the singular emergence of a discourse not yet articulated in the 1830s emerging out of the ruins of an older mode of perception and discourse, and 'whose unity is still *to come* on the basis of what is announced' (Derrida 1989, 53). If London erupts apparently, here and there, now and then, as provisionally monstrous, sublime, Gothic but ultimately at the edge of the ineffable; and if it remains undecidable as to its identity, being or meaning; then it enables, not a retreat from the political into a restatement of aporetic suspension, but rather – and herein resides its radical rupture with the conventions of representation and thus the equally radical emergence of a modernity, for which there is barely a language – a necessary abstention and so a break 'from . . . historicist empiricism' (Derrida 1989, 59). In this, it institutes a movement towards a truth in re-presentation, which 'is really that of a concrete and specific history – the foundations of which are a tempo-ral and creative subjectivity's acts based on the sensible world and the life-world as cultural world' (Derrida 1989, 60). Between London and its witnessing subject interconnections are originated, invented, inter-connections of 'what is, in the fullest sense of the word, *history itself*' (Derrida 1989, 59), the possibility of which is *language* (Derrida 1989, 60). Such a language, in looking back, gathers up in its folds the traces of a past discourse, transforming those, in the moment of experience and perception, into an opening, in response to the city's apparition, on to modalities of perception and re-presentation to come.

There is, then, no London as such, save for its appearance in the possibility of a language, and in, for, a subject which, paradoxically, the condition of the city calls into being. But if there is no *one* London, there is more than one London; there are Londons, each singular-plural – and *there*, the text of Dickens maps this, *there* is London for its (their) subject(s). Such Londons, such urban multiplicities are everywhere. In its / their instabilities (there is more than one), London(s) remain(s) as an experience for the subject of displacements and dispositions, dis-placements within disposition. London, to borrow a word of Nicholas Royle's, veers from within itself / theirselves; it is 'at once what writing [in the text of Dickens] is about and what the reader is drawn to in turn' (Royle 2011, 23), in the wake of the subject. London makes / Londons make possible the expression, through the agency of the modern urban sensibility expressed as an experiencing, perceiving subjectivity in its interconnection of the modes of documentary journalism and Gothic, 'the possibility of history as the possibility of language' enabling 'a phe-nomenology of historicity' (Mighall 1999, 69). Nowhere permanently, they / it erupt(s) and interrupt(s) with an insistent if irregular rhythm, like so many more obviously Gothic horrors. Reading / writing London risks everything on the Gothic trope in gestures that anticipate not only Husserl but also Joyce, in the expression of a will to 'awaken' from the nightmare of history, so as to 'master that nightmare in a total and present resumption' (Mighall 1999, 103). The 'urban Gothic', in excess of the merely factual and historicist empiricism to which later anthropo-logical and political writers such as Mayhew or Engels succumb, risks a phenomenological discourse that wakes the subject from the nightmare of the inescapably mimetic and realist, which merely reinscribes the political and social horrors it seeks to denounce.

Glancing over the titles of articles by Dickens from *Household Words* or *All the Year Round*, your eye, seeking out those occasional pieces in which London assumes a significant role as subject for the anonymous subject already described, might alight on the following examples: 'The

Streets—Morning', 'The Streets—Night', 'Scotland Yard', 'Seven Dials', 'Meditations in Monmouth Street', 'London Recreations', 'The River', 'Gin Shops', 'A Visit to Newgate', 'Spitalfields', 'A Nightly Scene in London' and, last, 'Wapping Workhouse'. London is to be found in many more places, of course, but the mere observation of titles, where the metropolis is dismembered and represented as a series of scenes, events and localities visited and reported on over a period of more than a quarter-century, confirms for us what many already know: that London is an inexhaustible resource. At the risk of generalisation, then, and to reiterate an observation central to this discussion, the city is figured through a number of recurring, iterable motifs or tropes, such as entertainments, the poor and criminality (the 'Seven Dials' essay conflates elements of all three). There are other 'worlds' also: the law, for example, the Civil Service and, in a phrase that yokes legal, political and economic institutions, 'Bar, Barnacles, and Bank'. One might argue, though, that the latter three belong to the novels and are principally, in their flows of power, read as exclusively discursive rather than material. This is not to say that the text does not figure the various material institutions. It is to contend, though, that such forces are most immediately known in the effects their invisible forces produce. Working-class London, criminal London and the London of entertainments constitute three alternative demi-mondes which to the Dickens reader become configured and refigured again and again, touching here and there on one another like three partially overlapping circles in a Venn diagram, each veering off into the other, folding back on one another, wherein the overlaps and folds are also spaces of transformation and translation. If 'London' names the enclosing or universal set, each of London's particular 'worlds' has an internal logic, and each shares with the other common elements, through that apperceived excess felt to be just beyond the limits of re-presentation.

Beyond or, perhaps more accurately, *before* re-presentation and the narrative that binds content in its subjective perception, though, there are those formal or structural aspects, constituent parts or facets that, in their complex formal relation, serve to constitute in turn that which makes certain manifestations of London Gothic peculiarly and singularly what it is: a Gothic, on the one hand, of complex, repeated formal structures, traces and interanimating architectural and topographical parts; and a Gothic, on the other hand, of affect, emotion, sensate apprehension and apperception. A topology is mapped therefore tending towards provisional ontological reinscription and the reading or interrogation through that topological and tropological formation of the translation or communication of the conscious experience of place and event. Within this, the event of encounter with what is objectively real is irreversibly interiorised as the phantasmic perception of the materiality of place in the phenomenal traces. Experience becomes, in this relation, revelation, and so illumination, for the experiencing and reading subject, of an aura of authenticity, of that which is London, appearing uniquely for the subject. The city is apprehended as the constellated auratic phenomena through 'appearances' to some perceiving subjectivity, 'manifestations according to the forms . . . of space and time . . . [and, as a result of this], all appearing . . . is necessarily a singularizing manifestation' (Gasché 1994, 187).

This broad sketch requires qualification in order that we continue. It is therefore necessary to explicate the relationship between a phenomenology of perception and those aspects of an ontology of the Gothic more explicitly where materiality of place and the concatenation of objects that constitute place overlap with the perception of what place might harbour, or which, immanent within its structures, might without direct revelation nevertheless cause to erupt within the subject as the anticipation of what is to come. 'Communication', writes Merleau-Ponty, 'is an appearance' (1981, 7), an appearance moreover implying the subject for whom the communication takes place. This is not to say that communication is, or can be, direct, straightforward or successful. Dickens's reading and writing of the city apprehends this question of causing to appear, and so communicate, and the fraught conditions under which it might occur. In order to cause the city to appear, not *as such* but *as it is*, the text of Dickens risks everything on communication in ruins filtered through the discourse of the Gothic, with its evasiveness, its fragmentation and its tantalising, yet addictive frustrations. Reading and writing the city in Dickens moves, therefore, through manifestations of the urban for a subject constituted by and placed within those manifestations, which present themselves sequentially and serially. An object, or fragment of an object, comes to present itself, to be re-presented, only to be supplemented by another, as each 'builds' in the imagination through a precarious concatenation not objectively explicit.

This is given us to read in 'Wapping Workhouse', published early in 1860. In directing himself towards the 'East-end of London' and on leaving Covent Garden, the imagined narrator, the Uncommercial Traveller, having 'got past the India House', is caused to reflect in desultory fashion on 'Tippoo-Sahib and Charles Lamb'. These phantasms are supplanted in turn by the little wooden midshipman, Aldgate Pump, the Saracen's Head, his already 'swarthy countenance' disfigured by an 'ignominious rash of posting bills' (*UT* 43). These phenomena are juxtaposed with an 'ancient neighbour', another Inn, the name of which is not to be remembered distinctly as a result of its having long disappeared and its becoming conflated with another coaching inn, The Bull, which was to be torn down six years after this article was published. While items, names, images and objects accumulate, already in meaningful ways, the journey moves forward but the narrating subject displaces himself from the present both spatially and temporally. Names and figures – India House, Tippoo-Sahib, the Saracen's Head – hint at an 'orientation' which is also a disorientation, the journey to the East of London invoking another, Orientalist East, and with that, other temporal and historical frames. Topographical motion brings about a slippage in the mind, into Gothic codes of 'the barbaric or Oriental' (Miles 1993, 144), as if the physical act of perambulation, in its causing the chance encounter with various signs of alterity, releases an unconscious desire, as language itself succumbs to an inadvertent revelation of the perception or anticipation of excess. A doubling temporality is opened from within the present for the subject, who later confesses himself, in another Orientalist turn, in a 'Turkish frame of mind' (*UT* 44), for he walks on quite blind to place and historical moment, lost in the pasts of coaching inns and a phantasmic, quite possibly Gothicised East, before emerging in both 'the age of railways' and Whitechapel Church (*UT* 43). The signs of the city lose the subject in a phenomenal miasma between Leadenhall Market and the church (St Mary Matfelon),[23] a distance of less than a mile.

In the presentation of objects, a street scene, the details of atmosphere, the listing of proper names by encounter and association, or, as elsewhere, details of a building or room, the object or group of objects being represented manifesting themselves through the communication of traces in an often febrile adumbration: all disappear in the phantasm woven out of the collective web of signs. Concomitantly, the urban subject, that anonymous 'traveller', finds himself lost, once more. As a similar figure had found himself involved in a disorientating experience in Seven Dials almost three decades before, so here it is confessed by the traveller that 'I gave myself up as having lost my way, and abandoning myself to the narrow streets in a Turkish frame of mind' (*UT* 44). As if to enforce the Gothic transformation of place and subject, the narrator then recounts how a young man is encountered, whose 'puffed sallow face, and . . . figure all dirty and shiny and slimy . . . may have been . . . the drowned man' of local advertising hoardings (*UT* 44). This 'figure', defined three times as an 'apparition' and having a ghastly grin and a watery gurgle for a laugh (*UT* 44), erases the narrator's own sense of individualism, causing the latter to feel himself to be anonymous, a 'General Cove, or member of the miscellaneous public' (*UT* 44). The subject is given up, giving himself up to the city. Being addressed by it, he becomes the place of its projections a psychic palimpsest of its structures, flows and manifestations. Objects and places are revealed as being veiled by the traces of themselves, traces which bespeak the tenor of other identities, meanings and times, and which in turn direct the subject away from the present materiality, through the lightning flash impressions that they leave perceptually. Moreover, the material form, belonging to the technique of urban re-presentation, is 'never grasped as distinct from what reveals it. 'In short,' observes Renaud Barbaras, 'the manifestation presents the object as what itself remains unpresentable' (Barbaras 2006, 14) – hence the fabricated Gothic East with its wild boar, dismembered Muslims and aqueous ghouls.

The figural urban mapping and representation here proceed by telegraphic shorthand and phatic adumbration. Simultaneously this outlines the experience and perception, while re-presenting that which is otherwise unavailable. That very act of sketching nevertheless captures the traces 'rigorously as what requires formulation': the subject's apperception of the truth of the urban, as London is transformed by subjective perception and memory, and as the subject must decipher both 'the manifestation and what appears, [as these are] affected by a double constitutive ambiguity' (Barbaras 2006, 14). Perception thus reveals itself as a reading, while being that writing effected by the city. The subject, in the revision of a reading that produces the world through the imaginary register, overcomes objective reality. And 'as for the object', Barbaras continues, 'it is [therefore] simultaneously present in the sense that it is attained in person and indefinitely absent in the sense that no series of adumbrations can exhaust the tenor of being.' Manifestations of London generated in fragmentary surges – themselves communicated through the fragment, the ruin, the otherwise unorderable collocation of traces, elements and aspects both structural and phantasmic – project or give, rather than represent, 'the identity of a coming to presence and a retreat into the unpresentable' (Barbaras 2006, 14). The subject sees the city. The subject *is* the city. Being is given; this, such being-given, is the gift of the other. Conscious experience becomes the place where, and the screen on which, the apparent unity of the urban is found and projected contingently, before giving way to the haunting implication, always at work, of 'an eidetic abyss between experience and reality' (Barbaras 2006, 14). Half-glimpsed, as it were, the city in full retreats, its various manifestations never coalescing into a whole but perceived as ungraspable totality, which can only be apprehended in the present if it is linked with a historical or fictive past – thus that drive we identify through the adjective *Dickensian*, that restless rapid pulse at the heart of urban re-presentation. And if 'the Gothic novel remains unhistorical precisely because it lacks this link' between the 'historical reality' of the past and 'the present' (Iser 1974, 84), then the text of Dickens situates the interconnection, to make this point once more, explicitly between historical reality and subjective historicity, through those Gothic tropes.

This somewhat modified Husserlian reading remains to be developed further. The phenomenon that is London, from the early nineteenth century onwards, causes or gives to be known a radically different mode of apprehension and representation, or, as I have been distinguishing, re-presentation. After Dickens, it is no longer possible to 'represent' the material world 'as if there were only a single manner of existing and therefore a single adequate modality of access to existing' (Iser 1974, 16). There is no objective truth available for 'representation'. It is this realisation which causes one to apprehend the radical effect on subjectivity and the birth of the modern that the city figured in writing and reading causes to be figured. London brings about the revelation of the ruin of conventional representation – its reduction to 'nothing other than the vital movement of the coexistence and the interweaving of original formations and sedimentations of meaning' (Husserl 1989, 174) – in terms of the limits of a purely presentist mimetic adequation, and so forces on the subject a new identity, with a historically and materially grounded urban specificity, from which must be generated an inventive 'idiocultural' writing. Such inscription, while grounded in empirical or historical fact, whether solicited 'in the present through experience or . . . as a fact in the past, necessarily has its *inner structure of meaning*' and thus is founded on an 'immense structural a priori', the disclosure of which gives to the act of writing its 'historical becoming' (Husserl 1989, 174). Such a writing is 'inventive' in the sense that the writing subject is forced by the object to find the trace of alterity within what is already there, rather than create some wholly new mode, in order to communicate perception and experience from its partial and subjective location as this takes place. And it is 'idiocultural', to borrow this term of Derek Attridge's, inasmuch as Dickensian urban invention, through its adumbrated and telegraphic phatic fluxes, attests in a performative manner to the 'individual's grasp on the world [of the modern city, as this] is mediated by a changing array of [historically given] interlocking, overlapping and often contradictory cultural systems' that mark the urban scene as a 'complex', and which therefore is 'necessarily unstable and subject to constant change' (Attridge 2004, 21).

The 'complexity of a cultural field or an idioculture [given singular expression as 'London in the nineteenth century'] is something we can barely fathom; it is certainly not something to which we can achieve direct access' (Attridge 2004, 22). This is affirmed in the reading / writing of London and the invention, the response, of a singular, modern metropolitan mode of re-presentation in the wake of perception. Anyone familiar with the city of Dickens's novels, early or late, will understand the validity of this claim. The description of Snow Hill and Newgate in *Nicholas Nickleby* (passage 3) draws on the already established register of the short texts from *Sketches* and elsewhere, giving expression to the unstable complexity and its power to confound, as it involves, the subject. Unfolded as an excessive countersignature to anything the name 'Snow Hill' might signify to someone not from London, the city gives itself in all its terrifying force as obviously a living and yet inhuman phenomenon, challenging both comprehension and the limits of representation, at a given historical instant. Though language may be indebted to Gothic or other literary registers and so riddled by an anachrony, the time can be no other than that *now* to which the subject is witness. London is to be felt as much as seen, and in this the text of Dickens appears to be anticipate Conrad's injunction that the reader should *feel* and *see*. (In the doubleness of the trope, Conrad anticipates Marion's investigation into those modes of vision announced by intuition and respect.) The narrative subject as individual form has disappeared, the subjects being both the city and those who inhabit the machine, the principal purposes of which are to replicate itself and execute the criminal. What is precisely disquieting here, and that which, I believe, gives access to that singular idiocultural mode of historical becoming referred to here as the urban Gothic, is that equivalent excess of violent motion; a body without a head, the capital city, swarms, roars and thrives, and yet, in this tumult of unthinking surfeit of dark energy, it targets destructively at a moment that appears engendered out of the fright and frightfulness of the 'excess of human life'. And, once more, we experience the performative; the sentence is entangled in itself, clause after clause, driving itself and being driven, as the written form offers a perception of the city through the analogy of its own excessive deformity in 'a complex relationship both to historical verisimilitude and to ... processes of authentication' (Robertson 1994, 93) through that performative becoming-monstrous.

Reading and writing London as the site of modernity and modern subjectivity 'comes into being as a challenge to cultural norms [of representation] and retain[s] that challenge ... because it is never fully accommodated' (Attridge 2004, 46). Yet, although it cannot be fully accommodated, there is, nevertheless, that strange, disquieting feeling of the 'experience of intimacy ... a sense that the work speaks to my inmost, most secret being', its haunting and uncanny singularity striking me 'afresh' (Attridge 2004, 78). At the same time, the demand made on me is clearly akin to the demand made on the modern subject by the city.

The demand that London imposes is also a demand that 'this specific collocation of words, allusions, and cultural references makes on me, in the event of my reading, *here and now*' (Attridge 2004, 67; emphasis added). I read the subject in Dickens encountering the city. I *am* that subject – or at the very least, phantasmically, it is *as if* I were that subject; mine is that subjectivity in the *here and now* of reading. This experience and perception are thus the manifestation of a haunting, iterable singularity, in which is given to me the following perception: 'experience of singularity involves an apprehension of *otherness*, registered in the event of apprehension' (Attridge 2004, 67). In this, we are simultaneously at a remove and yet impossibly close to the early nineteenth-century subject's encounter with that very opening of experience and perception which writing could never suture, and which intuition, in its givenness through that opening, may serve in part to explain the motivation at work in the invention of a specifically modern, idiocultural urban Gothic. Or, let us just suggest, the urban *was* Gothic inasmuch as Gothic was the only language appropriate to re-presentation. What was Gothic was precisely the apprehension of the difference of modernity, which drove the reading and writing of the city as a topography and architecture never to be known in full or directly, never mapped in its entirety for the imagination, never given totalised, finite representation. Reading Dickens on the city, there arrives the experience of a 'living through, of the invention that makes the work not just different but the creative re-imagination of cultural materials' and material culture (Attridge 2004, 67).

If I experience that sense of a 'living through' – in the sense of duration and its endurance – as vicarious, phantasmic event, it is in Dickens's creative re-imagining of various dimensions of the Gothic in culturally and historically specific terms iterable in the urban contexts. Additionally, my phenomenal, haunting experience is marked by both the replication and iteration of subjectivity's 'fall' into the world and anonymity. The anonymous narrator-effect delivers us at a threshold between subject and world. The Gothic is all the more immanently troubling, because on the occasions that London is figured under the heading of the Gothic, subjectivity is subsumed in the urban. The modern self is anonymous, haunted by subsumption into anonymity, 'the anonymous [being] a constitutive feature of the social' (Natanson 1979, 534). As the anonymous subject disappears into the urban, so I too experience this estranged, ironic displacement. Therefore, the anxiety in the face of London's haunting traces is more nearly felt, more intimately available, if not to perception then to apperception (a distinction I shall make clear shortly). For now, it is enough to remark that in indirect apprehension the city is experienced as a possibly occult threatening, inhuman, yet vital force, which can swallow us, suffocate us, lose us forever and prevent our escape. The flows of London consolidate around the nameless subject all too easily, being both material locations *and* Gothic structures of the imagination.

By the phrase 'Gothic structures' I want to suggest the forms of particular locations in Dickens's essays as simultaneously always real *and* imaginary, and I have in mind not only those aspects of setting and place that resonate with the more obvious settings of the Gothic narrative. As I have already intimated, I am also reading the various 'worlds' of Dickens's London as mappings of material structures, the streets, buildings and so on, which in their complexity, fragmentation, their 'barbarous' or 'rude' qualities, are suggestive often anachronistically of an otherness and also a tendency towards excess of detail and irrationality in design. There is always the sense, for example, in reading Dickens, of passages that lead nowhere and to nothing, whether those passages are narrative cul-de-sacs or dark streets (reflect once more on 'Seven Dials' or 'Wapping Workhouse'). The street may be found on the map, but its phenomenological phantasm, palimpsest and countersignature are not. If Dickens produces the city as always in some sense the obliquely significant labyrinth, this may well have to do with the abyssal immanence felt by the urban subject in the early nineteenth century. Nicholas Freeman remarks of tropic irregularity and Gothic excess in Dickens's text, 'the labyrinth encapsulates the bewildering confusion of proliferating and dangerously similar streets, engendering frightening claustrophobia or even deadening ennui . . . the city is a realm of tangled passages and monstrous artifice' (2007, 162). This is absolutely, undeniably so; but what Freeman also gestures towards here is that performative palimpsest of Dickensian writing, equally informed by 'tangled passages' of representation and 'monstrous artifice' in the conjunction of design and phenomenological effect, at the always moving centre of which is the urban subject. The subject is always there and always about to be swallowed.

Hence a passage such as our fourth extract, in which all estranges even as every detail feels uncannily familiar, and familiarly uncanny. The passage comes from the article 'Spitalfields', written in 1851 (*SJ* 294–305). After 'we cross a many cornered square and enter a sort of gateway', in which geometry and the threshold collude in our initiation, we encounter this 'Gothic structure'. What is given is merely part of a much longer, labyrinthine image. The monstrous growth of the sentence is so serpentine and excessive that the collective subject is all but lost, appearing only barely after what seem innumerable clauses. All the more remarkable in this ravelling up of subjectivity is the fact that the sentence or 'narrow passage' does not only distend itself disorientatingly, but its multiple clausal facets also lose the reader in the many-layered density of the structure. Intensity, density and duration combine to overwhelm, to lose, and to render space no longer clearly imaginable. How much time do we need to register all that is here, and all that combines to delay passage and yet impinge on perception with a sense of discontinuous but endless duration? So much does the city rely on the iterability of such effects and forms that the endlessness is itself suggestive that not only is London an unfathomable and illimitable labyrinth but that, formally, reiteration of device and aspect produces that type of 'ritualization of mystery' typical of Gothic fiction identified by Fiona Robertson (1994, 72). Arguably also, this London resembles the production of 'something irreducible, therefore perpetually to be interpreted; not secrets to be found out one by one, but Secrecy' (Kermode 1979, 143). There is nothing 'behind' or 'beyond' such iterable perceptions of the city. There is merely the one 'secret' that here and now, as everywhere, there and then, is London, irreducible to definition.

In part, proximity *and* distance, obsessive attention to detail and the impossibility of access to a greater definition: this is achieved through literary effects that generate a visual image: alliteration, consonance and dissonance play across the sentence structure, moving between and across clauses, picking up, as it were, the stitches of a labyrinthine network, in which the written passage and the topographical passage are mutual palimpsests, each an iterable figure of the other. From those instances of poetic device the subject's world emerges, but each serves in the maintenance of the image as brush strokes serve to present a visual figure, whilst remaining independent of content, merely formal markers. We may be in the silk warehouse, but the various elements obscure our vision, so closely are we *in*, so nearly are we involved in the elements, traces, tropes and phenomena of this world. Aural device, rhythmic motion, irregular and seemingly endless sentence structure perform the wayward diataxis moving in seemingly indiscriminate, not to say profligate fashion. There is to be experienced in this febrile perception a terrible pulchritude, terrible in that negation of all that is not what is immediately there, and in that tropological confusion. 'We' are pulled into the perception, losing ourselves in the motions, the echoes, and that pictorial economy in which the image is evoked 'explicitly or implicitly, and which is part of the very substance of the text' (Louvel 2011, 56) as the text is part of the substance of the image, as brush or pencil strokes are to a picture or painting. The strange is made familiar, the familiar strange, to paraphrase T. S. Eliot (1975, 169).

What is experienced and perceived does not give access to a world beyond; this is the world, and here subjective witness, response and re-presentation. There is a recursive waywardness here, as re-presentation presents representation of nothing other than representation's deconstruction of itself. It is this very irreducibility that drives the traveller, the stranger, the wanderer on, to describe, inscribe and reinscribe the ineffable and ineluctable performative of a tropic and topic manifestation of the same-everywhere and everywhere as other. In the combination of manifest labyrinth, replicated at and resounding between the levels of form, content and interpretation, the narrating figure in the text of Dickens opens the city on to 'the wider vocabulary of visionary experience' and the 'unsolved puzzle' (Freeman 2007, 163). For the reader of Dickens or the traveller in Dickens's London there is no 'outside' the city and, concomitantly, no solution, no relief and no possibility of freeing oneself from the simultaneously *material* and *phantasmic* vision in which one finds oneself involved.

In that understanding of the 'something irreducible . . . perpetually to be interpreted', we read the Dickensian anticipation of what Edmund Husserl was to call, in *Cartesian Meditations*, the experience of 'appresentation' or 'analogical apperception' (Husserl 1995, 108ff.). London in its Gothic presentation and its perception as such is not logical, it is analogical; one grasps it, if at all, indirectly through the limitless comparison between its singular sites, events and experiences, and the literary manifestation and invention of its phenomena. I grasp at the next image, and the next, even as sentences such as the one above to which I feel myself bound, in which I find myself enmeshed, and to which my subjectivity is sentenced, move, replicate, double and displace every element of themselves beside, within and from themselves. The text of Dickens does not so much present, represent, apprehend or invite the reader to perceive the city directly (this being impossible), as the city figures itself as an other through the apperceptive realisation of its immensity, its sublime terror and endless awful wonder. One's consciousness cannot grasp the whole, and so consciousness moves feverishly and with an anxiety of inadequacy, from sign to sign, the totality immanent and always at a remove, however proximate or intimate, from the street, the room, the shop window and so on. Modern urban narrative mediation therefore gives us to apprehend how 'experience is original consciousness' (Husserl 1995, 108), this consciousness being always consciousness of an other. In its encounter with alterity, consciousness has itself reflected back to itself as a '"there too"' (Husserl 1995, 109). Modern urban consciousness presents a focused reflection on the materiality of place and the (a)material traces that register on subjectivity.

To return to 'Spitalfields': in a gesture of parabasis, the reader is interrogated over his or her knowledge or experience of Spitalfields (*SJ* 294). Supposing the reader only to have a vague impression of a place never visited, the narrator proceeds to ask if the reader will accompany him there. Perceiving myself to be thus mediated by my experience of the other, I come to a mediated awareness of place, a being '"there too"'; but my consciousness of myself is simultaneously opened to me as never being capable of achieving a pre-originary sense of 'an "itself there"' (Husserl 1995, 109). In being made to perceive myself not as pure presence but as being made '"*co-present*"' (Husserl 1995, 109), I am presented to myself as an other; thus, I am conscious of myself through, in Husserl's word, an *appresentation*. Doubled and divided, I am haunted as much as I haunt myself. In pieces such as 'Spitalfields', the Dickensian narrator maintains this mode of appresentation and doubling after his initial rhetorical gambit by shifting to speaking of what 'we' observe: 'Turning . . . out of . . . Bishopsgate, we suddenly lose the noise that has been resounding in our ears' (*SJ* 294). Location and loss, placement and displacement mark the transition of the self and the experience of this district of London. The city as both material entity and experience and perception of a material entity thus breaks up irrevocably the Romantic compact between solitary consciousness and Nature, which simultaneously makes me at one with Nature whilst giving to my consciousness the illusion that I am in control, I master Nature in perceiving it for myself, and myself alone. Nature vouchsafes me the perception of an '"immanent transcendency"' (Husserl 1995, 110). But everywhere in the urban location I encounter others, like myself and yet not myself, urban subjects. I am thus reduced in relation to that something irreducible (recalling Kermode's phrase) to the situation of being an other – *comme les autres*, as it were – and yet other than each and every other. The city thus produces in my appresentative consciousness, inscribing in me indirectly, the analogical apperception of myself as one more urban subject, a fragment of an impossible, infinite and monstrous form. I enter into, and am found to myself, given subjectivity through my '"*analogizing*" apprehension' of my subjectivisation (Husserl 1995, 111).

This is not a 'thinking act' though. For,

> *Every* apperception in which we apprehend at a glance, and noticingly grasp, objects given beforehand—for example, the already-given everyday world—. . . points to . . . an *analogizing transfer* . . . [and] to the extent that there is givenness beforehand [given that we know the material world in which we find ourselves is always already there in its brute, mute materiality, a materiality the immensity of the city enforces with a particular violence in the first decades of the nineteenth century], there is such a transfer . . . (Husserl 1995, 111)

Such analogising transfer arrives between the discontinuous motion of object after object, clause after clause, experience after experience, and subject substituted for subject. Such transfer, such translation takes place in me through the iterable material condition translated as the equally iterable fragmentation and singular-seriality of the urban. Thus, the revelation is that the subject 'merely becomes conscious' of that which is always already at work, the narrative and constitutive 'creation' being 'only the explication of an already constituted concept' that is encountered (Derrida 1989, 40). This is witnessed also in the article and analogical transference of Spitalfields into the textual matrix of traces that bear its name as itself and not itself, and which, in turn, though irreducible to any given meaning, are simply the fragments that the subject shores against the ruin of representation. In this, the subject is responding rather than creating; he happens to be on hand in order to receive and so set free 'a possibility' in representation 'which is nothing less than historical, in order to hand it to us' (Derrida 1989, 39). If, as Husserl reminds us and as we see in this passage from 'Spitalfields', the '*radical differentiation of apperceptions*' as so many 'different levels' (Husserl 1995, 111) of the same experience comes down to the disappearance of any separable subjectivity into that anonymous doubled self haunted by the urban, by its irreducibility, then this phenomenal experience is already mapped in the broken heap of images.

Urban subjectivity, then, is constituted through its reception and grasping of phenomena, traces, signs and so on. In repeating them, in transferring them from their material historicity to the materiality of the letter, the subject constructs the labyrinth of urban subjectivity analogous with the labyrinth of the city through the transformation of objects into tropes. This, in turn, leads both nowhere and back to where one begins, where the subject finds him- or herself constituted. London is, therefore, invented through the mediation of the Gothic device of employing 'narrative and architectural [as well as topographical] passages which seem to lead nowhere [but which] in fact lead' (Robertson 1994, 74), if not to a secret past, then to the uncanny revelation of one's own fundamental relation to the modern world of London, *by the historical and material facticity of that world*. As in Gothic narrative, Dickens's London 'disrupt the reader's conventional expectations about the working of cause and effect' (Robertson 1994, 76). What is also achieved is the displacement of Gothic effect from the subject in the narrative to the reading subject. Whereas, in Gothic narrative, the protagonist's consciousness is represented as apprehensive and anxious, and whereas this is, in part, the effect that the text of Dickens reworks on its characters the reading subject is produced as anxious and

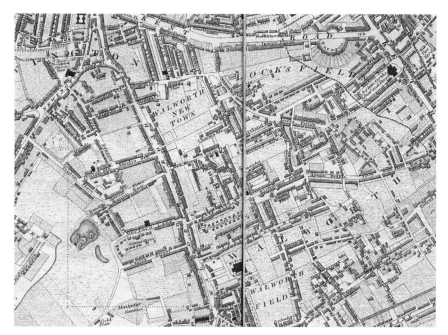

Walworth

apprehensive through the presentation of the particular areas of the city as labyrinthine, obscure and confusing, without the balm or false hope of a resolution.

Dickens's writing of London mediated through the Gothic serves, then, and in conclusion, two purposes at least. On the one hand, in its invention of an idiocultural discourse appropriate to time and place, it mediates the historically determined experience of the modern urban subject at the beginning of the nineteenth century, mapping this in a manner that, in its phenomenological dimensions, effectively rethinks subjectivity apropos the city through the close relation traced in representation, the memory of experience, writing translating walking. On the other hand, its revision of the Gothic in response to the urban condition as experience and perception of serial fragmentation, iterability, rhythm and irregular motion generates a performative and discontinuous subjectivity in prose, which has the possibility to assume 'limitless shapes of being [and] in the special way of responding and vibrating to the encounter of one's glance . . . [which in turn] evokes all sorts of variations' (Merleau-Ponty 1981, 62–3), causing to appear to the reader's perception the indirect manifestation of London's otherwise inaccessible reality.

In this, the subject's perception inaugurates an order of 'coherent deformation imposed on the visible' (Merleau-Ponty 1981, 91), precisely so that the truth of place is available to processes of perception that exceed the mere present and empirical. London needs a language equal to itself. Fashioning this from what is found in the cultural memory of literary and idiocultural formation, the text of Dickens enacts a mode of indirect and analogical appresentation and apperception in which communication, however ruinous, causes London to appear in its irreducible secrecy. Impossibly close but also at a remove, London is there, London gives itself for its subject as a place in which signs are given continually. Through the Gothic modality, there is only the haunting revelation and knowledge of 'the meaninglessness of association through contiguity' (Merleau-Ponty 1962, 15). What is all the more terrible here for the subject is that the immediate and local impression given the Dickensian subject can only arouse other images because it is 'already *understood* in the light of the past experience' of 'the psychic fact' (Merleau-Ponty 1962, 115) in which the 'I' finds itself ever involved within, and from which it speaks, this confounding place, time and again. Like the unfortunate freemason at the close of 'Wapping Workhouse', '"I am in this unfortunate position . . . [for there is never received] the countersign!"' (*SJ* 375).

Heart • St Paul's Cathedral

Master Humphrey's Clock

We lingered so long over the leaves from which I had read, that as I consigned them to their former resting-place, the hand of my trusty clock pointed to twelve, and there came towards us upon the wind the voice of the deep and distant bell of St. Paul's as it struck the hour of midnight.

'This,' said I, returning with a manuscript I had taken at the moment from the same repository, 'to be opened to such music, should be a tale where London's face by night is darkly seen, and where some deed of such a time as this is dimly shadowed out. Which of us here has seen the working of the great machine whose voice has just now ceased?'

Mr. Pickwick had, of course, and so had Mr. Miles. [. . .]

I had seen it but a few days before, and could not help telling them of the fancy I had about it.

I paid my fee of twopence upon entering, to one of the money-changers who sit within the Temple; and falling, after a few turns up and down, into the quiet train of thought which such a place awakens, paced the echoing stones like some old monk whose present world lay all within its walls. As I looked afar up into the lofty dome, I could not help wondering what were his reflections whose genius reared that mighty pile, when, the last small wedge of timber fixed, the last nail driven into its home for many centuries, the clang of hammers, and the hum of busy voices gone, and the Great Silence whole years of noise had helped to make, reigning undisturbed around, he mused, as I did now, upon his work, and lost himself amid its vast extent. I could not quite determine whether the contemplation of it would impress him with a sense of greatness or of insignificance; but when I remembered how long a time it had taken to erect, in how short a space it might be traversed even to its remotest parts, for how brief a term he, or any of those who cared to bear his name, would live to see it, or know of its existence, I imagined him far more melancholy than proud, and looking with regret upon his labour done. With these thoughts in my mind, I began to ascend, almost unconsciously, the flight of steps leading to the several wonders of the building, and found myself before a barrier where another money-taker sat, who demanded which among them I would choose to see. There were the stone gallery, he said, and the whispering gallery, the geo-metrical staircase, the room of models, the clock—the clock being quite in my way, I stopped him there, and chose that sight from all the rest.

I groped my way into the Turret which it occupies, and saw before me, in a kind of loft, what seemed to be a great, old oaken press with folding doors. These being thrown back by the attendant (who was sleeping when I came upon him, and looked a drowsy fellow, as though his close companionship with Time had made him quite indifferent to it), disclosed a complicated crowd of wheels and chains in iron and brass,—great, sturdy, rattling engines,—suggestive of breaking a finger put in here or there, and grinding the bone to powder,—and these were the Clock! Its very pulse, if I may use the word, was like no other clock. It did not mark the flight of every moment with a gentle second stroke, as though it would check old Time, and have him stay his pace in pity, but measured it with one sledge-hammer beat, as if its business were to crush the seconds as they came trooping on, and remorselessly to clear a path before the Day of Judgment.

I sat down opposite to it, and hearing its regular and never-changing voice, that one deep constant note, uppermost amongst all the noise and clatter in the streets below,—marking that, let that tumult rise or fall, go on or stop,—let it be night or noon, to-morrow or to-day, this year or next,—it still performed its functions with the same dull constancy, and regulated the progress of the life around, the fancy came upon me that this was London's Heart,—and that when it should cease to beat, the City would be no more.

It is night. Calm and unmoved amidst the scenes that darkness favours, the great heart of London throbs in its Giant breast. Wealth and beggary, vice and virtue, guilt and innocence, repletion and the direst hunger, all treading on each other and crowding together, are gathered round it. Draw but a little circle above the clustering housetops, and you shall have within its space everything, with its opposite extreme and contradiction, close beside. Where yonder feeble light is shining, a man is but this moment dead. The taper at a few yards' distance is seen by eyes that have this instant opened on the world. There are two houses separated by but an inch or two of wall. In one, there are quiet minds at rest; in the other, a waking conscience that one might think would trouble the very air. In that close corner where the roofs shrink down and cower together as if to hide their secrets from the handsome street hard by, there are such dark crimes, such miseries and horrors, as could be hardly told in whispers. In the handsome street, there are folks asleep who have dwelt there all their lives, and have no more knowledge of these things than if they had never been, or were transacted at the remotest limits of the world,—who, if they were hinted at, would shake their heads, look wise, and frown, and say they were impossible, and out of Nature,—as if all great towns were not. Does not this Heart of London, that nothing moves, nor stops, nor quickens,—that goes on the same let what will be done, does it not express the City's character well?

The day begins to break, and soon there is the hum and noise of life. Those who have spent the night on doorsteps and cold stones crawl off to beg; they who have slept in beds come forth to their occupation, too, and business is astir. The fog of sleep rolls slowly off, and London shines awake. The streets are filled with carriages and people gaily clad. The jails are full, too, to the throat, nor have the workhouses or hospitals much room to spare. The courts of law are crowded. Taverns have their regular frequenters by this time, and every mart of traffic has its throng. Each of these places is a world, and has its own inhabitants; each is distinct from, and almost unconscious of the existence of any other. There are some few people well to do, who remember to have heard it said, that numbers of men and women—thousands, they think it was—get up in London every day, unknowing where to lay their heads at night; and that there are quarters of the town where misery and famine always are. They don't believe it quite,—there may be some truth in it, but it is exaggerated, of course. So, each of these thousand worlds goes on, intent upon itself, until night comes again,—first with its lights and pleasures, and its cheerful streets; then with its guilt and darkness.

Heart of London, there is a moral in thy every stroke! as I look on at thy indomitable working, which neither death, nor press of life, nor grief, nor gladness out of doors will influence one jot, I seem to hear a voice within thee which sinks into my heart, bidding me, as I elbow my way among the crowd, have some thought for the meanest wretch that passes, and, being a man, to turn away with scorn and pride from none that bear the human shape. (*MHC* 106–9)

Custom House, Lower Thames Street, Houndsditch, Leadenhall Street, St Mary Axe, the Monument, Fish Street Hill, the Borough

Insolvent Court • Portugal Street, Lincoln's Inn, Houndsditch, Tyburn, Whitechapel, St George's Fields, Southwark

The Pickwick Papers

In a lofty room, badly lighted and worse ventilated, situate in Portugal Street, Lincoln's Inn-fields, there sit nearly the whole year round, one, two, three, or four gentlemen in wigs, as the case may be, with little writing-desks before them, constructed after the fashion of those used by the judges of the land, barring the French polish; a box of barristers on their right hand; an inclosure of insolvent debtors on their left; and an inclined plane of most especially dirty faces in their front. These gentlemen are the Commissioners of the Insolvent Court, and the place in which they sit is the Insolvent Court itself.

It is, and has been, time out of mind, the remarkable fate of this Court to be somehow or other held and understood, by the general consent of all the destitute shabby-genteel people in London, as their common resort, and place of daily refuge. It is always full. The steams of beer and spirits perpetually ascend to the ceiling, and, being condensed by the heat, roll down the walls like rain: there are more old suits of clothes in it at one time, than will be offered for sale in all Houndsditch in a twelvemonth; more unwashed skins and grizzly beards than all the pumps and shaving-shops between Tyburn and Whitechapel could render decent, between sunrise and sunset.

It must not be supposed that any of these people have the least shadow of business in, or the remotest connexion with, the place they so indefatigably attend. If they had, it would be no matter of surprise, and the singularity of the thing would cease at once. Some of them sleep during the greater part of the sitting; others carry small portable dinners wrapped in pocket handker-chiefs or sticking out of their worn-out pockets, and munch and listen with equal relish; but no one among them was ever known to have the slightest personal interest in any case that was ever brought forward. Whatever they do, there they sit from the first moment to the last. When it is heavy rainy weather, they all come in wet through; and at such times the vapours of the Court are like those of a fungus-pit.

A casual visitor might suppose this place to be a temple dedicated to the Genius of Seediness. There is not a messenger or process-server attached to it, who wears a coat that was made for him; not a tolerably fresh, or whole-some-looking man in the whole establishment, except a little white-headed apple-faced tipstaff, and even he, like an ill-conditioned cherry preserved in brandy, seems to have artificially dried and withered up into a state of preservation, to which he can lay no natural claim. The very barristers' wigs are ill-powdered, and their curls lack crispness.

But the attorneys, who sit at a large bare table below the Commissioners, are, after all, the greatest curiosities. The professional establishment of the more opulent of these gentlemen, consists of a blue bag and a boy: generally a youth of the Jewish persuasion. They have no fixed offices, their legal business being transacted in the parlours of public houses, or the yards of prisons, whither they repair in crowds, and canvass for customers after the manner of omnibus cads. They are of a greasy and mildewed appearance; and if they can be said to have any vices at all, perhaps drinking and cheating are the most conspicuous among them. Their residences are usually on the outskirts of 'the Rules,' chiefly lying within a circle of one mile from the obelisk in St. George's Fields. Their looks are not prepossessing, and their manners are peculiar. (*PP* 571–2)

The relation between subject and place is not always a material one, if ever. One need not be in a particular locale in order to apprehend or remember its effect, the experience of having stood in that place, or the memory of perception. Some places give themselves, they 'call', if you will, in the imagination, by virtue of what takes place in a name, even though you may never have visited them at all. To offer one obvious example: Whitechapel. The very idea of 'Jack the Ripper' and all such a thought entails is, for some, the *sine qua non* of the site. A memory which is not mine, it nevertheless imposes itself, or can do so. After a particular historical moment, it remains the persistent tattoo on the site. Of course, this could not have been the case for Dickens, though for some of his readers, Whitechapel would have been synonymous with crime, vice, poverty and, for some, the Ratcliffe Highway murders of 1811. More generally, a condition of modernity (implied in the idea of the haunting of subject by place as one dimension of a particular phenomenal modern condition) is a sense of 'historic temporality' allied anachronistically to 'those passions or situations that repeat themselves, that come back' (Agacinski 2003, 107). The text of Dickens is enmeshed within the ravel of such anachronic iterability; it is reliant on that sense of the past of a place having an iterable, phenomenal force. Such energy may emerge through the most minimal of openings, the cultural past, cultural memory and the anachronic flow arriving in a brief moment of presentation; such is the case before us, in the Insolvent Court.

Wigs and writing-desks, boxes of barristers, inclosures of insolvent debtors, the 'lofty room' of the Insolvent Court, Portugal Street, Lincoln's Inn Fields, is understood not simply in itself but through a number of comparisons and allusions. Additionally, its singular condition is discerned in its being frequented by a regularly large number of people who have nothing to do with insolvency. Even the attorneys are 'curiosities', in that they appear to do little in the Insolvent Court but, as we are assured, having no 'fixed offices', they conduct the law either in public houses or prison-yards. Given the present tense of the passage, it might be observed that, like the poor, the law is always with us, always before us – as is insolvency, though that is a different matter. Beginning, as it were, in alliteration, pausing along the way to observe that 'curls lack crispness', and concluding with alliteration, beyond the court and its immediate, mappable location into those gathering places of the working classes – the one perhaps helping to lead to the other, in the world of Dickens's London – the passage conjures through its poetics a formal architextural analogue between the smaller and the larger world, thereby tracing a relation between each of the smaller worlds. Alliteration brings to the fore a formal mapping of relation, addressing an economic inter-dependency that defines parts of the modern urban condition and its subjects. It is the thread which stitches place to place, this network re-enforced through the aural play on the Commissioners, whose peripatetic practice of the law works through 'crowds', in which are found 'custom-ers' for whom they 'canvass', in a manner similar to 'omnibus cads'.[24]

Though everything about the place gives itself to be seen, yet there is little of purpose or utility, and barely a narrator; any hypothetical *flânerie* is that of the 'casual visitor', who might speculate on the identity, if not the nature of this location, had he wandered into the Court. Present, given phantasmal presence and giving in turn the discourse on the Court, which is to give the Court to be seen, there is no narrator as such. Only *there*, only as a medium through the agency of projection afforded the veils of language, the narrator-effect is to transform, or at least merge or submerge, the equally phantasmal witness, the subject of the scene into that place; I is the site. Or, as close as one can be to the place one is in, and to which one gives testimony, as it is possible to be, whilst still main-taining that differentiation that allows one to speak, observe, record.

Perhaps more than place, therefore, 'I' becomes – is always already – a site of translation, from the materiality of place to the materiality of the letter. This leaves the reader to judge, but in a manner called by Kant reflective judgement: that is to say, judgement without preconditions, parameters, regulation or criteria.[25] Frequently, in Dickens, the reader, or the subject of the city, is called on not only to give testimony, but also to do so without prior evidence, theoretical model, or paradigm for judging. This is why London calls the subject, the narrator, the reader to a halt before a given scene, maintained in a narrative suspension of topo-analytical re-presentation. This occurs through not infrequent intensi-fication caused by a shift from past to present tense; on occasion, this is abetted by the increased frequency of semi-colon use, the (implied) erasure of adverbial modification indicating place ('there is'), in order that the distance between the subject / narrator and location diminishes, and the occasional parenthesis or apostrophe addressed directly to a 'you', singular or plural, the reader as audience. In order to maintain the novelty of re-presentation, the Dickens text augments the force of simile or metaphor, shifting towards catachresis. (Or it might be, catachresis is already at work, invisible performative in the troping of language, deformation as the condition appropriate to a discourse of re-presentation, apropos London's modernity for its subject.) There is thus at work in such passages not a reading of place organised around a politics of identity, but one organised by, and around, a politics of difference. This, as Thomas Docherty suggests, causes reading to become uncomfortable, inasmuch as it produces, or aims to engender, a new experience, as if one had never seen this, or seen something in this manner. From within representation, out of history, comes the re-presentation of subjective perception enabled by an 'exogamy of language', which signifies a desire 'to escape from the sphere of what is always the same, the spell of what one is and knows anyway' (Adorno 1991a, 187).

To return to detail in the image of the Insolvent Court: the senses are challenged, confronted, from the outset, the vision of place variable, 'as the case may be', the wigs ('ill-powdered') and the writing-desks being the most immediately determined objects at hand. Barristers and debtors oppose one another, between whom, below the wigs and writing-cases, are the 'dirty faces' of the Commissioners. Everything about the Court tends to dirt, destitution, shabbiness and seediness, steam and condensation, unwashed skin and unshaven visages. At inclement times, the atmospheric conditions worsen outside this dismal room, and so does the aura within, the 'vapours' becoming 'like those of a fungus-pit'; while the appearance of Commissioners is further expatiated on, their appearance denoted as 'greasy and mildewed', conditions of appearance – and appearance is that which Being gives, what is shown, and, therefore, the phenomenal essence of what is seen – contributing to the sense of unprepossessing peculiarity in this legal cabinet of singular curiosities.

At the same time, though, that which is within has its corollary beyond the walls of this disquieting image. Vapours, steam, dirt, rain; the shabby gentility of the visitors, whose purpose remains unknowable, and more particularly their clothes, which invoke the second-hand shops and stalls of Houndsditch; the Court, the public house, the prison, the 'Rules' – every place is implied as a partial figural and phenomenal palimpsest of every other; what is given is suggested elsewhere. That which connotes 'greasy and mildewed appearance' before us finds, whether on human being or object, a relation beyond. To remind ourselves of what takes place, what Jean-Luc Marion calls the 'mode of *givenness*' (2002b, 19), we should note how, through the givenness of the collected phenomena present in the image, there are gestures towards other worlds outside the Court, as we have already argued. In part, this takes place because of that 'exogamy of language'. The auratic modality common to things and people as so many privileged tropes of presentation causes us to see beyond the mere depiction, and to apperceive an other London; the discourse of damp, mildew, steam, grease and 'ill-conditioned' presentation gives us to see in a more authentic light, by which 'the given, givens, and the datum, even reduced to their brute factuality, still bear in themselves the ambiguity constitutive of givenness' (Marion 2002b, 62); wherein, in the very disappearance in the given, of truth of that to which we are subject is all the more visibly there. This is the work of language. Such work, such exogamic revelation works not only through adjectival embellishment, which is at once 'factual' after a manner, but also discursively, if not ideologically, 'inappropriate' to the representation of the law. Language, the servant of the law, in providing evidence, giving testimony, transgresses the bounds of 'proper' representation, admitting the world beyond. Language, if we open ourselves, becoming subject to its play, enables an 'essential phenomenological operation of . . . reduction' to arrive 'beyond objectness and beingness – at pure givenness' (Marion 2002b, 17–18) And this too is what takes place in the proper name, as the figure of phenomenological immanence *par excellence*, whereby the immanence of historicity is given.

The proper name is as much a detail in the image as is any description of the contents or inhabitants of the Court. Language gives to place co-ordinates, rather than simply 'context'. Indeed, the name within the frame of reference that is the image belongs to the indexical function that persists in the image, even as language strives to escape from the sphere of the same. In belonging to this indexical modality, it hints that, on the one hand, there is both more than one context and that context is infinite, in principle; on the other hand, there is nothing other than context, and it is only in the act of reading selectively that we delimit what we choose to see as centre or periphery, *ergon* or *parergon*. We had observed already how the extract is determined before us through comparison with the larger world: Houndsditch, Tyburn, Whitechapel and St George's Fields. There is something rather more complex at work, though, to which we should attend. The question of place in this instance of adumbrated chorography offers at once a mapping through implied inversions and analogues, whilst also being a medium for meditation on a network of places as a collective site of memory. While the Insolvent Court and Lincoln's Inn Fields might be said to provide the present nexus in this topoanalysis, its subjects are connected through matters of both law and economics in the present, but also in a relation between the law at, or possibly as, the imagined or desired centre of the *polis* and more generally modern urban culture, and a lawlessness associated with poverty, criminality, insurgency and, generally, an urban proletariat. Dickensian chorography serves to trace a cultural memory of attempted control and rebellion, which, belonging to cultural anamnesis, produces this particular re-presentation of the Court as a mnemotechnic, the poetics of which cause to appear memory of the city itself, as well as a certain mapping effect. With Tyburn to the east, Whitechapel and Houndsditch to the east, and St George's Fields south of the river, on what would have been the Surrey side in Southwark, 'modern' London finds itself haunted at its juridical centre by memories of what forms and informs the identity of that centre. Centre and margin, present and past are inverted, as the periphery and what is absent determine London through a poetics and politics of difference.

In such a chorography, what I have described as an adumbrated technique amounts to a phenomenology of the name, place reduced to signature. The proper name gives. There – on the page, on the map – it is, it calls as, the signature of 'things past', of events and experiences, if one shares or has access to certain histories or cultural memories. The name stands as countersignature to what is merely observed. A quantum trope, the name gives on to the difference and other of the Court.

Thus Tyburn is the site of the 'first permanent gallows' (Porter 1994, 153), set up in 1571, but also a place of transgression, apprentices being 'allowed a "Tyburn Fair" holiday', with the victims of executions regarded as 'heroes' (Porter 1994, 153). Large crowds could often be depended on at such holidays, often exceeding 30,000, with the largest recorded as around 80,000 in the eighteenth century (Inwood 1998, 308). As early as 1388, though, it was a place associated with executions, Sir Nicholas Brembre, previously Mayor of London until 1386, being 'dragged to Tyburn on a hurdle and hanged, drawn and quartered as a traitor' (Inwood 1998, 79); in May 1535, 'three Carthusian priors . . . were executed . . . before a vast crowd for denying royal supremacy', to be followed a few months after by the exaction at Tyburn of more 'London Carthusians' (Inwood 1998, 151). Servants were frequently hanged there, for stealing from their employers (Inwood 1998, 341), and Jonathan Wild, the 'hero' of Henry Fielding's novel, *Jonathan Wild the Great* (2004), and the model for Peachum in John Gay's *Beggar's Opera* (Inwood 1998, 374), was executed at Tyburn in May 1725. Tyburn was, then, a 'favoured site for a hanging', the earliest recorded being in 1196 (Ackroyd 2000, 291; see 291–3, and 295–6), but also a place of semi-licensed and sanctioned release for the working classes, through a particularly secularised form of carnival, law and order in London having taken the place of the church in the authorised discourse of transgression (Stallybrass and White 1986, 1–79 *passim*). And, of course, as the West End spread for the upper- and upper-middle classes in the late eighteenth century, Paddington became referred to as 'Tyburnia' 'after public executions had ended at Tyburn in 1783' (Porter 1994, 212; see Inwood 1998, 575, 576).

Houndsditch, a road running along the boundary of the City wall, and the area adjacent, was also an ambiguous location dating back to the Middle Ages and the early modern period. In his *Survey*, John Stow records that 'Houndes ditch' was a place of 'much filth (conveyed forth of the city), especially dead dogs' (Stow 1956, 116; see Ackroyd 2000, 22); however, by Stow's time, the area was already built up, to the extent that many inhabitants 'suffered severely' as a result of plague, with a common burial pit holding over 1,000 corpses being nearby (Weinrebb and Hibbert 1995, 396–7). The areas of Spitalfields and Whitechapel, 'from Houndsditch in the west to Vallance Road in the east' (Inwood 1998, 414), have always been associated with the poorest members of London society, criminality and immigration. Most immediately, though, and this is what the passage from *Pickwick* signals, the 'market' and second-hand clothing spread along the 'eastern edge of the City, especially along Houndsditch, the . . . centre of second-hand clothes dealing' (Inwood 1998, 453).

The last proper name to invoke memory of place, or to signify a site of memory, is that of St George's Fields. Invoked through the reference to the obelisk at St George's Fields, this location south of the Thames is the site of what is known as the massacre of St George's Fields (1768), where the Gordon Riots are said to have begun in 1780. There is thus something of an irony in that this is the place of the 'Rules', where the Commissioners are said to live, that 'circle of one mile' from the Obelisk taking in, to the south-west, the Marshalsea Debtors' Prison, which would, of course, still be in full operation at the time of *Pickwick*. That aside for the moment, St George's Fields, generally a site with a particular history of lawlessness, offers recorded scenes of what Stephen Inwood terms 'popular unrest', dating back at least to 1640. The site was used as a gathering point for 'City apprentices, suburban leatherworkers and watermen' (Inwood 1998, 221), in order to march on Lambeth Palace. Not only a convening point for radicals and dissenters, the Fields was also the working-class equivalent to Ranelagh and Vauxhall, with the Apollo Gardens and the Dog and Duck popular places of amusement, as well as being (allegedly) the 'resort of low and vicious characters'

St George's Circus (previously Fields)

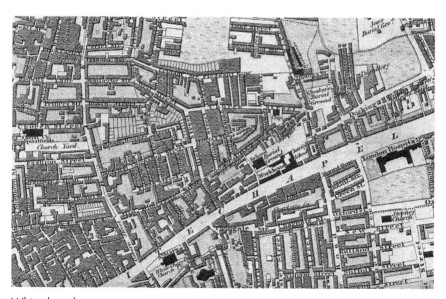

Whitechapel

(Walford 1878, 347). Though, for many generations, the Fields was a locus of recreation and popular assembly, by the time of Samuel Pickwick – and Sam Weller – the area had already been subsumed by the spread of suburbanisation, the location having been chosen in 1815 as the site of the new Bethlehem Royal Hospital (Bedlam) (Inwood 1998, 308). Of the area, in 1812, James and Horace Smith wrote, satirically, 'St George's Fields are fields no more, / The trowel supersedes the plough; / Huge inundated swamps of yore / Are changed to civic villas now' (Smith 1879, 4).

History remains immanent, though, in the name. If the extract gives in a particular fashion more than it shows, this at least illustrates for us the manner in which, while place can always be an archive or repository, that which is erased or lost, in leaving traces what takes place in a given locus always exceeds any representation of a given experience. Perception is otherwise, and if there is that which is clearly given, givenness is also obscure, calling for the subject to read closely. Critically, the Dickens text situates itself apropos London in relation to its reading subject, calling for the subject who knows how to read and distinguish the literary difference within descriptive, realist or mimetic surface-fidelities. Close reading attends to difference; any other kind of reading misses the literary. It is in the poetics of figuration that opens, resonates with that 'temporalized delay' externalised in the dualism of place and subject, or location and narrator. In this delay, the effect of close reading, the Dickens text would have us understand as we loiter in the place of an other – as if we could be there and as if that place were there for our perception – there takes place the 'strictly phenomenological conversion of what gives itself (the call) into what shows itself (the responsal). The conversion', Marion continues, 'imposes a delay – a slowness, but a ripening slowness . . . The visible' – that is to say, the truth of the image, of historicity – only has its chance of coming to light 'in this very delay. Temporality itself delays only in order to attest it' (Marion 2002b, 296). In this, the idea of the narrator or the subject are merely mediums; for what arrives, what calls, that which gives itself in short, is nothing other than London, the multiplicities of the city. Perhaps, it might be worth hypothesising, this is why that suspension in, and of, the Dickensian present tense, the shift of focus effected by semi-colon following semi-colon, the abandonment of the objectifying adverbial modifier and verb, the Dickens-machine idles, resonating at certain frequencies, demanding in the process that from the temporality of delay, we see exactly what calls, and what is given.

Jaggers's House • Gerrard Street, Soho

Great Expectations

[Mr Jaggers] conducted us to Gerrard-street, Soho, to a house on the south side of that street. Rather a stately house of its kind, but dolefully in want of painting, and with dirty windows. He took out his key and opened the door, and we all went in to a stone hall, bare, gloomy and little used. So, up a dark brown staircase into a series of three dark brown rooms on the first floor. There were carved garlands on the panelled walls, and as he stood among them giving us welcome, I know what kind of loops I thought they looked like.

Dinner was laid in the best of these rooms; the second was the dressing room; the third, his bedroom. He told us that he held the whole house, but rarely used more of it than we saw. The table was comfortably laid—no silver in the service, of course—and at the side of his chair was a capacious dumb-waiter, with a variety of bottles and decanters on it, and four dishes of fruit for dessert. I noticed throughout, that he kept everything under his own hand, and distributed everything himself.

There was a bookcase in the room; I saw, from the backs of the books, that they were about evidence, criminal law, criminal biography, trials, acts of parliament, and such things. The furniture was all very solid and good, like his watch-chain. It had an official look, however, and there was nothing merely ornamental to be seen. In a corner, was a little table of papers with a shaded lamp: so that he seemed to bring the office home with him in that respect too, and to wheel it out of an evening and fall to work. (*GE* 211)

It is unremarkable. There is nothing to be remarked.

The introduction to Mr Jaggers's home is one of Dickens's more economical impressions of architectural and topographical space. More than economical, it is reserved; it reserves to itself that which would otherwise be traced with simultaneously minute and hyperbolic attentiveness. In part, this has to do, undoubtedly, with the fact that Pip is the narrator. However, Pip's imagination elsewhere in the text can take powerful hold of a passing image and make a great deal of it, to the degree that the absence of any fanciful projection is notable. Perception is therefore understood as always subject to place to some degree, rather than having any autonomous agency. Jaggers's home has the power to curtail the imagination's flight. Pip notices all there is to see, or seems to do so. He remembers, at least, those phenomena that work, in memory of the visit, to produce Mr Jaggers's house in such a way that is significant for Pip. Such significance as there is resides in circumscribing Pip's analogical associations. As narrator, Pip's memories of place constitute a field of significance, constructing the image of place so as to give to it a meaning in denying Pip's literary phantasies (his associations are driven often by what he has read, to which 'reality' is compared), but also for Pip's audience, whilst withholding direct observation of Mr Jaggers's character. Mr Jaggers is behind the impression of the dwelling space, the god in the machine, in a manner analogous to those rooms at which Jaggers hints but rarely uses. To an extent, therefore, place stands in for person, the attributes of the architecture, its colouration and the combinations in representation tend toward reception of an indirect portrait of the lawyer, behind all of which there is always the law, inevitably.

There is, in effect, the work of implied layering here – implied only inasmuch as every surface suggests something beneath, below or behind it; but once passed, that surface gives way to yet another surface. The spatial and architectural image moves from outside to inside, as we travel with Pip through the areas of the *topos*, shifting through the initial perceptions of gloom, dirt, lack, bareness and neglect. There is an entire house beyond the hall and the three rooms employed by Jaggers, but this is as little seen as it is employed. In contrast, the table is 'comfortably laid', and there is a 'capacious' dumb-waiter, with four dishes of fruit alongside a number of bottles and decanters. Four? Is there an opulence, a hint of decadence or exoticism in such a display of fruit? It is impossible to know, but the perception of the detail remains none the less. It remains as a small enigma of representation, not unlike what appear to be oranges (or are they apricots?) on the cabinet top and window ledge in the Arnolfini Portrait (1434) by Jan Van Eyck, the significance of which is in the undecidability concerning whether such details are symbolic. The house appearing to be 'stately', the furniture offers an echo in its solidity, 'good', in Pip's assessment, like the lawyer's watch-chain. There is no waste, no silver (of course) in the service, and nothing 'merely ornamental'. The books are of a piece, or a family at least, being solely concerned with the law, criminality, justice, legislature and so forth. Finally, Jaggers's work table, which reproduces the workplace in the domestic scene, reiterates the functionality of the dumb-waiter. In effect, this is a portrait: the Jaggers Portrait, by Philip Pirrip, exact date unknown. A Portrait of the Lawyer, by a Young Man.

All of which gives me to ask, what is this place? What kind of place, and what kind of a portrait, are these? If, as Marc Augé asserts, following the work of Jean Starobinski and Jean Baudrillard on modernity, a 'place can be defined as relational, historical, and concerned with identity' (Augé 1995, 77), what precisely is given here? All relation refers to Jaggers: the 'historical', such as it is, is inscribed in the books that make up Jaggers's library, the identity of place determined by the occupant. The house – and the image – is nothing so much as a rhetorical and tropological site, in which the paucity of descriptive sustain serves in the manner of phenomenological reduction, leaving everything as a mystery, undecidable as to symbolism beyond the obvious – is there anything beyond the obvious here? How could we tell, how do we know? – and all the more immediately before the reader as a result. Pip's gaze and Pip's narrative, the consciousness which these two constitute, read place as identity, but not the identity of *topos*. There is little in the way of identity for the house. However, its very anonymity, its secrecy and being enclosed on itself serves as a palimpsest of Jaggers, in much the same manner as his office does for Pip, on Pip's first encounter with the lawyer (*GE* 164–5). The difference between the two experiences for Pip is that the first affords much greater play of the imagination.

Note how the recurrence of tropes occurs. The parallelism between seemingly distinct phenomena informs the movement through the passage, into the house and through to the different aspects of the room. The further we follow Pip, the closer we observe, after him; we learn only what has already been conveyed. Passing one surface, one layer of description, we find another, the purpose of which is to keep us from moving any deeper into the identity or meaning of either the house or Jaggers, as I have already intimated. The very move from house front to room, to dinner, to bookcase, to work table, is one of the avoidance of choices, for each move results only in another impenetrable surface. The house is 'stately', each room, the image of the others, being dark and brown; the dinner table is 'comfortably laid', the furniture 'solid and good', reminiscent (once again) of the watch-chain. The office is brought home. Wherever Jaggers is, everything is the same, all is 'under his own hand'. In one sense, then, as I have already remarked, Pip's imagination is defeated, even though he does observe, somewhat enigmatically, that he knows what kind of loops the carved garlands on the hall panels resemble.

What does this all have to do with London, though? A detour is necessary, in order to arrive at our destination; if, as Paul de Man has commented, literary language is definable as a 'nonconvergence between the stated meaning and its understanding', then reading, as de Man continues, has to 'begin in this unstable commixture of literalism and suspicion' (1979, 57–8). Pip's presentation of the lawyer's dwelling – and, we speculate, the lawyer also – gives to us little more than the bare scene, and yet it is because of this relative poverty of interpretation that we should be suspicious of Pip's rather banal observations. There are already two readings at work here, if not more. There is – there *was* – Pip's initial perception; this has then been filtered through his memory, to appear in the form of the reading / writing, the composition or portrait we have before us, poised carefully between seemingly minimal interpretation and the odd moment of departure into embellishment. Following in the wake of these, we find ourselves in the position of the first Pip, seeing through the hindsight of the second. Thus far, the motion of the reading has been one of entry, interiorisation and increasing attention to detail, albeit attention without embellishment, rather than taking in the whole, but all the while assuming association, relation and identity, so as to appear to give meaning to place, even as other significations appear suspended, through a speculative symbolism that in no way can be confirmed – *or denied*. Pip, as subject, is not positioning himself, though, at least not directly. It may be that a reading of Pip's subjectivity is available from the manner of his narrating self's representation of his narrated self's perceptions. Interestingly, though, the reading has tended towards an analogical excavation of the meaning of Mr Jaggers. Mr Jaggers is aligned with the house, the house an image of the lawyer, giving little away, having the promise of sequestered spaces, abstract because occluded and definable only in their impenetrability.

To approach this problem in representation differently, if the office can be transposed on to the home; if each trope is a figure for every other, all folded on to one another through the implication of iterability; if Mr Jaggers's hand is on everything, in control, and everything thereby remains solid, stable, never merely ornamental but, at bottom, useful, serving a purpose within a system of purposes; then Pip's reading cannot enter the penetralia, either of the house or Jaggers, but must live on the surfaces, each supplementing the others, to come back to this point. Moving out from the hand, the table, the dumb-waiter, the rooms, the hall, the house, there is the city, or a secret city at least, the city of the law, before which Pip must always remain; as with every reader, Pip is always before the law. There is here the hint of a London, not available, to which one never has access. Beyond fantasy, story-telling, the flights of the imagination that colour Pip's imagination in his reading of situations, events and experiences, there is a world for which he never comes to terms. Jaggers is the guardian of that world; gatekeeper and symbol, his house thus the most typical. Pip, perhaps the most typical reader in the world, has to stay before what is given. The world for Pip is a mystery not to be solved, of which London is the greatest enigma, Jaggers its representative. But this is not a limit of Pip's. Rather, his inability to perceive beyond what is shown is typical of us all, and in this he is reminiscent, however accidentally, of no one so much as the figure of the man from the country who comes seeking the law, who waits all his life but who cannot get past the first doorkeeper, in Kafka's parable, *Vor dem Gesetz.*

Besides showing what is there, this passage offers its effect, that effect being occlusion, the hidden, the absent and silent, or rather all that cannot be said, all that remains the other side of narration. Addressing Pip's mediated re-presentation and returning to the bareness of the scene, it has to be suggested that here is a narrative of *topos* which is reduced to absolute effect: not a pure phenomenality perhaps, but, in its reduction, what is given to Pip, and so to us, is the 'bracketing of [the phenomena's] mundane beingness and reality' (Marion 2002b, 52). Pip is confronted, as are we, with an absolute and unconditional require-ment that we accept what there is, as the assertion of a universal author-ity, given the forms of Jaggers and his house. Thus we remain before a mystery, a conundrum not to be solved. Indeed, the enigma of place must remain in place, a problem not to be solved but maintained. This is the categorical imperative, if you will, to which Pip is subject. In what is seemingly the most direct re-presentation, the most allusive expression might be heard. For '[i]mage, the equivocity of language, and metaphor, all escort and authorize the saying of the True' (Badiou 2008, 38). The house in Gerrard Street is an analogue for Jaggers, Jaggers, the analogue of the city's impenetrability. Both are analogues that speak enigmati-cally because allusively, but always with the authority and truth of the law, of the ultimate inaccessibility of the meaning of London as a whole. All that is perceived, all that is shown, is *there* before the subject, in its givenness. There is thus nothing other; this remains before the subject, who remains before the place in which he finds himself, seeing but not understanding. No Ariadne will appear to solve the riddle of London's labyrinth, which the Dickens-machine so effectively constructs.

Krook's • by Lincoln's Inn

Bleak House

I was ... sufficiently curious about London, to think it a good idea on the part of Miss Jellyby when she proposed that we should go out for a walk.
[...]
  ... I admired the long successions and varieties of streets, the quantity of people already going to and fro, the number of vehicles passing and repassing, the busy preparations in the setting forth of shop windows and the sweeping out of shops, and the extraordinary creatures in rags, secretly groping among the swept-out rubbish for pins and other refuse.
[...]
  Slipping us out at a little side gate, the old lady stopped most unexpectedly in a narrow back street, part of some courts and lanes immediately outside the wall of the inn, and said, 'This is my lodging. Pray walk up!'
  She had stopped at a shop, over which was written, KROOK, RAG AND BOTTLE WAREHOUSE. Also, in long thin letters, KROOK, DEALER IN MARINE STORES. In one part of the window was a picture of a red paper mill, at which a cart was unloading a quantity of sacks of old rags. In another, was the inscription, BONES BOUGHT. In another, KITCHEN STUFF BOUGHT. In another, OLD IRON BOUGHT. In another, LADIES' AND GENTLEMENS' WARDROBES BOUGHT. Everything seemed to be bought, and nothing to be sold there. In all parts of the window, were quantities of dirty bottles, medicine bottles, ginger-beer and soda-water bottles, pickle bottles, wine bottles, ink bottles: I am reminded by mentioning the latter, that the shop had, in several particulars, the air of being in a legal neighbourhood, and of being, as it were, a dirty hanger-on and disowned relation of the law. There were a great many ink bottles. There was a little tottering bench of shabby old volumes, some outside the door, labelled 'Law Books, all at 9*d*.' Some of the inscriptions I have enumerated were written in law-hand, like the papers I had seen at Kenge and Carboy's office, and the letters I had so long received from the firm. Among them was one, in the same writing, having nothing to do with the business of the shop, but announcing that a respectable man aged forty-five wanted engrossing or copying to execute with neatness and dispatch: Address to Nemo, care of Mr Krook, within. There were several second-hand bags, blue and red, hanging up. A little way within the shop-door, lay heaps of old crackled parchment scrolls, and discoloured and dog's-eared

law papers. I could have fancied that all the rusty keys, of which there must have been hundreds huddled together as old iron, had once belonged to doors of rooms, or strong chests in lawyers' offices. The litter of rags tumbled partly into and partly out of a one-legged wooden scale, hanging without any counterpoise from a beam, might have been counsellors' bands and gowns torn up. One had only to fancy ... that yonder bones in a corner, piled together and picked very clean, were the bones of clients, to make the picture complete.

As it was still foggy and dark, and the shop was blinded besides by the wall of Lincoln's Inn, intercepting the light within a couple of yards, we should not have seen much but for a lighted lantern that an old man in spectacles and a hairy cap was carrying about in the shop. Turning towards the door, he now caught sight of us. He was short, cadaverous, and the breath issuing in visible smoke from his mouth, as if he were on fire within. His throat, chin, and eyebrows, were so frosted with white hairs, and so gnarled with veins and puckered skin, that he looked, from his breast upward, like some old root in a fall of snow. (*BH* 63, 66, 67–8)

Reading / writing London opens the fixed, the stable identity, or any objective assumption thereof, to a question concerning what is seen, the modality in which it is given visibility through the response of the subject, and a concomitant, subjective destabilisation, leading to that 'reduction' through subjective perception. The possible apprehension of an urban abyss is maintained at a distance through the registration of experience in response to phenomena, which is detailed, iterable in its rhythms, syntax, grammar and tropic play, and which, as we have had occasion to observe elsewhere, is informed by a proximity in the re-presentation of the trace. The syntax of Krook's window is thus governed, obviously, by Esther Summerson's being both subject of the vision, the subject for whom the window comes to be visible in this particular way, and no other, and the narrating subject, for whom the experience and perception has now been translated into the syntax that follows in the wake of experience, thereby reiterating the visible 'order' of presentation.

This is Esther's first excursion on foot in London in *Bleak House*. Hitherto, she had seen the city only as a succession of 'vignettes' through a carriage window, stereotypes or the slides of a magic lantern show or phantasmagoria. In moving on foot, Esther enters into the flow of the city, wherein matters are no longer presented *in extremis*, in a 'distracting state of confusion' (*BH* 42) tending towards a collective loss of the senses, as Esther supposes, but instead are apprehended with 'admiration' as a long succession of crowds defined by the double motion of moving 'to and fro' and in the 'passing and repassing' of the vehicles. Whether defined as pedestrians or passengers, Esther encounters and experiences the anonymous urban mass initially as being a collective, already underway. Movement is of the initial perception of London (recall Nicholas Nickleby's arrival with Smike), motion being the quality of both those subjects moving about but also as a condition of place, that which is given to the senses, that which shows itself. Even the 'extraordinary creatures in rags' are perceived to be active.

Happening to meet Esther, Caddy, Richard and Ada, Miss Flite introduces Esther to the window of Krook's shop. The initial impression of the shop front and its windows conveyed by Esther, and that which leaves its trace most insistently on her memory, is of writing, architecture transformed into text. The capitals of the inscriptions tend towards a blurring rather than a clarification of vision, while the general initial sense being conveyed is that of the affirmation of transaction, through the reiteration of the term *bought*. The shop front, its signs, its windows filled with signs, and the objects appearing in the windows present a disparate, not to say heterogeneous collection, a concatenation of signs to be read, which is precisely what Esther attempts to do. Rendered passive, motionless, by the plenitude of phenomena, Esther cannot but seek to read. The experience of the window is thus analogous with the experience of reading London for its new subject. In the perception there is sense to be made, at the local, or perhaps *microlocal* level, whereby, for the subject, syntax, tropological geometry and architecture bring together a focus on one location in a more generalised space, which offers itself as the apprehensible figure for that which is only indirectly available to the imagination; but the enormity and complexity, the multiplicities coming together in the constellated image, promise to overwhelm the senses. Krook's shop is perceived and received as both singular and manifold, having a topology, the coherence of which relies not on a logic but on the subject's perception of the whole. Perception and re-presentation are, in effect, *of* the world, inasmuch as, in giving itself to the subject, the window serves to disclose the subject as an extension of the world perceived and in the process of being read. And this extract is very much one of process rather than finished object; for as Esther's eye moves from sign to sign, bottle to bottle, books to papers, so too does the shop front – which is never given as a whole but only seen part by part – become available to the reader, who assumes Esther's position, becoming the subjective palimpsest of Esther's re-presentation. All observation, we may learn if we read carefully, taking note from Esther's process, is a reading, which, in turn, is also a writing, the one slightly out of time with the other, and thereby marked by that difference that makes its motion possible.

If London cannot be seen whole, this is only to reveal the limits of a certain reading, and, equally, the necessity for a different reading, a reading of difference rather than of identity. In order for such a reading to be possible, perception has to shift its ground. We must, of necessity, begin with our experience because, as Kant has shown, the *a priori* is not knowable, as Merleau-Ponty argues, ahead of experience (1962, 220). Without knowing Kant, Esther, as the good reader, begins with experience. Unlike either of her first-person narrating counterparts, Pip and David, her impression, her perception – and hence her revelation of the authentic facticity of her being-in-the-world – begin from the very experience of the world *as* an experience of reading. More than this, Esther's patient, attentive and detailed re-presentation of the shop front before her serves to project Esther as being always in a process of self-constitution through a perceptual field which is, at once, the world of London in this instance and also her own world, herself, the field of vision being the field of her historicity. In this, Esther shows herself; and she shows herself, furthermore, as the figure of the London subject, the modern subject of the modern city, *par excellence*. Having suspended her initial orientation to the world of the capital, as presented in her carriage journey to Kenge and Carboys, she begins a process of reflecting on the condition of her perception through that acknowledgement of the phenomenal flow that constitutes London and its subjects. From this, she arrives before Krook's shop, which immediately presents itself as a problem and a limit: of legibility and comprehension. Before this, Esther remains still, accommodating herself to what is apprehended in the field of vision, thereby giving expression not only to her experience but also to the world as it shapes that experience. In one sense at least, it may be argued that Esther is the paradigmatic modern London subject. Like those strangers, walkers, travellers and other anonymous *flâneurs*, Esther embodies, if not the 'painter', then at least the reader and writer, the interpreter of modern life.

In part, Esther's ability to read is grounded in memory, the memory of letters from Kenge and Carboy's, and it is this that carries over into her perception of Krook's in the enumeration, as she describes it, of various inscriptions, presented in 'law-hand'. Esther finds herself involved, in her relation to place which is seen from within as also a temporal relation, concerned with learning how to read and to discern modes and forms of textual presentation, assuming to herself, her subjectivity a disposition and comprehension that neither makes greater claims, nor aims to imply meanings larger than those at hand. In this – a resistance to attempt a movement beyond what is *there* for the subject – Esther's reading, so inescapably the affirmation through her perception of her being involved in – 'engrossed', as it were, in and by – the world, she disappears, save for the rhythm of her narration, becoming in the process the place on which the shop front, its window, its signs, the bottles and books, become written and imagined, projected in the place of Esther, for the reader of the text of Dickens to receive. As I have suggested elsewhere, in this re-presentation, Esther's narrative becomes the window, a translation of its traces at least, the window becoming narrative and narration. To figure each element is to compose the shop window, to trace for the reader form and vision, as the eye alights as if by chance, on the multiple and heterogeneous phenomena (Wolfreys 1998, 148). Esther's eye moves over the window, its rhythm of observation the 'rhythm of subjectivity' (Louvel 2011, 174). Such rhythmic play dances between writing and image, subsuming both in its general motion whereby the 'movement in space and language' finds itself reiterated as a 'movement of approximation both in perception and in knowledge' (Louvel 2011, 175). Subjectivity, given 'voice' through the rhythm of the eye – as the optical, though invisible analogy for the verbal 'I' – marks the place 'materializing the exchange which keeps having to be renegotiated' (Louvel 2011, 175) in a disposition of subject. This renegotiation introduces into the rhythm a temporal flux as well as a spatial motion that completes the rhythm, seen 'as a moving and fluid form . . . [given] in a syncopation of the visible' (Louvel 2011, 175).

Esther's 'vision' is, then, in addition, a picture, as well as an interpretation. If, as Edward Said observes, writing 'cannot represent the visible' it can 'move toward the visible' (1983, 101); or, as with this interpolated vision of Esther's, it can bring the visible to us, however much a phantasm the 'picture' may be. In doing so, it erases the metaphoricity implicit in the Horatian truism, *ut picture poesis*. Furthermore, Esther's vision reminds us, *contra* Said, that, in the words of Roland Barthes, '[a]ll literary descriptions are *sights*' (1970, 61).[26] It is at once a reading / writing of the image, and a pictorialisation of verbal text, in between which her subjectivity mediates between the two, making both known. Between Krook's signs and his bottles, his mouldy books and the uncollected but heaped papers, there is in play the motion between image and word, the visual and the verbal text. What Esther's reading and revelation of the world gives us to apprehend is that, on the one hand, the text of the world and the world of the text are interchangeable, the one is the other, albeit in an exchanged, re-presented form; on other hand, the verbal, legible, written text presents images for deciphering, the pictorial text presents an image remaining to be read. Esther's reading become writing become image of the shop front, with Esther before the shop front, in turn becomes this image, before the reader, on the page of *Bleak House*, for us to remain still before, to look at, examine, decipher and become subsumed within. If no larger image, no transcendent reading is there, this is because there is no transcendent image, no text of

London at which one can arrive. *A priori* London is a fiction, a fantasy, the mistaken projection on to the real of textual worlds, which are found wanting, whereby London evades the reader, hiding behind the illegibility of a totality that has never existed. The *a posteriori* London is equally unavailable, having no textual equivalent that can figure it once and forever, *in toto*. It is a fantasy beyond legibility, beyond comprehension, inscription or possibility. In Esther's passage, there is London, and there, also, is the transcendent realisation of the impossibility of a transcendent, or final reading, writing or image. There is, however, the transcendent realisation that the invention of London is the invention of the subject. There is in Esther's extract the awareness that 'I can experience more things than I represent to myself, and my being is not reducible to what expressly appears to me concerning myself' (Merleau-Ponty 1962, 296), and in this subject and city accommodate one another, even as the verbal and visual exchange places in the dance of perception and re-presentation.

Life and Death • Snow Hill, the Saracen's Head, Smithfield, Saint James's Parish, Saint Sepulchre's Church

Nicholas Nickleby

Snow Hill! What kind of place can the quiet town's-people who see the words emblazoned in all the legibility of gilt letters and dark shading on the north-country coaches, take Snow Hill to be? All people have some undefined and shadowy notion of a place whose name is frequently before their eyes or often in their ears, and what a vast number of random ideas there must be perpetually floating about, regarding this same Snow Hill. The name is such a good one. Snow Hill—Snow Hill too, coupled with a Saracen's Head: picturing to us a double association of ideas, something stern and rugged. A bleak desolate tract of country, open to piercing blasts and fierce wintery storms—a dark, cold, and gloomy heath, lonely by day, and scarcely to be thought of by honest folks at night—a place where solitary wayfarers shun, and where desperate robbers congregate;—this, or something like this, we imagine must be the prevalent notion of Snow Hill in those remote and rustic parts, through which the Saracen's Head, like some grim apparition, rushes each day and night with mysterious and ghost-like punctuality, holding its swift and heading course in all weathers, and seeming to bid defiance to the very elements themselves.

The reality is rather different, but by no means to be despised notwithstanding. There, at the very core of London, in the heart of its business and animation, in the midst of a whirl of noise and motion: stemming as it were the giant currents of life that flow ceaselessly on from different quarters, and meet beneath its walls, stands Newgate; and in that crowded street on which it frowns so darkly—within a few feet of the squalid, tottering houses—upon that very spot on which the vendors of soup and fish and damaged fruit are now plying their trades—scores of human beings, amidst a roar of sounds to which even the tumult of the great city is as nothing, four, six, or eight strong men at a time, have been hurried violently and swiftly from the world, when the scene has been rendered frightful with excess of human life; when curious eyes have glared from casement, and house-top, and wall and pillar, and when, in the mass of white and upturned faces, the dying wretch, in his all-comprehensive look of agony, has met not one—not one—that bore the impress of pity or compassion.

Near to the jail, and by consequence near to Smithfield also, and the Compter and the bustle and noise of the city; and just on that particular part of Snow Hill where omnibus horses going eastwards seriously think of falling down on purpose, and where horses in hackney cabriolets going westwards not unfrequently fall by accident, is the coachyard of the Saracen's Head Inn, its portal guarded by two Saracen's heads and shoulders, which it was once the pride and the glory of the choice spirits of this metropolis to pull down at night, but which have for some time remained in undisturbed tranquillity; possibly because this species of humour is now confined to Saint James's parish, where door-knockers are preferred, as being more portable, and bell-wires esteemed as convenient tooth-picks. Whether this be the reason or not, there they are, frowning upon you from each side of the gateway, and the inn itself, garnished with another Saracen's Head, frowns upon you from the top of the yard; while from the door of the hind boot of all the red coaches that are standing therein, there glares a small Saracen's Head with a twin expression to the large Saracen's Heads below, so that the general appearance of the pile is of the Saracenic order.

When you walk up this yard, you will see the booking-office on your left, and the tower of Saint Sepulchre's church darting abruptly up into the sky on your right, and a gallery of bedrooms on both sides. Just before you, you will observe a long window with the words 'coffee-room' legibly painted above it ... (NN 88–90)

Melancholy • Leadenhall Street, Newgate, Lant Street, Borough, St George the Martyr

Our Mutual Friend / The Pickwick Papers / Nicholas Nickleby

A grey dusty withered evening in London city has not a hopeful aspect. The closed warehouses and offices have an air of death about them, and the national dread of colour has an air of mourning. The towers and steeples of the many house-encompassed churches, dark and dingy as the sky that seems descending on them, are no relief to the general gloom; a sun-dial on a church-wall has the look, in its useless black shade, of having failed in its business enterprise and stopped payment for ever; housekeepers and porters sweep melancholy waifs and strays of papers and pins into the kennels, and other more melancholy waifs and strays explore them, searching and stooping and poking for anything to sell. The set of humanity outward from the City is as a set of prisoners departing from gaol, and dismal Newgate seems quite as fit a stronghold for the mighty Lord Mayor as his own state-dwelling. (*OMF* 386)

There is a repose about Lant Street, in the Borough, which sheds a gentle melancholy upon the soul. There are always a good many houses to let in the street: it is a bye-street too, and its dullness is soothing. A house in Lant Street would not come within the denomination of a first-class residence, in the strict acceptation of the term; but it is a most desirable spot nevertheless. If a man wished to abstract himself from the world; to remove himself from within the reach of temptation; to place himself beyond the possibility of any inducement to look out of the window, we should recommend him by all means to go to Lant Street.

In this happy retreat are colonized a few clear-starchers, a sprinkling of journeymen bookbinders, one or two prison agents for the Insolvent Court, several small housekeepers who are employed in the Docks, a handful of mantua-makers, and a seasoning of jobbing tailors. The majority of the inhabitants either direct their energies to the letting of furnished apartments, or devote themselves to the healthful and invigorating pursuit of mangling. The chief features in the still life of the street, are green shutters, lodging-bills, brass door-plates, and bell-handles; the principal specimens of animated nature, the pot-boy, the muffin youth, and the baked-potato man. The population is migratory, usually disappearing on the verge of quarter-day, and generally by night. His Majesty's revenues are seldom collected in this happy valley, the rents are dubious, and the water communication is very frequently cut off. (*PP* 417)

The square in which the counting-house of the brothers Cheeryble was situated, although it might not wholly realise the very sanguine expectations which a stranger would be disposed to form on hearing the fervent encomiums bestowed upon it by Tim Linkinwater, was, nevertheless, a sufficiently desirable nook in the heart of a busy town like London, and one which occupied a high place in the affectionate remembrances of several grave persons domiciled in the neighbourhood, whose recollections, however, dated from a much more recent period, and whose attachment to the spot was far less absorbing, than were the recollections and attachment of the enthusiastic Tim.

And let not those whose eyes have been accustomed to the aristocratic gravity of Grosvenor Square and Hanover Square, the dowager barrenness and frigidity of Fitzroy Square, or the gravel walks and garden seats of the Squares of Russell and Euston, suppose that the affections of Tim Linkinwater, or the inferior lovers of this particular locality, had been awakened and kept alive by any refreshing associations with leaves, however dingy, or grass, however bare and thin. The city square has no enclosure, save the lamp-post in the middle: and no grass, but the weeds which spring up round its base. It is a quiet, little-frequented, retired spot, favourable to melancholy and contemplation, and appointments of long-waiting; and up and down its every side the Appointed saunters idly by the hour together wakening the echoes with the monotonous sound of his footsteps on the smooth worn stones, and counting, first the windows, and then the very bricks of the tall silent houses that hem him round about. In winter-time, the snow will linger there, long after it has melted from the busy streets and highways. The summer's sun holds it in some respect, and while he darts his cheerful rays sparingly into the square, keeps his fiery heat and glare for noisier and less-imposing precincts. It is so quiet, that you can almost hear the ticking of your own watch when you stop to cool in its refreshing atmosphere. There is a distant hum—of coaches, not of insects—but no other sound disturbs the stillness of the square. The ticket porter leans idly against the post at the corner: comfortably warm, but not hot, although the day is broiling. His white apron flaps languidly in the air, his head gradually droops upon his breast, he takes very long winks with both eyes at once; even he is unable to withstand the soporific influence of the place, and is gradually falling asleep. (*NN* 552–3)

London and the experience of London are, if not wholly inseparable, then inescapably bound one within the other, to the extent that it can be difficult to discern where melancholy is a condition of the city's disposition or the perception of its subject, as that perception's modality of giving itself. In the three extracts here, the atrabilious phenomena of the city present themselves in markedly different ways. There are distinct modalities of melancholia, which manifest themselves in human attitude, as the sensible apprehension of the urban effect on the 'soul', and in the forms of architectural and topographic constitution aiding the reflective exploration of melancholy. Melancholy is related to retirement, repose, resignation, stillness, ennui; but also, it is the manifest and determining phenomenal condition of waifs and strays. The phenomena of melancholy are, therefore, discernible in others, in the situation or circumstance, both as the expression of out-of-the-way and neglected spaces, and as one sensible orientation of the narrator's perception, in response to that which presents itself, appearing before him. Melancholia, it might be said, gives expression to the numinous, not in the aspect of *mysterium tremendum*, that force which causes fear and trembling, but in the perception and apprehension of a *mysterium fascinans*, the capability of attracting or fascinating. Through the examples of reflective melancholy that informs the image of certain parts of the city, the condition of contemplation and meditation invoked is suggestive of a mode of communion with whatever is felt to be wholly other in London, but which is neither revealed nor capable of direct perception, only analogical apperception, that process by which the subject makes sense of the sensate apprehension through pursuing a relation with ideas already understood.

In the passage from *Our Mutual Friend*, two 'types' of waifs and strays are melancholy: material and human. A relation between the two is traced in the latter observed searching through the former. However, it is in the paper and pins' abandonment and random motion caused by the grey and dusty wind circulating through Leadenhall Street that lies our perception of that which gives to us that understanding of the human 'detritus' of the city its abject quality. The paper and pins are property cast away, 'property' being in legal discourse that which is thrown away, found by chance and unclaimed. As the eye moves over the scene, though, it also chances on the human figures searching through their material counterparts, as so many unclaimed, discarded 'products' of this particular London. While the human examples may manifest signs of melancholy to the eye, this being a condition of their appearance, the other windswept 'property' of the street can have no such constitution, melancholy here being that phenomenon apprehended by the subject. In this moment of the passively directed eye, we see the establishment of 'relations between differences' (Arsic 2003, 13), relations in the absence of relation, which is crucial to the apprehension of the modern city, and equally to the constitution of the modern urban subject, if subjectivity is to find its place within London. The difference without relation is formed through the copula of the perceiving subject, as this makes itself known through the iterability that marks the resemblance as one. Such movement of the 'eye', which reads, and which, in its wake, trails the conscious reflection of writing as what it sees, gathers together, within the location of the experience, the finite phenomena and objects; and in doing so, there is mapped that sense of relation and connectedness through the sensory awareness of melancholy.

Here is the work of urban re-presentation unveiled, as the materiality of the text traces and gives phenomenal form to the materiality of the city, as this comes to be revealed in turn through that reading / writing of eye / consciousness. Melancholy is that which focuses and serves as the sensate copula of the image; it informs, and is mediated by, greyness and dustiness of that 'withered evening' in London, to which there is no 'hopeful aspect'. This last word doubles itself, figuring both that which appears to perception, and also that which the subject considers; it signifies an appearance or quality, and a disposition, a face directed towards the subject's gaze. It is what looks back at one, that which captures one's attention, and that towards which one turns one's eye. Melancholia is anticipated also in that 'air of death', that 'air of mourning'. Once more, *air* is a doubled and divided trope, being both the impression given by some thing, some other, and also that which is assumed in consciousness. There too, to be seen, are darkness, dinginess, failure, uselessness, the appearance of descent, and with all a dismal pall.

The melancholy of Lant Street, in the Borough, is not that of Leadenhall Street and Newgate Prison, south London being distinctly its own place, singularly other. Dickens knew Lant Street well, having lodged there in 1824, during his father's incarceration in the Marshalsea. Lant Street's qualities are those of repose and a gentle 'air' of dullness, soothing in its absence of energy or excitement. Repose is the condition of the street's presentation to the eye, and it is from this phenomeno-topographic constitution, or, perhaps, 'temperament' that there arises, through the subject's perception, the apperception of the melancholy 'shed' on the spirit. From a discernible *there* to the appreciation of that which, *here*, touches one in a marked way, I find myself involved in the world, not separate from it, simply observing. The self comes to apprehend that which appears from within the present scene, experience translated into perception, in a passage from world to being, from the visible to the invisible.

As a result of this analogical apperception (the relation of non-relation between architecture and topography and the soul), the 'spot' is considered 'desirable', a 'happy retreat' and a 'happy valley'. Melancholia enables the possibility of making oneself, if not invisible, then at the very least occluded from any greater public eye. So in retreat, in repose, abstracted from urban energies in general, are Lant Street and its inhabitants that the scene is apprehended as a still life. The subject's gaze transforms the world before it into a pictorial arrangement – a particular genre, moreover; this is, however, to conflate images if not confuse them, for equally, in its arrangement of workers and inhabitants, in the observed pursuit of mangling, and in this instance of *enargia*, the reader finds him- or herself before a textual example of genre painting, being clearly a scene of everyday life, uninvolved in all but the most minimal narrative interest.

It is through the phenomenon of melancholy, and in that double register, of external scene and conscious reflection, that the image-text as example and illustration of *enargia* is grounded. Though not a material property, melancholy is of the material and immaterial, inextricably; it gives to the image and the reading of place its animation, such as it is. As such, it gives to the image and its re-presentation that sense of 'lustre', which, according to George Puttenham, in *The Arte of English Poesie*, is a constituent element of *enargia* (1968, 119). Though in repose, though gentle, the image of quotidian existence in a bystreet of the Borough is vividly drawn nevertheless. That this is an example of *enargia* – indeed, that many of the images of London in the text of Dickens may be considered as at once examples of iconotexts and yet instances of *enargia* or *hypotyposis* – is understood if we appreciate fully the work rhetorically in the passage in its uniting the 'outward shew . . . upon the matter with wordes' and the 'sence of such words . . . inwardly working a stirre to the mynde'. Thus the image performs rhetorically that which, in its figurative trace of the play of phenomena, opens access from place to subjectivity, already acknowledged. Such 'ornament poeticall', as Puttenham calls it, is what creates the efficacy of such passages for us; we stand before the image, standing in for the narrating subject, becoming that subjectivity momentarily, or perhaps coming to have that subjectivity occupy us, becoming haunted in turn by the re-presentation of the perception of place.

The image does not exist in the same sense as the thing, of course. The former remains as phantasm, the latter as material object. However, as the three passages treating of melancholy give us to reflect through the acknowledged relation constituted through the fictive and phantasmal 'eye' of an equally phantasmal 'subject' – and by which, in turn, the apparition of place makes itself felt both *for* and *in* us, here, appearance produces the impression that we are as much 'in' that world as it comes to be 'in us', as Merleau-Ponty suggests (1968, 158). The motif of vision, of visibility and of the optical possibility as that which the written text mediates is therefore more than merely a rhetorical device. It serves to direct our reading of the city as if mediated through a visual modality without which the textual presentation cannot return, with that immediacy of involvement. Reliant on the illusion of visual elements, imitations of the material, the architectural, topographical, illumination or lack thereof, and so forth, the textual image of place is equally dependent on the play of phenomena, conveyed in particular verbal tropes, such as 'melancholy'. Writing the city thus directs the reader to look where we do not; that is to say, it works on the reading subject to make him or her conscious of what takes place in our conventional or habitual experience of the world. In those suspensions of narrative, in order that one's vision may be redirected, there is a concomitant phenomenological suspension of habit, a bracketing of our unthinking relation to reality.

Thus, the final passage, from *Nicholas Nickleby*, in which the narrator directs the sight of others from the outset, moving the expectations of sight from the grand squares of London to 'this particular locality'; removed from the West End and London's more upmarket nooks, the reader is directed to the City square, both in particular and in general. The 'stranger' in the Dickensian text, the figure who often stands to look at the city, and through whom the effect of place on its subject is imagined, appears briefly, a marginal focal point, but also that figure through which we come to see, and to see, moreover, in a manner that is perhaps somewhat disappointed. Disappointment might be said to arise as a result of the disparity between Tim Linkinwater's 'fervent encomiums' and the 'sanguine expectations' of the stranger, which are not 'wholly realize[d]', when presented with the reality, for which Tim's words stand in as subjective projection.

In the registration of this gap, we might read the singularity of place, and the wholly subjective turn of mind in re-presentation by which that singularity comes to be conveyed. London can only be known, specific places throughout the capital can only be perceived authentically, if felt. The experience that inscribes the city in the subject and the subject in the city is that which only returns, if at all, in the mnemotechnic work of the image-text that evokes the very thing by which it has been marked: 'affectionate remembrances', 'recollections' and, thereby, 'attachment'. All else is mere surface detail, historical or social fact. The city only assumes its force, its singularity, through the realisation of a subjectivity as singular as its own.

The City square is presented principally in negative comparison, therefore, through what is absent, at least with regard to the models already advertised, but also implicitly in the disappointed perception of the urban 'stranger' – indeed, the eyes 'accustomed' to the general leafiness of Fitzrovia, Mayfair and Bloomsbury. The distinction made between districts and their perception is not insignificant, and serves in part to explain the impossibility of knowing or representing London *in toto*. Given that there is nothing of the residential square conventionally understood to be seen, what does the eye of the stranger, or that other *flâneur* observed, the 'Appointed', who 'saunters idly by the hour', *see* exactly? That the square has little traffic, is quiet and retired as a consequence. In these qualities, it lends itself to melancholy, reflection and waiting. The City square is a place defined by the implied lack of extremes of condition, all being once more silent, or if not, then informed only by a 'distant hum'. The melancholy disposition is here allied implicitly with languidness and a propensity towards sleep, as imagined in the figure of the idle ticket porter, in whom, in turn, this condition is a result of the influence of place. Melancholy, idleness, silence and quiet, languid motion, lingering snow, refreshment, sauntering perambulation: in effect, one is given to see little, unless *seeing* is understood as insightful perception into the concatenated phenomena of place, which, through the marking of the yearly cycle, are assumed to define the square. The visible world appears largely, if not solely, then, through the association in the mind's eye of all that is invisible, but which touches the subject all the more intimately for that. Through that melancholy and contemplation, encouraged in the passage by languid heat and quiet, we come to interrogate 'our experience precisely in order to know how it opens us to what is not ourselves . . . if only in order to see these margins of presence', through fixing our perception on 'what is apparently *given* to us' in the absence of all else (Merleau-Ponty 1968, 159).

Nocturnal • Millbank

David Copperfield

We were now down in Westminster. We had turned back to follow her [Martha], having encountered her coming towards us, and Westminster Abbey was the point at which she passed from the lights and noise of the leading streets. She proceeded so quickly, when she got free of the two currents of passengers setting towards and from the bridge, that, between this and the advance she had of us when she struck off, we were in the narrow water-side street by Millbank before we came up with her. At that moment she crossed the road, as if to avoid the footsteps that she heard so close behind; and, without looking back, passed on even more rapidly.

A glimpse of the river through a dull gateway, where some waggons were housed for the night, seemed to arrest my feet. I touched my companion without speaking, and we both forbore to cross after her, and both followed on that opposite side of the way; keeping as quietly as we could in the shadow of the houses, but keeping very near her.

There was, and is when I write, at the end of that low-lying street, a dilapidated little wooden building, probably an obsolete old ferry-house. Its position is just at that point where the street ceases, and the road begins to lie between a row of houses and the river. As soon as she came here, and saw the water, she stopped as if she had come to her destination; and presently went slowly along by the brink of the river, looking intently at it.

All the way here, I had supposed that she was going to some house; indeed, I had vaguely entertained the hope that the house might be in some way associated with the lost girl. But that one dark glimpse of the river, through the gateway, had instinctively prepared me for her going no farther.

The neighbourhood was a dreary one at that time; as oppressive, sad, and solitary by night, as any about London. There were neither wharves nor houses on the melancholy waste of road near the great blank Prison. A sluggish ditch deposited its mud at the prison walls. Coarse grass and rank weeds straggled over all the marshy land in the vicinity. In one part, carcases of houses, inauspiciously begun and never finished, rotted away. In another, the ground was cumbered with rusty iron monsters of steam-boilers, wheels, cranks, pipes, furnaces, paddles, anchors, diving-bells, windmill-sails, and I know not what strange objects, accumulated by some speculator, and grovelling in the dust, underneath which—having sunk into the soil of their own

THE PENITENTIARY, MILLBANK.

Millbank, from the Surrey side of the Thames

weight in wet weather—they had the appearance of vainly trying to hide themselves. The clash and glare of sundry fiery Works upon the river-side, arose by night to disturb everything except the heavy and unbroken smoke that poured out of their chimneys. Slimy gaps and causeways, winding among old wooden piles, with a sickly substance clinging to the latter, like green hair, and the rags of last year's handbills offering rewards for drowned men fluttering above high-water mark, led down through the ooze and slush to the ebb-tide. There was a story that one of the pits dug for the dead in the time of the Great Plague was hereabout; and a blighting influence seemed to have proceeded from it over the whole place. Or else it looked as if it had gradually decomposed into that nightmare condition, out of the overflowings of the polluted stream.

As if she were a part of the refuse it had cast out, and left to corruption and decay, the girl we had followed strayed down to the river's brink, and stood in the midst of this night-picture, lonely and still, looking at the water. (*DC* 625–6)

Obstructive • Tower Street Ward

No Thoroughfare

In a court-yard in the City of London, which was No Thoroughfare either for vehicles or foot-passengers; a court-yard diverging from a steep, a slippery, and a winding street connecting Tower Street with the Middlesex shore of the Thames; stood the place of business of Wilding & Co., Wine Merchants. Probably as a jocose acknowledgment of the obstructive character of this main approach, the point nearest to its base at which one could take the river (if so inodorously minded) bore the appellation Break-Neck-Stairs. The court-yard itself had likewise been descriptively entitled in old time, Cripple Corner.

Years before the year one thousand eight hundred and sixty-one, people had left off taking boat at Break-Neck-Stairs, and watermen had ceased to ply there. The slimy little causeway had dropped into the river by a slow process of suicide, and two or three stumps of piles and a rusty iron mooring-ring were all that remained of the departed Break-Neck glories. Sometimes, indeed, a laden coal barge would bump itself into the place, and certain laborious heavers, seemingly mud-engendered, would arise, deliver the cargo in the neighbourhood, shove off, and vanish; but at most times the only commerce of Break-Neck-Stairs arose out of the conveyance of casks and bottles, both full and empty, both to and from the cellars of Wilding & Co., Wine Merchants. Even that commerce was but occasional, and through three-fourths of its rising tides the dirty indecorous drab of a river would come solitarily oozing and lapping at the rusty ring, as if it had heard of the Doge and the Adriatic, and wanted to be married to the great conserver of its filthiness, the Right Honourable the Lord Mayor.

Some two hundred and fifty yards on the right, up the opposite hill (approaching it from the low ground of Break-Neck-Stairs) was Cripple Corner. There was a pump in Cripple Corner, there was a tree in Cripple Corner. All Cripple Corner belonged to Wilding and Co., Wine Merchants. Their cellars burrowed under it, their mansion towered over it. It really had been a mansion in the days when merchants inhabited the City, and had a ceremonious shelter to the doorway without visible support, like the sounding-board over an old pulpit. It had also a number of long narrow strips of window, so disposed in its grave brick front as to render it symmetrically ugly. It had also, on its roof, a cupola with a bell in it. (*NT* 7)

Poverty • Angel, Islington, St John's Road, Sadler's Wells Theatre, Exmouth Street, Coppice Row, Hockley-in-the-Hole, Saffron Hill, Field Lane

Oliver Twist

They crossed from the Angel into St John's Road; struck down the small street which terminates at Sadler's Wells Theatre; through Exmouth Street and Coppice Row; down the little court by the side of the workhouse; across the classic ground which once bore the name of Hockley-in-the-Hole; then into Little Saffron Hill; and so into Saffron Hill the Great, along which the Dodger scudded at a rapid pace, directing Oliver to follow close at his heels.

Although Oliver had enough to occupy his attention in keeping sight of his leader, he could not help bestowing a few hasty glances on either side of the way, as he passed along. A dirtier or more wretched place he had never seen. The street was very narrow and muddy, and the air was impregnated with filthy odours. There were a good many small shops; but the only stock in trade appeared to be heaps of children, who even at that time of night, were crawling in and out of the doors, or screaming from the inside. The sole places that seemed to prosper amid the general blight of the place, were the public-houses; and in them, the lowest orders of Irish were wrangling with might and main. Covered ways and yards, which here and there diverged from the main street, disclosed little knots of houses, where drunken men and women were positively wallowing in filth; and from several of the door-ways, great ill-looking fellows were cautiously emerging, bound, to all appearance, on no very well-disposed or harmless errands.

Oliver was just considering whether he hadn't better run away, when they reached the bottom of the hill. His conductor, catching him by the arm, pushed open the door of a house near Field Lane; and, drawing him into the passage, closed it behind them. (*OT* 102–3)

The map is drawn, co-ordinates given in the form of street names; but for whom? The streets are not yet known to Oliver, his attention in these moments directed to other concerns, but in this extract a distance of between 1 and 1.5 miles is charted, moving across London from north to south. We know – or can ascertain – the shape of the journey, perhaps also knowing Field Lane to be, in the first half of the nineteenth century, synonymous with extreme poverty and the domestic overcrowding that accompanied such conditions for London's poor.

The journey, starting out at around 'eleven o'clock when they reached the turnpike at Islington', objections having been raised to 'entering London before nightfall' (*OT* 102), relies upon the distinction between night and relative lack of visibility, as well as the precision of naming as a mode of sketching the plan of this part of London on the one hand, and Oliver's unfamiliarity with the districts of Islington and Clerkenwell, causing his perception to be of an impressionistic and necessarily hurried nature, on the other. The narrative functions between precision and imprecision; or, more accurately, on the knowable and that which is largely, if not unknown, then 'invisible' to those able to afford a plan, or a copy of Greenwood's 1827 map of the capital. Looking at that map, one will observe a sharp distinction between Islington and those parts of the city through which the Dodger and Oliver pass (see Fig. 16.) Though covering only a short distance, the journey moves from fields to densely built-up neighbourhoods.

An incommensurability, and with that a frame, resides at the heart of the extract's play, and the tensions that arise from out of this. Either one is outside the place, above the streets as one would be above the map; or one is in the streets, passing through each location, at ground level, without overview. Street names may identify, or serve as points of reference, but they give nothing away, unless our knowledge is of a different kind, where the name, no longer simply a reference, works through association, chiefly at the time of *Oliver Twist* for many, if not from first-hand familiarity, then with journalistic reports. Street names and route construct a frame, a form of enclosure; they limit the area. Inside the frame, Oliver is contained, so to speak, enclosed. But there is also the Dodger. His familiarity with the area is that of being habituated to place; his is the ability to 'scud' at 'a rapid pace', to take short cuts through small streets and little courts, to cut across areas. The rapid motion, during which he directs Oliver, gives Oliver no time other than to observe, having, as the narrative time, 'enough to occupy his attention in keeping sight of his leader'.

Yet Oliver cannot 'help bestowing a few hasty glances on either side of the way, as he' passes through. The movement of the head and eyes is fleeting, images of the world presumably rapidly essayed. Oliver's perceptions must, therefore, be cursory and yet also, given the narra-tive representation, of the most intense kind. That negative, by which Oliver is acknowledged as turning his gaze here and there, is doubled in the following statement on the degree of dirt and wretchedness, the observation being comparative; Oliver has never seen anything quite so filthy or in such a condition of squalor. Sight and smell simultaneously present themselves with an inescapable intimacy to Oliver, followed

Islington Turnpike Gate (1819)

Islington Toll Gate (1829)

immediately by the impression that the innumerable shops on every side trade in children, whose crawling motion resembles nothing so much as larval life, while to the sights and smells are added screams, in the overall suggestion of 'blight'. There is only to be added filth, drunkenness, the

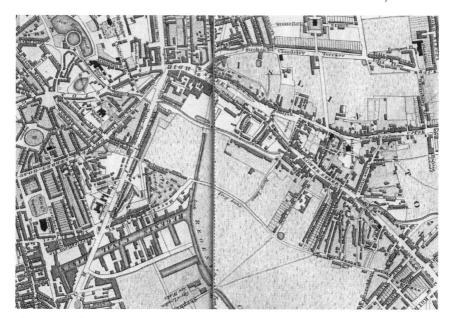

Islington, with City Road and Windsor Terrace

'lowest orders of Irish' glimpsed fighting in public houses, and figures with the suggestion of criminal intent – an intent signalled indirectly through another negative grammatical formation – emerging from door-ways. As Oliver moves through the scene, the movements around him are of a constant counter-motion; neither with or against the direction of Oliver and the Dodger's passage, a transverse animation proceeds, repeatedly, in and out of doors while, all around, life within buildings and on the streets maintains a collective animation.

Oliver perceives the phenomena of Islington and Clerkenwell as a choreographed and iterable motion, poverty giving the impression of an organic condition, through the agency of which humanity is all but negated. The only 'positive' condition of existence is 'wallowing'. Sound and odour confront Oliver with as much immediacy as the visible world, and though the boy sees only rapidly; yet the impression has an obviously greater affective density than the velocity of the subject – the mapping of the territory is marked through being 'crossed', 'struck down', 'through', 'down', 'across', 'then into', 'along', 'passed along' – might initially suggest, a speed already marked by the brief naming of streets and their grammatical sequence hurried along through the use of semi-colon in conjunction with the serial prepositional flight. The collective, contrapuntal activity – the urban 'swarm' offering a countersignature to

Oliver's motions through his perceptions, which, in the narrative, distinguish between the modalities of representation employed here – is signified not only through those negative subjective comparisons, but also in the following tropes: 'dirtier', 'more wretched', 'narrow', 'muddy', 'impregnated', 'filthy odours', 'heaps', 'crawling', 'screaming', 'wrangling', 'wallowing', 'filth', 'emerging'. Produced through perception, place is generated so as to suggest that which is more immediate than mere representation; poverty is written into the very production of place and thus politicised for the reader – although, of course, not for Oliver. It is, indeed, his subjective presence and his unknowing, hasty, ineluctable reception and re-presentation of place that engender the political from within the poetics of place. The phenomenal effects cause an immediacy of perception and, with that, presentation, the image taking on, in a performative manner, the very motions it figures. Real life, as Henri Lefebvre has it, thus 'appears quite close to us. We feel able, from within everyday life, to reach out and grasp it, as though nothing lay between us' (Lefebvre 1991, 189) and the mediated reality of the scene, to which we are afforded witness. Less a representation, more a gesture, Oliver's grasp of the real strikes the reader with as much energy as if the perception were our own.

Quiet • Soho Square, Lincoln's Inn Fields, Old Square

Bleak House

At last we came to Soho Square, where Caddy Jellyby had appointed to wait for me, as a quiet place in the neighbourhood of Newman Street. (*BH* 373)

We drove slowly through the dirtiest and darkest streets that were ever seen in the world (I thought) and in such a distracting state of confusion that I wondered how people kept their senses, until we passed into sudden quietude under an old gateway and drove on through a silent square until we came to an odd nook in a corner, where there was an entrance up a steep, broad flight of stairs, like an entrance to a church. (*BH* 42–3)

Here [in Lincoln's Inn Fields], in a large house, formerly a house of state, lives Mr Tulkinghorn. It is let off in sets of chambers now, and in those shrunken fragments of its greatness, lawyers lie like maggots in nuts. But its roomy staircases, passages, and antechambers still remain; and even its painted ceilings, where Allegory, in Roman helmet and celestial linen, sprawls among balustrades and pillars, flowers, clouds, and big-legged boys, and makes the head ache—as would seem to be Allegory's object always, more or less. Here, among his many boxes labelled with transcendent names, lives Mr Tulkinghorn, when not speechlessly at home in country-houses where the great ones of the earth are bored to death. Here he is to-day, quiet at his table. An oyster of the old school, whom nobody can open.

Like as he is to look at, so is his apartment in the dusk of the present afternoon. Rusty, out of date, withdrawing from attention, able to afford it. Heavy, broad-backed, old-fashioned, mahogany and horse-hair chairs, not easily lifted; obsolete tables with spindle-legs and dusty baize covers; presentation prints of the holders of great titles in the last generation or the last but one, environ him. A thick and dingy Turkey-carpet muffles the floor where he sits, attended by two candles in old-fashioned silver candlesticks that give a very insufficient light to his large room. The titles on the backs of his books have retired into the binding; everything that can have a lock has got one; no key is visible. [. . .]

Here, beneath the painted ceiling, with foreshortened Allegory staring down at his intrusion as if it meant to swoop upon him, and he cutting it dead, Mr Tulkinghorn has at once his house and office. (*BH* 158–9)

He passes out into the streets and walks on, with his hands behind him, under the shadow of the lofty houses, many of whose mysteries, difficulties, mortgages, delicate affairs of all kinds, are treasured up within his old black satin waistcoat. He is in the confidence of the very bricks and mortar. The high chimney-stacks telegraph family secrets to him. Yet there is not a voice in a mile of them to whisper, 'Don't go home!'

Through the stir and motion of the commoner streets; through the roar and jar of many vehicles, many feet, many voices; with the blazing shop-lights lighting him on, the west wind blowing him on, and the crowd pressing him on, he is pitilessly urged upon his way, and nothing meets him murmuring, 'Don't go home!' Arrived at last in his dull room to light his candles, and look round and up, and see the Roman pointing from the ceiling, there is no new significance in the Roman's hand tonight or in the flutter of the attendant groups to give him the late warning, 'Don't come here!'

It is a moonlight night; but the moon, being past the full, is only now rising over the great wilderness of London. [. . .]

A fine night, and a bright large moon, and multitudes of stars. Mr. Tulkinghorn, in repairing to his cellar and in opening and shutting those resounding doors, has to cross a little prison-like yard. He looks up casually, thinking what a fine night, what a bright large moon, what multitudes of stars! A quiet night, too.

A very quiet night. When the moon shines very brilliantly, a solitude and stillness seem to proceed from her, that influence even crowded places full of life. Not only is it a still night on dusty high roads and on hill-summits, whence a wide expanse of country may be seen in repose, quieter and quieter as it spreads away into a fringe of trees against the sky with the grey ghost of a bloom upon them; not only is it a still night in gardens and in woods, and on the river where the water-meadows are fresh and green, and the stream sparkles on among pleasant islands, murmuring weirs, and whispering rushes; not only does the stillness attend it as it flows where houses cluster thick, where many bridges are reflected in it, where wharves and shipping make it black and awful, where it winds from these disfigurements through marshes whose grim beacons stand like skeletons washed ashore, where it expands through the bolder region of rising grounds, rich in corn-field windmill and steeple, and where it mingles with the ever-heaving sea; not only is it a still night on the deep, and on the shore where the watcher stands to see the ship with her spread wings cross the path of light that appears to be presented to only him; but even on this stranger's wilderness of London there is some rest. Its steeples and towers and its one great dome grow more ethereal; its smoky housetops lose their grossness in the pale effulgence; the noises that arise from the streets are fewer and are softened, and the footsteps on the pavements pass more tranquilly away. In these fields of Mr Tulkinghorn's inhabiting, where the shepherds play on Chancery pipes that have no stop, and keep their sheep in the fold by hook and by crook until they have shorn them exceeding close, every noise is merged, this moonlight night, into a distant ringing hum, as if the city were a vast glass, vibrating.

What's that? Who fired a gun or pistol? Where was it?

The few foot-passengers start, stop, and stare about them. Some windows and doors are opened, and people come out to look. It was a loud report and echoed and rattled heavily. It shook one house, or so a man says who was passing. It has aroused all the dogs in the neighbourhood, who bark vehemently. Terrified cats scamper across the road. While the dogs are yet barking and howling—there is one dog howling like a demon—the church-clocks, as if they were startled too, begin to strike. The hum from the streets, likewise, seems to swell into a shout. But it is soon over. Before the last clock begins to strike ten, there is a lull. When it has ceased, the fine night, the bright large moon, and multitudes of stars, are left at peace again.

Has Mr Tulkinghorn been disturbed? His windows are dark and quiet, and his door is shut. (*BH* 747–50)

Have you ever paused to consider how *quiet* a novel *Bleak House* is, its complex narrative threads resulting in a nuanced, complex web of diverse, but muted resonances?

No one has, to my knowledge, written or considered a phenomenology of quiet; less still has there been a study of quiet in relation to either space or place, or that which passes between space, place and subject. Yet there it is, *there* in places in the city, quiet gives itself; not an 'it', a 'thing', barely this liminal quality, immeasurable save for its taking place, as and between gradations of noise, sound and silence: quiet remains; it remains to arrive, and so to define. Opening its taking place, quiet enfolds, gives the disposition of phenomena to the world, to be experienced by the subject in such a manner that the perception of quiet can always become a determining quality or disposition of subjectivity. Though mentioned neither in Wordsworth's 'Composed Upon Westminster Bridge, September 3, 1802' nor Arnold's 'Dover Beach', published in 1867, quiet is there, belonging to place and time, whether morning or evening, but also to the calm and repose of the subject – until, of course, for Arnold at least, beneath the susurration of the waves there are heard the note of sadness, the melancholy roar, the confused alarms, and clash of armies. Beneath the quiet, below the repose, there is to be imagined the returning tumult. Quiet is escape or retreat, a hide, but it also is a defence, a bulwark, a dam already cracked.

Phenomenological reduction being, as Renaud Barbaras suggests, the 'suspension of natural attitude' revealing to consciousness the 'world's existence' as 'a unique spatiotemporal reality subsisting in self', which suspends the thought of existence 'so as to allow an inquiry into its sense of being' that comes in turn to question the 'very structure of . . . appearance' (Barbaras 2006, 44); then, we can suggest, quiet might be apprehended as the *sine qua non* of such a reduction. With that, to continue, it may be taken equally as the *sine qua non* of such a moment of *épóché*, and consequently the revelation of the structure of appearing. Where the text of Dickens suspends narrative – principally, though not exclusively, through the shift to present tense in order that the presentation of place become all the more immediate, closely perceived, and felt by the reader – there, in that suspension is the reduction given to be read, London revealing itself through the mediation of the writer in an authentic disposition for the subject involved in that spatiotemporal reality, and the narrated mnemotechnic of its presentation. Quietness, quietude, quiet places: these are found, they give themselves everywhere in London, throughout the text of Dickens, in the midst of noise, confusion, within, hidden from, physical and phenomenal tumult, a world of motion, auscultation, and other sensory assaults, such as the press and imagined overflow of crowds, masses, the throng.

Although the notion of quiet has come to signify the absence, as the *Oxford English Dictionary* (OED) has it, of excessive motion, noise or bustle, yet the word's earlier connotations bespeak freedom from agitation, peace of mind, rest or repose, whether physical or emotional, release from work. Quiet can define, or at least determine, the mode of givenness for a particular location, at a certain moment in the day or night, simply through its being noted. Quiet is not silence, not quite. The world remains, as if with the immanence of a roar, not yet the other side of silence, at the borders between quiet and noise, quiet and disquiet, repose and dis-ease. Quiet is also the phenomena, it is that which 'shows' itself in its givenness, as, on the one hand, a quality of place or what takes place (such as the passage through a site, or the presentation of the subject in a specific locus), or, on the other hand, as that which shows itself in a person, often in an echo, or as a response to the quiet that is given, which is found. Passing from place to subject, mediated by subjective perception at a given moment, in the experience of that quiet location, quiet is that which comes to consciousness as well as being a condition of that consciousness. Moreover, quiet is that modality of *épochè*'s occasion in consciousness and in the re-presentation of experience and perception, whereby the phenomena of the text, figural or literal, are 'bracketed', as Husserl terms the process, and examined as they are, for every image in a text is always the constellated presentation of the traces of phenomena revealing the unity of a consciousness, and the 'unique spatiotemporal reality subsisting in self'. That the subject is subject to quiet as a condition of conscious reflection as well as a conscious awareness of the disposition of the world in consciousness makes apparent Merleau-Ponty's insistence, *contra* Husserl's 'naïve' phenomenology (the insistence on the possibility of eidetic reduction so as to give access to the essences of any phenomenon), that 'essence proceeds from experience and never absorbs it completely' (Barbaras 2006, 45).

This is noted in the first passage above. Soho Square is marked off in

Esther's perception as a quiet place, even though in the midst of London. Quiet, with solitude and stillness, marks Tulkinghorn's nocturnal passage. Quiet is of the essence to the narrative subject's experience of nocturnal London, legal London. Indeed, as Esther observes in her first experience of Kenge and Carboy's, '[e]verything was so strange—the stranger for its being night in the day-time, and the candles burning with a white flame' (*BH* 43). Legal London is *always* a nocturnal place; there is always something 'dark', to use that delightfully imprecise word. That Esther's experience and subjective impression, the memory of her initial perception, dominate here, is captured in the fact not only that the image proceeds from experience, but that, in re-presenting this, Esther finds a formal means of tracing that experience in the parallel between her 'thinking, thinking, thinking' and the fire's 'burning, burning, burning' (*BH* 44). Consciousness precedes and gives shape to the world, even as the former mirrors the latter, illuminating for the reader that inextricable relation between the interior of the subject and the interior of the office. Before this moment of suspended reflection, with its reduction of the structure of appearance, as the world is given for the subject, there is the arrival at Kenge and Carboy's. The quietude of Old Square, Lincoln's Inn, is arrived at, in distinction to the dirt and dark, and the distracting state of confusion that troubles Esther Summerson, as if entering a different realm situated between Chancery Lane and High Holborn, with its 'old gateway', 'odd nook', its 'silent square' and 'steep broad flight of stairs', giving to the lawyer's chambers the appearance of a church. The repeated insistence of age in name and definition, curiosity, silence, regularity and the sharp angle of the stair well collude in the impression of quiet, a sibilant institutional susurration running through Esther's perception, as the quiet insistence in her memory of place. This impression is confirmed elsewhere as a condition of the city. 'Stir and motion', 'roar and jar', these belong to 'commoner streets', just beyond Tulkinghorn's final walk home. To the quiet places, out of the sight of 'blazing' illumination found in the city's thoroughfares, where 'many . . . many . . . many' traces in the image the press of the people, belong secrets, affairs kept in confidence between lawyers and the architecture.

Tulkinghorn, speechless in the houses of others, quiet in his own, is the silent centre of legal secrecy and discretion. If *Bleak House* is 'ababble with speaking, writing, preaching, gabbing scribbling characters' (Budd 1994, 196), Tulkinghorn remains quietly observing – as, in her own way, does Esther. Tulkinghorn takes quietude to an entirely different level from Esther, who describes herself as 'timid and retiring' and 'retired and quiet'; she spends 'six happy, quiet years' at Greenleaf, as she remarks herself telling us twice (*BH* 28, 31, 39). Even Tulkinghorn's bows are 'quiet' (*BH* 24). To consider briefly the initial representation of the solicitor through the configuration of his essential qualities, he is 'rusty to look at', appears as if having an aureate glow constituted through confidences which repose in him, and of which he is 'known to be the silent depository', an archive so large that it is also analogous with the greatest of mausoleums. The solicitor, perceived in different ways as a vessel of sorts, is 'of the old school', a nebulous definition, and he is 'mute, close, irresponsive to any glancing light'. A black hole, so to speak, his black, unreflective clothes are simply the outward image of Tulkinghorn. The reader is also informed that he 'never converses' unless on a professional topic, and is 'found sometimes, speechless but quite at home', in 'great country houses'. So quiet, so retired within himself is the solicitor that the subjective perception given is one tending towards undecidability, given that, in Sir Leicester's opinion, it is impossible to tell whether Tulkinghorn has 'any idea': 'It may be so, or it may not' (*BH* 23–4). Tulkinghorn's quiet is professional, confidential, discrete. His disposition toward the world is one of quietude, to pick up on Esther's word; the lawyer maintains himself in a condition of stillness and calm.

While Budd's observation that quiet is a positive quality attributed to women and is desirable from a patriarchal perspective, that the principal lawyer and the places of the law are also quiet suggests something that exceeds questions of gender. That quiet, with its close relation, silence, and, equally, with that rare quality in the novel, repose – Lady Deadlock is, from the first, disturbed by ennui, unrest, anxiety and apprehension – is in some manner associated with, or suggestively hints at, secrecy is, again, indicative of matters beyond concerns with gender. Considering the impression of Tulkinghorn from those qualities of his character already commented on, it becomes apparent that quiet is never just a simple or single quality. Tulkinghorn's quiet is the quiet of secrets, of appearing everywhere quietly, and thereby revealing through the quietness and silence the keeping of secrets *as* secret. There is to Tulkinghorn an essential solitude, 'solitude itself and the secret itself' (Derrida 2005, 96). These are not silent; they 'appear', as it were, they sound in the depths of the solicitor's quiet, his secrecy that is everywhere on display, and in his solicitude to remain the mute witness for others. The perception of Tulkinghorn is that, in revealing his 'mask as a mask, but without showing' (Derrida 2005, 96) or presenting himself; in a mode of 'non-presentation' to which quietness attests, the solicitor speaks 'by keeping quiet, keeping something quiet' (Derrida 2005, 96), he still addresses us, if not those before whom he stands. He speaks the quietude, the confidence and repose of the law in its authority and mystery, its essentially *nocturnal* bearing, but also the quiet with which authority is given.

A question as to the relation between the quiet and quietude of the law in the figure of Tulkinghorn arises, only partly addressed in passing, and then chiefly through Esther's perception of Old Square and the rooms of Kenge and Carboy's. In itself, this is not without significance because it extends the matter of legal authority, secrecy, confidence, witness and quiet beyond Tulkinghorn, so that the good reader does not mistake these interlinking traces as being essential to him, and to him alone. There is to Tulkinghorn something 'architectural'. Already seen as a species of mausoleum, Tulkinghorn is related to other structures also. He is, the narrator confides in us, 'in the confidence of the very bricks and mortar', the chimney-stacks 'telegraph[ing] family secrets'. As he is the repository of family secrets, so the 'lofty houses' store their 'mysteries, difficulties, mortgages, delicate affairs of all kinds' in his 'old black satin waistcoat'. The solicitor is a retainer and container, a receptacle who lives amongst receptacles, his 'many boxes labelled with transcendent names'. His apartment, which is also his office, is itself a storage place, for those boxes as well as for Tulkinghorn, who sits 'quiet at his table', an 'oyster of the old school'. The quietness is maintained by the heaviness of the furniture, and the 'thick and dingy Turkey-carpet', which 'muffles' the floor. Minimal sound, minimal light, boxes surrounded by caskets, in containers, surrounded, enclosed, confined, retained. This is Tulkinghorn, this is his apartment, this is the house of the law. If Allegory looks down on Tulkinghorn, so Tulkinghorn in his mode of appearing, and his disposition in the world, is allegorical; or rather, the visible appearance of Tulkinghorn, in the impression it gives, is allegorical, the solicitor and his chambers an allegorical performative and a performative allegory. But he, his waistcoat, his boxes, and those metaphors of containment and enclosure that surround the solicitor, all belong to an economy of allegory in which the allegory is that of secrecy, silence, repose, confidence, occlusion, mute witness.

There is nothing behind in the phenomena of this appearance. Here we have the law of structural appearance that is at the heart of phenomenological reduction and the appearance of that law as the structure of re-presentation and perception. As everything is absorbed – engrossed – in the dark, non-reflective non-presentation of Tulkinghorn, so the passage concerning Tulkinghorn's apartment is both engrossing and a gesture of engrossing, that type of writing which produces, through reproduction (every figure a figure of all else, an iterable copy), a legal statement in its final form. There is, in the appearance of the structures of the law and the chiastic law of structures, perceived from the vantage point of a phenomenological reduction – such as I am suggesting, but which, I argue, is also that which the text of Dickens presents, and which

I am merely tracing, following along in the wake of – the appearance of the inessential condition of the law. There is no essence to the law, only the subject's apprehension of the endless substitution (allegorical) of trope for trope. What is the relation here to quiet? To recall those earlier senses of the word, here, in Tulkinghorn's apartments, everything is at rest, in repose, free from agitation. All is contained, self-contained. For everything that is perceived, even though no one is there, with Tulkinghorn, there is always another figure in a process of supplementary iteration. Herein resides the confidence, and the quietude of the law. Having no essence as such, no final object, nothing is available to a final determination, an ultimate meaning. To remind ourselves of the significant condition of quiet, as there is no essence to the perception and re-presentation of the law, so quiet is without a final determination, its appearance defining but also a condition of that which is given in any 'encounter between "us" and "what is"' (Merleau-Ponty 1968, 159).

But as Tulkinghorn's quiet – a quiet residing hidden in plain sight everywhere in the law, in its offices, its architecture, its structures and institutions – is not quite Esther's, it is also not that quiet that 'engrosses' him and engulfs him, obscuring him from the general view, as he passes towards home. There is that quiet of the night belonging to the great wilderness of London. The reader is told this is a 'quiet night', a 'very quiet night', with a 'solitude and stillness'. This is not a silent night, for just at the limits of perception remain that roar and that glare of the busy thoroughfares less than a mile from the places traversed by Tulkinghorn. The houses that entrust their mysteries to Tulkinghorn are noted for their mute witness to the solicitor's passage, as they refrain repeatedly from saying 'Don't go home!' or 'Don't come here!' The country may be seen, were we there to see it by the agency of the moon, as 'in repose, quieter and quieter', but that moonlight is also what illuminates Tulkinghorn's way. What is to be seen is presented *as if* for a solitary viewer. Moonlight illuminates nothing quite so much as the auto-affirmation of the subject to himself as the controlling, the universal eye to which the scene presents itself, from which vision flows, as if Lincoln's Inn Fields were some Romantic landscape with its echoes, in which repose and quiet rest. Quiet in the scene is implied by those minimal sounds that cannot be heard in town, the 'murmuring weirs, and whispering rushes'. It is figured more immediately in the perception that 'even in this stranger's wilderness of London there is some rest', and the experience of sound's diminution: 'noises that arise from the streets are fewer and are softened, and the footsteps on the pavements pass more tranquilly away.' 'Every noise', we are invited to imagine, 'is merged, this moonlight night, into a distant ringing hum, as if the city were a vast glass, vibrating'. That one gunshot, a loud, heavily rattling report, shatters the quiet, as it breaks the image of the city as a huge glass vessel, thereby opening the scene to barking, howling, the striking of clocks, and the 'swell' of the streets' hum, all of which noises appear to emerge from their containment beneath the vast glass momentarily to the senses, before the quiet closes again around the instance of violence, leaving only Tulkinghorn's windows 'dark and quiet'.

Quiet is a trope for all that hovers, passing almost imperceptibly. It may suggest suspension, and from within that the possibility of authentic reflection, perception, and a subjective consciousness meditating on the conditions of being in the world. It is, in its admission of watchfulness, perception and temporality, a condition that reminds us that absolute silence is impossible, but also that there is impermanence. Not 'quietness' (to call it this would be to raise it to the level of a concept) nor 'the quiet' (the definite article implies certainty of meaning and definition), the figure traces relatively an aural experience or attitude, without being confined to this. Nothing as such in a literary text – quiet can only be indirectly assumed – quiet is suggestive of undercurrents, murmurings, low resonances. That quiet is associated at all with a site such as nineteenth-century London appears, at first sight, counterintuitive. It is for that reason perhaps that the moment of the picturesque night-scene adverts to a Romantic and 'natural' representation, in order to bear witness to what is unnatural, what is unavailable to direct presentation, such as murder, beyond which is not quiet but a quietus, death as a radical quiet. In the city, violence breaks out from within the perception of quiet, much as secrets eventually break the bounds of containment in *Bleak House*. All the subject can do, like Esther, is remain passively, quietly awaiting the revelation. London makes possible revelation, eruption, but this is not in the subject's control, and the city thus teaches us to read what we are reading, in Hugh Kenner's phrase on what he calls part of the business of *Ulysses* (1977, 382). *Bleak House* teaches us to read for what is not spoken directly or out loud, what is not in plain sight or daylight, what resides on the margins, in the quiet passages we pass by, in the quiet delivery of phrases that say one thing and mean another. If quiet is the phenomenal emblem for the law's work, it is also other, it is the place in which the subject – Esther Summerson – resides, learning how to become the good reader, but knowing that reading does not always proceed in the most clearly articulated ways. Quietness, not simply a supposedly positive attribute, but also a commodity at a premium in the capital, teaches the subject to habituate herself to patience and attentiveness, and to differentiate those phenomena that are barely discernible. This is all the more important once we recall that London, and the novel, are immersed in '[i]mplac-able November weather', enveloped in a miasma of smoke and fog, fog, as we are told 'everywhere, . . . up the river . . . down the river, . . . on the Essex marshes, . . . on the Kentish heights' (*BH* 13). So poor is the visibility at the heart of London that dogs are indistinguishable, horses barely so, and there is doubt, at least regarding visible evidence, whether day has broken (*BH* 13). Like Esther, we have to be quiet, in order to hear whatever there is to hear muffled and muted, in an otherwise nearly invisible world.

Resignation • Todgers's, somewhere adjacent to the Monument

Martin Chuzzlewit

Surely there never was, in any other borough, city, or hamlet in the world, such a singular sort of place as Todgers's. And surely London, to judge from that part of it which hemmed Todgers's round, and hustled it, and crushed it, and stuck its brick-and-mortar elbows into it, and kept the air from it, and stood perpetually between it and the light, was worthy of Todgers's, and qualified to be on terms of close relationship and alliance with hundreds and thousands of the odd family to which Todgers's belonged.

You couldn't walk about in Todgers's neighbourhood, as you could in any other neighbourhood. You groped your way for an hour through lanes and bye-ways, and court-yards and passages; and never once emerged upon any-thing that might be reasonably called a street. A kind of resigned distraction came over the stranger as he trod those devious mazes, and, giving himself up for lost, went in and out and round about, and quietly turned back again when he came to a dead wall or was stopped by an iron railing, and felt that the means of escape might possibly present themselves in their own good time, but that to anticipate them was hopeless. Instances were known of people who, being asked to dine at Todgers's, had travelled round and round it for a weary time, with its very chimney-pots in view; and finding it, at last, impossible of attainment, had gone home again with a gentle melancholy on their spirits, tranquil and uncomplaining. Nobody had ever found Todgers's on a verbal direction, though given within a single minute's walk of it. Cautious emigrants from Scotland or the North of England had been known to reach it safely by impressing a charity-boy, town-bred, and bringing him along with him; or by clinging tenaciously to the postman; but these were rare exceptions, and only went to prove the rule that Todgers's was in a labyrinth, whereof the mystery was known but to a chosen few.

Several fruit-brokers had their marts near Todgers's; and one of the first impressions wrought upon the stranger's senses was of oranges—of damaged oranges with blue and green bruises on them, festering in boxes, or mould-ering away in cellars. All day long, a stream of porters from the wharves beside the river, each bearing on his back a bursting chest of oranges, poured slowly through the narrow passages; while underneath the archway by the public-house, the knots of those who rested and regaled within, were piled from morning until night. Strange solitary pumps were found near Todgers's, hiding themselves for the most part in blind alleys, and keeping company with fire-ladders. There were churches also by dozens, with many a ghostly little churchyard, all overgrown with such straggling vegetation as springs up spontaneously from damp, and graves, and rubbish. In some of these dingy resting-places, which bore much the same analogy to green churchyards, as the pots of earth for mignonette and wall-flower in the windows overlooking them, did to rustic gardens—there were trees; tall trees; still putting forth their leaves in each succeeding year, with such a languishing remembrance of their kind (so one might fancy, looking on their sickly boughs) as birds in cages have in theirs. Here, paralysed old watchmen guarded the bodies of the dead at night, year after year, until at last they joined that solemn brotherhood; and, saving that they slept below the ground a sounder sleep than even they had ever known above it, and were shut up in another kind of box, their condition can hardly be said to have undergone any material change when they, in turn, were watched themselves.

Among the narrow thoroughfares at hand, there lingered, here and there, an ancient doorway of carved oak, from which, of old, the sounds of revelry and feasting often came; but now these mansions, only used for storehouses, were dark and dull, and, being filled with wool, and cotton, and the like—such heavy merchandise as stifles sound and stops the throat of echo—had an air of palpable deadness about them which, added to their silence and desertion, made them very grim. In like manner, there were gloomy court-yards in these parts, into which few but belated wayfarers ever strayed, and where vast bags and packs of goods, upward or downward bound, were for ever dangling between heaven and earth from lofty cranes. There were more trucks near Todgers's than you would suppose a whole city could ever need; not active trucks, but a vagabond race, for ever lounging in the narrow lanes before their masters' doors and stopping up the pass; so that when a stray hackney-coach or lumbering waggon came that way, they were the cause of such an uproar as enlivened the whole neighbourhood, and made the very bells in the next church-tower vibrate again. In the throats and maws of dark no-thoroughfares near Todgers's, individual wine-merchants and wholesale dealers in grocery-ware had perfect little towns of their own; and, deep among the very foundations of these buildings, the ground was undermined and burrowed out into stables, where cart-horses, troubled by rats, might be heard on a quiet Sunday rattling their halters, as disturbed spirits in tales of haunted houses are said to clank their chains.

To tell of half the queer old taverns that had a drowsy and secret existence near Todgers's, would fill a goodly book; while a second volume no less capacious might be devoted to an account of the quaint old guests who frequented their dimly-lighted parlours. These were, in general, ancient inhabitants of that region; born, and bred there from boyhood; who had long since become wheezy and asthmatical, and short of breath, except in the article of story-telling: in which respect they were still marvellously long-winded. These gentry were much opposed to steam and all new-fangled ways, and held ballooning to be sinful, and deplored the degeneracy of the times; which that particular member of each little club who kept the keys of the nearest church, professionally, always attributed to the prevalence of dissent and irreligion; though the major part of the company inclined to the belief that virtue went out with hair-powder, and that old England's greatness had decayed amain with barbers.

As to Todgers's itself—speaking of it only as a house in that neighbourhood, and making no reference to its merits as a commercial boarding establishment—it was worthy to stand where it did. There was one staircase-window in it; at the side of the house, on the ground-floor; which tradition said had not been opened for a hundred years at least, and which, abutting on an always-dirty lane, was so begrimed and coated with a century's mud, that no pane of glass could possibly fall out, though all were cracked and broken twenty times. But the grand mystery of Todgers's was the cellarage, approachable only by the little back door and a rusty grating: which cellarage within the memory of man had no connexion with the house, but had always been the freehold property of somebody else, and was reported to be full of wealth: though in what shape—whether in silver, brass, or gold, or butts of wine, or casks of gunpowder—was matter of profound uncertainty and supreme indifference to Todgers's, and all its inmates.

The top of the house was worthy of notice. There was a sort of terrace on the roof, with posts and fragments of rotten lines, once intended to dry clothes upon; and there were two or three tea-chests out there, full of earth, with forgotten plants in them, like old walking-sticks, Whoever climbed to this observatory, was stunned at first from having knocked his head against the little door in coming out; and after that, was for the moment choaked from having looked, perforce, straight down the kitchen chimney; but these two stages over, there were things to gaze at from the top of Todgers's, well worth your seeing too. For first and foremost, if the day were bright, you observed upon the house-tops, stretching far away, a long dark path: the shadow of the Monument: and turning round, the tall original was close beside you, with every hair erect upon his golden head, as if the doings of the city frightened him. Then there were steeples, towers, belfreys, shining vanes, and masts of ships: a very forest. Gables, housetops, garret-windows, wilderness upon wilderness. Smoke and noise enough for all the world at once.

After the first glance, there were slight features in the midst of this crowd of objects, which sprung out from the mass without any reason, as it were, and took hold of the attention whether the spectator would or no. Thus, the revolving chimney-pots on one great stack of buildings, seemed to be turning gravely to each other every now and then, and whispering the result of their separate observation of what was going on below. Others, of a crook-backed shape, appeared to be maliciously holding themselves askew, that they might shut the prospect out and baffle Todgers's. The man who was mending a pen at an upper window over the way, became of paramount importance in the scene, and made a blank in it, ridiculously disproportionate in its extent, when he retired. The gambols of a piece of cloth upon the dyer's pole had far more interest for the moment than all the changing motion of the crowd. Yet even while the looker-on felt angry with himself for this, and wondered how it was, the tumult swelled into a roar; the host of objects seemed to thicken and expand a hundredfold; and after gazing, round him, quite scared, he turned to Todgers's again, much more rapidly than he came out; and ten to one he told M. Todgers's afterwards that if he hadn't done so, he would certainly have come into the street by the shortest cut: that is to say, head-foremost. (*MC* 132–4)

Resignation is an odd word, even when one recalls that it means, less frequently today, the act of giving oneself over, of surrendering or suffering passively the force of another. From the Latin, meaning cancellation or unsealing, it signifies the removal or subtraction of authority and control. In essence, you give yourself over to the other. The subject abandons the illusion of autonomy, mastery and anything amounting to control. This is not least the case with regard to perspective. Classical representation, aiming at mimetic fidelity and the fiction of an objective world separate from the self, places the viewing subject, the reading subject, at the centre of its worldview. The subject has the world he or she sees, over and against that seemingly controlling subjectivity. There is no view save for the one I see, no interpretation so valid as mine. Yet my perspective is merely a perception, a condition of my subjectivity and my being situated in the world at a given angle, or oriented in a particular direction. What takes place when that view becomes fragmented, when there are competing claims for my attention and when there is nothing on which my vision can fix, my interpretation can command, and to which it might give fixed or purposeful meaning? What occurs in the field of vision to perception, when the world resists, when it challenges? What takes place when there is more than one vision within any view? In the face of such challenges, classical, ordered representation no longer holds; falling apart, it reveals the differing facets, the heterogeneous perspectives, the irreconcilable positions, which do not reconcile themselves into a single image. As subject of that which is in fragments, which engages in an act of affirmative resistance by refusing to coalesce before me, for me, I must *resign* myself, I must resign the self that would separate the world from subjectivity, maintaining it in the fiction of objectivity. I must surrender myself, my *self*, to the other.

In what might be read today and retrospectively as an unconscious – how could it be otherwise? – anticipation of certain of the effects and devices of impressionism and post-impressionism, the opening pages of Chapter 8 of *Martin Chuzzlewit* posit such questions and problems for the subject. Or rather, they posit the possibilities of subjective resignation, and offer the reader the chance to rethink the question of narrative representation, which always puts into play the temporal and spatial phenomena of difference and deferral implicit in any image, if we read them carefully, and not think them merely a sustained passage of 'typical' Dickensian description. If such anticipation troubles the reader as retrospective anachrony on the part of the critic,[27] one might approach 'what Dickens does' (that is to say, what is put to play, and what produces in a given reader certain responses, if the reader is open to the other, which, here, is the singular instance of the experience of the text) from the other 'end', historically speaking. Baudelaire observes that Romanticism, in painting at least, 'is precisely located neither in the choice of subject nor in exact truth [this being, if you will, the 'accidental' of particular modes of presentation], but in a mode of feeling'; and moreover, 'Who says romanticism, says *modern art* – that is intimacy, spirituality, color, aspiration towards the infinite' (1987, 222). In its responses to, and experiences filtered through perception of, the city, Dickens's reading / writing of London aspires in its Romanticist vision towards the modern; always mediated by sensuous modalities, as befits an authentic unfolding of subjectivity's orientation, situation and determination, such reading bridges the Romantic and the modern. And while not all those qualifiers framing the idea of the modern necessarily leap from the page in the passage on Todgers's and its environs, not a few are already to be found at work.

A quite astounding passage, and perhaps one of the most sustained passages presenting London in any of the novels or essays, this study of place is as exhausting as it is exhaustive. It opens in abyssal fashion and hems one in, enclosing the reader on all sides with its idiosyncrasies of detail and observation. It is at once dizzying and claustrophobic, closely worked and yet proscriptive of positive or stable definition, save that in which affirmation of perception resists mimetic convention or adequation. In Dickens's generation of the city, his memory and apperception of London, these several paragraphs serve analogously as keystones and keys, in a re-presentation that is also a projection of remembered perception of the arche-textural and the founding of modern urban subjectivity attendant on this. Thus, the city drifts in and out of our vision – and with this motion, the viewer, the walker, the subject of the city, drifts also – as a series of 'phantasmagoria – now a landscape, now a room', as Benjamin puts it of Baudelaire's Paris (*SW3* 40). 'The modern is the accent' (*SW3* 40), that accent being a matter of reciprocity, inversion, iterability and recursion in presentation, and what one is given to read of the city is its ability to consume and overwhelm one, to lose the subject, but without trauma, even as the subject resigns himself to the experience, coming to reflect on what the urban location already reflects back – a series and sequence of seemingly endless locations of enclosedness or abyss. The opening of Chapter 8 thus forms itself as so many projections of 'the phantasmagoria of [a] "cultural history"' of urban modernity and its relation to the subject (*SW3* 41).

The presentation of Todgers's tends from its outset, with its hyperbole and negations, its intimacy and its intimations of enigmatic obscurity, to inculcate, in the winds and folds of its labyrinthine, not to say abyssal detail, that sense of disorientation tending to vertigo for the subject, that perhaps not so hypothetical stranger, who, though unable to find the way to Todgers's from the street, finds himself on its roof, overshadowed, quite literally, by the only nominally given location, the Monument on Fish-Hill Street, to which the reader might go. That one reference to 'real' London only serves in the general sense of disorientation, to the extent that all else remains a projection of the imagination, a perception of the city-rhizome, its concatenated phenomena impressing the senses with an immediacy from all aspects, causing one to reside in a *kind of resigned distraction* as much in the reading as in the subjective experience, were such an experience possible. Thus it is that the narrator can introduce the reader into the passages around Todgers's and, at the same time, open to our view the passages that inaugurate the chapter, with the confident affirmation – against which nothing remains to be said – that surely there never was, in any other borough, city or hamlet in the world, such a singular sort of place as Todgers's. Everything comes down to the name, which signals nothing so much as a sense of self-possession, and with that, of being closed off from access or comprehension. Singularity of place is all; it is a measure of Todgers's singularity that London itself takes its tone, as it were, from Todgers's affirmed being. For, in a moment of reciprocity, which moves from the specific to the general, proving singularity through the immanence of urban iterability, we read:

> And surely London, to judge from that part of it which hemmed Todger's round, and hustled it, and crushed it, and stuck its brick-and-mortar elbows into it, and kept the air from it, and stood perpetually between it and the light, was worthy of Todgers's, and qualified to be on terms of close relationship and alliance with hundreds and thousands of the odd family to which Todgers's belonged.

Todgers's being singular, it remains nevertheless in close relationship with *hundreds and thousands* of buildings and dwelling places. Though singular, Todgers's belongs, kinship being signalled. In its belonging, Todgers's singularity is affirmed. Though there are, as yet, no human beings, that the house has a name, and this is given each time as a possessive noun; this implies, if not ownership, then a given relationship between the human and place. Place has meaning through the name. In this, the structure is analogous with those other houses that surround it and extend beyond it. More – and more uncannily, perhaps – than this, though, is that the house, in having a name, not only takes on a particular human aspect; but also it shares with those other houses, those *hundreds and thousands*, with whom it is *on terms of close relationship* – and who are reciprocally *on terms of close relationship and alliance* with Todgers's – certain anthropomorphic phenomena, already foreshadowed in that allusion to London as a whole, which has *brick-and-mortar elbows*, and which hustles, crushes and intercedes between Todgers's and light and air. London defines Todgers's; but Todgers's, we might risk, in this perception of relation, offers to us what Gaston Bachelard terms a topoanalysis (1994, 8) of place by which meaning comes to light.

In short, Todgers's *is* London. *Surely*: that refracting pair of confident adverbs create the idea of place as if between two mirrors and their abyssal reflections. Not merely reciprocal reflections, the adverbial affirmations cause place to fragment into its myriad details, and so disperse across the capital in its entirety. Nowhere as such, utopian in one sense, and at least nowhere that can be found, Todgers's remains in its occlusion by virtue of a singularity that defies absolute generalisation but which, in turn, none the less makes available a kind of transcendental idea of the city to the subject's imagination, Todgers's can no more be 'seen' or 'represented' than can London as empirical entity. Instead, like London, Todgers's is available only as a series of sensory impressions, perceptions, which one has to arrive at in a spirit of passive openness, a *kind of resigned distraction*. Affirmation, singularity and inexplicable apperception open 'the space of an [otherwise] inextricably convoluted tangle of traits' (Weber 1996, 27), if we are prepared to accept these as the conditions of approaching Todgers's. Less a place than an idea, Todgers's comes to be apprehended, if at all, only through the work in re-presentation of the idea through its myriad traits, which in turn serve as 'countless intermediaries between reality and [those] symbols' (Bachelard 1994, 11) by which we grasp the sense of reality that shapes our impression.

Asserted through negative definition is the indisputable singularity of place, which, as we have argued, guarantees a generative iterability; further negation proving singularity is given – 'You couldn't walk about in Todgers's neighbourhood, as you could in any other neighbourhood.' Such a combination of the singular and the negative arises as the mode of urban perception and re-presentation in the text of Dickens in response to the modernity of the capital, a response marked by the historicity of the moment in its formation of its subject in the act of reading / writing. The subject has made available to him a mode of perception – the subject / place relationship analogous with that which is put in play between the two adverbial affirmations, and by extension from this formal reciprocity the material relationship between 'town and

Todgers', as the title of Chapter 8 has it – that enables re-presentation in an act (as in all the other *enargia*) of 'exemplary originality' (Kant 2007, 146; see also 136–7, 146–7). Kant's phrase, 'exemplary originality', is employed to define artistic genius, which, for Kant, is the intuitive, that is to say pre-cognitive ability to present or re-present materiality so as to embody or produce the aesthetic expression of a concept. There is in this process a 'subjective purposiveness' (146) in response to the world; but purposiveness is what one is given to see, determined here in the text of Dickens in the response that is the subject's becoming-historical, inasmuch as the moment *as* re-presentation – the *now* in the process of becoming past – leaves 'images comparable to those registered by a light-sensitive plate' (*SW4* 405).

Thus, 'genius' does not then create *ab nihilo* but rather, in the relation between being and world, being and the event of experience of that world; genius *invents*, finding what is given by the other – hence the trace of historicity in the re-presentation of the material – and shapes it in an originary manner, as if seeing for the first time, and giving in the process to the trace of the past moment the 'now of recognizability' in a 'visionary gaze' (*SW4* 316). All 'aesthetic' re-presentation bears the trace of this historicity (it could not have taken place at any other time) but also the memory of the subject who invents. As observed elsewhere, London in all its modernity demands a response, an invention, on the part of someone whose perception presents and re-presents to readers to come the place, and the relation between subject and site, being and event (the event of the experience of modernity and the shaping force it imposes on subjective intuition). Apropos urban modernity and the reader, the city's subject that the proper name 'Dickens' engenders, on whom the name calls, and who in turn responds in reading / writing London *as if* for a first time, is thus the name of this 'exemplary originality'. It is in the name of Dickens that the subject comes into being, a subjectivity appropriate to its subject.

Who, and where, though, is the subject in this particular passage? There is – but again, where? – the 'narrator', that phantasmic projection, the screen as well as the projection, but the projector also. However, introduced into the second paragraph, initially as someone incapable of or barred from action, is another subject: you, the one who *couldn't walk*, as you would in any other neighbourhood. Instead, 'You groped your way for an hour through lanes and bye-ways, and court-yards and passages; and never once emerged upon anything that might be reasonably called a street.' *You* are recalled, even as the narrator imagines *you* remembering. Less or more than a subject? What we read is the impossibility of assigning a stable place to any 'one' subject; memory of the subject re-presents the experience as a perception of 'groping', as if unable to see clearly, if at all. It could hardly be otherwise here, for Todgers's is so hemmed in, we will recollect, that neither light nor air can find its way to this location. Thus far, few if any details are given; there are the impressions of lanes, bye-ways, court-yards and passages, and, of course, impressions must be for someone; there are those brick-and-mortar elbows, but little resembling direct or straightforward mimetically or objectively faithful representation, merely an impression.

No sooner have *you*, the memory of you, or your memory been apostrophised, returned to the scene, recollected in the experience, than *you* disappear, giving way to a stranger, whose mental condition subsumes him:

> A kind of resigned distraction came over the stranger as he trod those devious mazes, and, giving himself up for lost, went in and out and round about, and quietly turned back again when he came to a dead wall or was stopped by an iron railing, and felt that the means of escape might possibly present themselves in their own good time, but that to anticipate them was hopeless.

That fragmentation of image initiated in the opening paragraph, finding its corollary in the displacements from within the instability of the second person singular, becomes the principal aspect of the stranger's passive, confused sense of self and place, distraction being a condition of being pulled apart or being pulled in different directions. The stranger surrenders to the experience of being lost, to suffering the event in something approaching a sublime reverie, as a condition that determines not only the phenomena of the city but the experience of those phenomena, and thus, indirectly, the apperception of London.

The (admittedly naïve) question might be asked, how does the narrator know the experience of the stranger, or the emotion and perception that are 'yours'? The most immediate response must be that the narrator, though a fictive projection of some subject, or otherwise the manifestation, the 'effect', if you will, of some narrating subjectivity irreducible to any one person, has experienced London in the manner being foregrounded, and responded in this way. Memory makes possible the re-presentation of the perceptual encounter with the urban phenomena. What returns here of the city is the result of 'putting the imagination into a play which is at once free and adapted to the understanding [of] . . . determinate ideas [received as] sensations', these being narrated, in the re-presentation of memory from the '*lasting* impression' (*SW*4 158) effected in subjective experience. A self – the condition of modernity – is performed as memory, as *you* and as stranger, estranged from selfhood in the encounter with urban phenomena. It is only in this manner of provisional re-presentation and its play that a true or authentic experience of London's modernity – and thus to unveil indirectly the historicity of the encounter – has the chance to be communicated. In this way, the reader may, in turn, intuit the pleasure of an experience otherwise anticipated as traumatic or baffling.

As if to illustrate the truth of this, other people come into the picture, as it were, serving indirectly as witnesses, their own experience being evidence:

> Instances were known of people who, being asked to dine at Todgers's, had travelled round and round it for a weary time, with its very chimney-pots in view; and finding it, at last, impossible of attainment, had gone home again with a gentle melancholy on their spirits, tranquil and uncomplaining. Nobody had ever found Todgers's on a verbal direction, though given within a single minute's walk of it. Cautious emigrants from Scotland or the North of England had been known to reach it safely by impressing a charity-boy, town-bred, and bringing him along with him; or by clinging tenaciously to the postman; but these were rare exceptions, and only went to prove the rule that Todgers's was in a labyrinth, whereof the mystery was known but to a chosen few.

The evidence amounts to a collective attestation regarding the difficulty, if not the impossibility of finding the location, but with that, equally, a shared sense of 'gentle melancholy', and 'tranquillity' in defeat. The lugubrious sense shared by those admitting of defeat is made all the more comically poignant by virtue of apparent proximity to the seemingly mythical location, given the greater frisson by virtue of the appearance of the chimney-pots. This single architectural feature does nothing to reassure, only serving in the general sense of frustration implicit here. Nothing else is to be seen, but the sense gained by those defeated is of a labyrinth, even though the idea of a labyrinth with chimneys is not a little odd. The very architectural incommensurability between what is seen and what is felt serves to construct an enigma in representation, as well as being expressive of that hieratic topographical conundrum. Those who do reach Todgers's allegedly are the stuff of urban legend, doxical knowledge affirming that they had 'been known to reach it'. Such a statement is mere word of mouth, with nothing to support it. In this way, the text comes to perform rather than describe the experience and the attendant memory of the subject's perception. For the narrative 'does not aim to convey an event per se, . . . [but to embed the event . . . in order that this be passed on] as experience to' the reader (*SW*4 316). Given that information is not being communicated, save for knowledge of the impossibility of 'knowledge transference' in the modish language of Higher Education documents today, there is a comic inutility to representation. However, something else takes place; inasmuch as there is a performative aspect to be read, which is not simply concerned with representation of experience so much as the translation of the experience into the materiality of language, the text of Dickens may be read as conveying what George Eliot describes in *The Mill on the Floss* as 'the "transferred life" of human sympathy and identification' (Eliot 1997, 634; Stewart 2010, 179). There is thus construed an immersive transference of feeling, from navigating the passages around Todgers's, to navigating the (written) passages *about* Todgers's. The memory of resigned distraction, gentle melancholia and weariness becomes ours, during and following the process of reading, as if the experience of the city's phantasmagoric parade were ours. In reading, I become the subject, as Georges Poulet puts it, 'of thoughts other than my own' (1969, 56), though whose thoughts – and more significantly, whose perceptions, whose intuitions, whose feelings – these may be one is not quite sure, given the transference and transposition between 'narrator', the 'stranger' and 'you' (I?), singular or plural. If 'my consciousness behaves as though it were the consciousness of another' (1969, 56), that other's consciousness is one engendered by London in the early part of the nineteenth century, felt as if for a first time, returning with the haunting force of its modernity.

Todgers's is there – as an enigma, or shibboleth perhaps. If you know how to navigate the area, no direction is necessary; you are a Londoner, of the city, one of its subjects or initiates. If, on the other hand, you do not know where Todgers's lies, no amount of information will make that plain to you. You do not belong, and cannot become part of this area of London, or, by extension, any other. Todgers's remains to be read, but is there affirming nevertheless its illegibility, its resistance to any mode of epistemological or, for that matter, topographical transcription. Knowing where the Monument is will not save you. All that you might receive, if you are 'the stranger' imagined as one of London's lost souls, is an impression:

> Several fruit-brokers had their marts near Todgers's; and one of the first impressions wrought upon the stranger's senses was of oranges—of damaged oranges with blue and green bruises on them, festering in boxes, or mouldering away in cellars. All day long, a stream of porters from the wharves beside the river, each bearing on his back a bursting chest of oranges, poured slowly through the narrow passages; while underneath the archway by the public-house, the knots of those who rested and regaled within, were piled from morning until night.

Strange impression this, at once – seemingly – olfactory and visual, or perhaps the phenomena belong to some synaesthetic or hallucinatory condition; though whether that is the stranger's or an effect produced in the stranger by the city can hardly be decided, given that the impressions are wrought upon the stranger's senses. The perception of 'festering' and 'mouldering' is an apperception, properly speaking, because the alleged oranges, belonging to nothing other than sensory apprehension, are conceived of as being secreted away in cellars. The reality that accompanies the impression is no less surreal to the already disturbed senses of the stranger, for there passes before him an endless, slowly moving stream – figuratively, of course, a human tributary of pouring trade from the river, bearing on its current 'bursting chest[s]' of oranges. In counterpoint to this diurnal, iterable flow are those congestive gatherings, the human knots.

That we are implicated in sensory apperception with the intimacy implied by the sense of rotting scent associated by damaged, overripe fruit is clear enough – our consciousness desires to attribute particular determinations; but the immediacy of experience is itself a determination that is illusory because, as readers, we are no further forward than the stranger. Apprehending all there is, or all that there appears to be, yet there is nothing concrete, nothing that grounds. Even work and rest take place, and come to pass as zones of the text and zones of the location, forming the structure of perception.

The 'resigned distraction' of the subject, causing, in turn, the simultaneous condition *and* perception of 'giving' oneself 'up for lost', or 'never once emerg[ing into] anything that might be reasonably called a street', within a labyrinth – or, more accurately, the apprehension of the city appearing to one as a labyrinth – are symptoms, it has to be stressed, not of a distressing quality; this is not the representation of some existential crisis. In our readerly perception of the stranger's perceptions – or the narrator's hypothetical speculation of the stranger's apprehension perhaps being a result of the narrator's own haunting memories; let us not forget we are the folds of a labyrinth produced as a result of the singular modality of presentation, in which this passage encloses us – we find ourselves suspended, within, and subject to, subjects of, a stability of world that is also the experience of a suspended animation. We are *in* a world we cannot fully comprehend, and yet everything there is to apprehend is there, immediately. The various phenomena, those which reveal and those which occlude, those which enlighten as well as those which confuse, all are 'conjoined to my vision only by the nil value of appearing' (Badiou 2009, 128–9). In this world, which is all the world of the urban that there is, 'the being-there' of the impression of festering or mouldering oranges has '"nothing to do"', and thus gives nothing to be seen, as Badiou has it, 'with the being-there' of chimney pots, porters, court-yards, 'strange solitary pumps' or any of the other observed details. There is, therefore, no trauma, no disjunction from the world, because the question is one 'of the nil value of a conjunction, and not of a dislocation of the world'. To put this another way, the determination of the passage to which one is led is not a crisis of or in representation but, simply, the transcription – the reading / writing – of one's being a subject of the modern. The meaning just is the conflation, the constellation of unrelated appearances, to which one's attention becomes 'situated', to appropriate Badiou's word, to, and by, phenomenon after phenomenon. Simply put, this is how one reads and writes London; there is nothing frightening, overwhelming, Gothic, traumatic and so forth in the experience of the city as such, if one's apprehension is of a piece with the modernity of the urban, and its phenomenological perception.

Importantly – and this might serve to explain why the passage is of such length – the text of Dickens constructs the modality of apprehension and experience as if it were a first time, as if one were coming to terms with London. Being lost, becoming lost is a mode of Being in itself, and resigning oneself to this one enters into a modernity that one barely understands, but which one senses, and which determines one's relation as the subject moves through the world. It is, therefore, necessary that the passage begin with negation, in a movement of presentation analogous with phenomenological reduction, in order to displace the false colouring of interpretive comparison, and thereby re-presenting the memory of the authentic event. From this, the reader, shadowing the narrator, and subsequently the second-person figure addressed and the 'stranger', moves without apparent purpose, without certainty of an end or any knowable goal, and without making connections, as the sustained scene, in which the furtherance of plot has no place, invents London. The city becomes a text to be read, 'a series of . . . images, of ideas, which in their turn begin to exist' (Poulet 1969, 54); and to do so, not 'in external space' but 'only', as Georges Poulet asserts of the experience of reading, in 'my innermost self . . . dependent on my consciousness' (1969, 54–5).

Though these are the perceptions, memories and the 'thoughts of another, . . . yet it is I who am their subject. The situation is even more astonishing' (Poulet 1969, 55) because I am perceiving, as the other perceives, memories which have never been mine arriving as if for a first time. Thus, we move on, moving spectrally, as it were, through 'a congeries of mental objects in close *rapport* with my own consciousness' (Poulet 1969, 55), a consciousness the *doppelgänger* of the narrator, the *you*, the stranger. Reading for a sign, reading the phenomena of the world, but not knowing how (yet) to navigate such a world in all its strangeness, you, the stranger estranged in the act of reading, enclosed by the signs and yet distanced from comprehension, are conscious of having to take on a 'humble role, content to record passively all that is going [on] in me' (Poulet 1969, 59). Thus, it is little wonder that 'Strange solitary pumps were found near Todgers's, hiding themselves for the most part in blind alleys, and keeping company with fire-ladders.' While the notion of an alley's 'blindness' might be common enough, metaphorically, the anthropomorphised aspect of the pumps – having reclusive personalities and the ability to 'hide', apparently of their own volition – does not give itself to any normative or naturalising recuperation. The subject is conscious of what is seen, but the perception, its modality implicit in the 'translation' from world to word, maintains something approaching uncanniness, albeit of a non-threatening kind. The prose of Dickens's London thus performs that urban site in its re-presentation of an experience that has inscribed within it the memory of an initial encounter. This is not a matter of style, or of style alone; for, were that so, then, the 'strangeness' would be presupposed, the assumption resting in the *a priori* determination of 'some exterior model' (Merleau-Ponty 1981, 59). Such presupposition, or at least the modality of representation that employs presuppositions concerning a particular fashioning of the world, might be seen to be at work in *fin de siècle* representations of London, with their reworked, overheated Gothic tropes. But London in the text of Dickens is still modern, if not new exactly, and it is the encounter with, and experience of, urban modernity that the memory work of the Dickens text attempts to re-present and give to the reader to experience. The world thus emerges, phenomenon by phenomenon, as these are experienced, as if at what Merleau-Ponty describes, in talking of the act of painting, as the 'point of contact' between the subject and the world, 'in the hollow . . . of perception, and as an exigency which arises from that perception' (1981, 59). This is the genius of Dickens's textual fashioning of London – that the reader experiences in him- or herself a phantasmal encounter commensurate or analogous with the experiential moment, as if the prose were the material of the world, to stress this once more.

It is all too much, or almost too much, and we have not yet begun to reach the beginning of an ending to this passage from *Chuzzlewit*. From such closeness of observation, the presentation of place opens, perhaps unexpectedly, as the following one-and-a-half paragraphs show. What they also indicate is that if subjectivity is always tied to place, as I have argued, and if, moreover, place is not fixed as a series of objects but is protean according to the subjective response to the motions, rhythms and energies of place as these come to be apprehended, then it follows that subjectivity is also unstable, 'neither thing nor substance but the extremity of both particular and universal' (Merleau-Ponty 1964a, 153); and it is this polarity and mutability that comes to be reflected in, mediated by, the ever-changing perception of 'town and Todgers'– two terms, as we have suggested, that signify relation, iterability and flux in exchange, reciprocity and synecdoche or metonymic supplement:

> There were churches also by dozens, with many a ghostly little churchyard, all overgrown with such straggling vegetation as springs up spontaneously from damp, and graves, and rubbish. In some of these dingy resting-places, which bore much the same analogy to green churchyards, as the pots of earth for mignonette and wall-flower in the windows overlooking them, did to rustic gardens—there were trees; tall trees; still putting forth their leaves in each succeeding year, with such a languishing remembrance of their kind (so one might fancy, looking on their sickly boughs) as birds in cages have in theirs. Here, paralysed old watchmen guarded the bodies of the dead at night, year after year, until at last they joined that solemn brotherhood; and, saving that they slept below the ground a sounder sleep than even they had ever known above it, and were shut up in another kind of box, their condition can hardly be said to have undergone any material change when they, in turn, were watched themselves.
>
> Among the narrow thoroughfares at hand, there lingered, here and there, an ancient doorway of carved oak, from which, of old, the sounds of revelry and feasting often came; but now these mansions, only used for storehouses, were dark and dull, and, being filled with wool, and cotton, and the like— such heavy merchandise as stifles sound and stops the throat of echo—had an air of palpable deadness about them which, added to their silence and desertion, made them very grim. In like manner, there were gloomy court-yards in these parts, into which few but belated wayfarers ever strayed, and where vast bags and packs of goods, upward or downward bound, were for ever dangling between heaven and earth from lofty cranes. There were more trucks near Todgers's than you would suppose a whole city could ever need; not active trucks, but a vagabond race, for ever lounging in the narrow lanes before their masters' doors and stopping up the pass; so that when a stray hackney-coach or lumbering waggon came that way, they were the cause of such an uproar as enlivened the whole neighbourhood, and made the very bells in the next church-tower vibrate again. In the throats and maws of dark no-thoroughfares near Todgers's, individual wine-merchants and wholesale dealers in grocery-ware had perfect little towns of their own; and, deep among the very foundations of these buildings, the ground was undermined and burrowed out into stables, where cart-horses, troubled by rats, might be heard on a quiet Sunday rattling their halters, as disturbed spirits in tales of haunted houses are said to clank their chains.

Following those solitary pumps, a difference is to be noted inasmuch as the narrator's perspective broadens, as if a camera sought to pull back, transforming the image into a more comprehensive urban landscape. If 'perception is always action', then it is at this point that perception and the action it describes 'becomes praxis', so that the value of phenomena comes to reside in 'their capacity for composing all together, even in their intimate texture, a valid emblem of the world with which we are confronted' (Merleau-Ponty 1981, 64). The reader must refocus, as Dickens maintains the movement away from classical representation, knowing that spectacle has no place in introducing 'the allusive logic of world' (Merleau-Ponty 1981, 65), if, by 'world', we understand this to signify London, in all its modernity. The multiple churches, with their churchyards and the mouldering vegetable over-growth; the anthropomorphised trees with their enfeebled memory; the figures of the watchmen, who 'guard the bodies of the dead at night' until 'they 'join that noble brotherhood', serve as so many examples of the temporality of place: perception also takes in the historicity of locus, as this is made manifest, albeit allusively, in decay and the intima-tion of the subject, placed in such a landscape, as both himself and as a *memento mori*; 'material change' is the perceived condition of every-thing, and so the sign of the authenticity of the image, history 'flattened out' in the perceived scene (Merleau-Ponty 1981, 65). The temporal and historical give to our reading a sense of 'sublimated existence', which is 'more true' than 'lived experience' (Merleau-Ponty 1981, 66), because of the access it gives to consciousness of one's Being. For the moment, there is no stranger at this point, no 'you' to whom the passage is explic-itly apostrophised. The reader is left with the immediacy of the ghostly apperception, as if there were no mediation at work.

Death, time, decay and 'deadness' maintain the tenor of the image in the subsequent paragraph. Carved doors are synecdochic material fragments of the past, signifying the past of architectural forms while giving access to collective memory of past lives, haunted by sound, indi-rectly received by the silence of the present. Indeed, it is the presence of the past in the present which helps define the *topos* of Todgers's as an exemplary place of modernity; for the 'presence of the past in a present that supersedes it but still lays claim to it' is, in this 'reconciliation', the 'essence of the modernity' (Augé 1995, 75) as mapped by the polytem-poral traces that mark the surface of narrative presentation. Dickens figures the cultural memory of place through memories of shadows, wood and stone, human lives and their material dwelling places inter-twined and interanimated, much as the graveyards figure the living and the dead, the not so recently alive and those soon to be dead living on only through memory, perception and re-presentation. In the absence of knowing how to navigate this corner of the city, the subject has opened by place the possibility of reflection and attestation. Such present as there is appears in the form of merchandise. Juxtaposed to the revelry and vivacity of those imagined pasts, which haunt the imagination, merchandise, singularised as cotton, has to be read as the none-too-subtle figure of the modern world.

It also stands as the material reminder, on the one hand, of slavery and colonial enterprises, and, on the other hand, the capital on which the modern is constructed, even as it serves a more murderous purpose, shifting in parenthesis to present tense, 'stif[ling] sound and stop[ping] the throat of echo'. The world of Todgers's has about it an air of 'palpable deadness', 'silence and desertion'; the court-yards are 'gloomy', the aspect 'grim', and the packs on their gibbets appear to figure nothing so much, 'dangling between heaven and earth', as material supplements for the damned. This 'Faustian image', coupled with the sense of historicity of place, the phenomena of gloom and death, the Ovidian echo – itself a classical allusion finding its own echo in the figures of labyrinth and maze, which serve as architectural forms of abyssal undecidability that 'define' the area around Todgers's – and the spectres of revelry, collapses worlds and times. If this is modern London, it is also a pre-modern place. Before the reader, one world emerges from within the other, the two in intimate relation and the intervening centuries erased in what might be called a temporal cathexis invested in the double image.

In the transposition between imagined revelry 'of old' and the quiet of the present, the transformation of lively mansions into dull warehouses and storage places, there is to be read something powerfully anachronistic at work, apropos historicity; possibly, this is the image of the modern out of time with itself; or, modernity is definable provisionally through the appearance of anachrony. Here, in surges, we read the re-presentation of past moments, allusively indebted to particular symbolic tropes, which fragment the present from within itself, and as the condition of its presentation. Anachrony works here in *Chuzzlewit* to render 'history-as-it-has-always-been-known' in ruins (Kates 2008, 203). As a result, every subjective experience and perception of the present, the presence of a present moment in relation to a particular site, 'becomes internally fragmented ... even as each [site or event] ceases to be linked in any necessary or causal way to the other moments putatively surrounding it'. Thus, every 'present, every moment ... is radically singular and unique', history, as a result, becoming 'located [albeit indirectly] in these otherwise dispersed moments' (Kates 2008, 203). The historicity of the passages and their traces becomes marked by, and offers a countersignature to, that double force of closure and opening, history being 'closed up in each present, even as this moment never closes upon itself' (Kates 2008, 203), due to that mediation on the part of an explicitly modern, urban

sensibility, and transmitted from the narrator in this openness of experience as if for a first time, to the reader. Furthermore, sound is cognate
with the visionary and imagination here, serving in the consciousness of
the reader to prompt the imagined aural signal, as the traces of the past
are conjured through what can be heard or imagined as having been
heard where now there is only silence. Horses troubled by rats in the cellarage are suggestive, sonically, of haunted houses, the purpose of aural
stimulation being to offer counterpoint and spur to the imaginary juxtaposition of different imagined temporal moments. In this, there appears
an 'understanding of forms', in which one might sense an injunction
not to limit 'itself merely to the recording of their objective aspects . . .
there is a "life of forms" perceptible not only in the historic development which they display from epoch to epoch, but within each single'
figure (Poulet 1969, 67), and 'in the movement by which forms tend . . .
sometimes to stabilize and become static, and sometimes to change one
another' (Poulet 1969, 67). What Poulet defines as the simultaneous
'contradictory forces . . . the will to stability and the protean impulse'
(1969, 67) is fully at play in Dickens's figures of the urban experience
and the interaction between subject and place, through the mediation
of the subject's perception of what haunts and resonates in place, to
displace the present through the trace of the past, with what remains,
what persists, and what comes to pass. In this, the rhetoric of the subjective reception and translation of urban modernity, the subject's reading
/ writing the city, we are enabled to perceive, in turn, 'by their interplay
how much forms are dependent on . . . a shaping power which determines them, replaces them and transcends them' (Poulet 1969, 67).[28]

From that momentary double vision where the 'throat of echo' is
countersigned by the 'the throats and maws of dark no-thoroughfares',
a somewhat more benign, if still melancholic, world returns. So, yet
another motion is discerned. The world of Todgers's contracts to
confine, and yet expands so that the subject's place gives away to
another situation. Across the lengthy introduction to the location and
its reciprocal relation to the larger world of the city, so there is a process
in re-presentation of experience, whereby, on the one hand, determination takes part in an infinite expansion, while, on the other, there is
constantly what Coleridge calls a 'force' – and perhaps this might be
the appropriate trope to supplement the notion of narrator-as-subject
– striving to 'apprehend or *find* itself in this infinity' (Coleridge 1983,
297). The double principle replays itself spatially and temporally in a
series of becomings across the text of Dickens. I say *becomings*-plural,
for, if this is not yet apparent, there are multiple worlds ('individual
wine-merchants and wholesale dealers in grocery-ware had perfect little

towns of their own'), temporally and spatially inhabiting the same place, the same realisation or cognisance; the urban space produced in the Dickensian imagination is, to borrow a singularly appropriate phrase of Coleridge's (in one of his more Kantian moments), 'inexhaustibly re-ebullient' (1983, 300).

From whence does this inexhaustibility, which nevertheless exhausts the subject, leaving him or her in a condition of ennui, arise? If 'to tell' is to describe, to enumerate and represent; and if such an action would 'fill a goodly book', while equally necessary would be a 'second volume no less capacious' concerning the guests of the 'queer old taverns'; then the matter is one of generation, attestation, reading and writing. It is not merely a matter of space, but of the interaction with space, and the relation of subjectivity to this. Apprehending this, we have to see how space is not just a neutral zone before us. The idea of space *is* an idea – that is to say, space is a conception, given concrete form in narrative as place. Space is a means to think the world architexturally, it is 'the means whereby the position of things becomes possible', invested with that power or force 'enabling them to be connected' (Merleau-Ponty 1962, 243). Narrative reveals a mode of reflection on the part of the subject, which causes the world to appear in a number of modalities, translated through that process of anthropomorphisation and abstracted as moods: resignation, melancholy, and so forth.

> To tell of half the queer old taverns that had a drowsy and secret existence near Todgers's, would fill a goodly book; while a second volume no less capacious might be devoted to an account of the quaint old guests who frequented their dimly-lighted parlours. These were, in general, ancient inhabitants of that region; born, and bred there from boyhood; who had long since become wheezy and asthmatical, and short of breath, except in the article of story-telling: in which respect they were still marvellously long-winded. These gentry were much opposed to steam and all new-fangled ways, and held ballooning to be sinful, and deplored the degeneracy of the times; which that particular member of each little club who kept the keys of the nearest church, professionally, always attributed to the prevalence of dissent and irreligion; though the major part of the company inclined to the belief that virtue went out with hair-powder, and that old England's greatness had decayed amain with barbers.

Here, the narrator appears to pause. The world and its forms promise to overwhelm, and the only recourse is to admit, however indirectly, the impossibility of representation faithfully rendered and, instead, to imply, if not an endless reading / writing, one at least which, out of the imagination, gestures towards an abyssal unfolding. Book upon book, text within text: the dynamic of space considered as the interconnection between mutable forms, opens to consciousness the promise of a potential infinity of narrative, remaining to be written but hinted at here by the sketched tales of 'opposition to steam', 'new-fangled ways', the sins of 'ballooning', the abandonment of 'hair-powder' as an essential cosmetic of civilised society, produced in response to the 'degeneracy of the times' by 'old guests', 'ancient inhabitants' and members of 'each little club'. Each narrative is a manifestation of memory, various pasts so many revenant instances belonging to others, the city's innumerable subjects. The multiplicity of worlds is conjured by, and in turn conjures and conjectures, equally, on the proliferation of story, and innumerable inhabitants. With this understanding, the narrating consciousness opens itself to the narration of countless others. The condition of the city is such that there can be no single, controlling subjectivity, no simple, sole position or perspective.

As the vision of the urban location unfolds, so too do its many traces call attention to themselves. The temporal opens from within the present, even as the space of narrative, and the place it strives to figure, expands all efforts towards offering greater detail and so the completion of representation inaugurating a gesture towards infinity and against stability. As the narrator admits to the reception of other narrations, other lives, other subjectivities – in this recognition, mimetic representation is defeated, objective vision of the world made impossible – so, here, we find two figures for the act of reading and writing London. On the one hand, the narrating machinery traces what it replicates, an ineluctable proem to urban modernity and the concomitant fluctuations of subjective reflection. The only authentic way that one can re-present the city is to generate a double act of reading and writing in which the subject is only ever a provisional figure, giving place to other subjectivities, other times and other narratives. On the other hand, as a corollary, any veridical apprehension or perception of, and response to, London perceives how the self is always situated by the world and appears in it and to him- or herself, as the world, as place appears. (On the situation of Being, see Badiou [2009, 113–18].) What the opening of 'town and Todgers' suggests is that Being does not have a world, as a stable object to which subjectivity bears witness. Instead, the being appears in a given place, or world, in its being situated by the given, singular locus. In short, subjectivity is always situated, and the situation being always more than one, so too is the urban subject.

Yet, what marks the subjectivity of the narrator in relation to place as singular, is that making exotic or strange the familiar, the otherwise unremarkable, and to excavate from within this material archive the historicity of place, without the programme to write a history of locale, as if from the outside. Here, the text of Dickens presents London, from the inside, with the perception of the 'native', the London subject. Such a fiction, a construct – and, it must be remembered, there is no such thing, no such person as that which we call 'narrator', this being merely the phantasmal projection, a situation of subjectivity in the text – is motivated by what Walter Benjamin calls 'journeys into the past'; as a result of which, the 'account of a city given by a native will always have something in common with memoirs' (*SW2* 262), which in turn narrate rather than describe (to make a distinction of Benjamin's). Even more, such native narrative drive, for Benjamin, and this is certainly true in the doxical orientation of a Dickens narrative, the narrator-effect functions through what has been heard, the text becoming 'an echo of the stories the city has told him ever since he was a child' (*SW2* 262). This produces an 'epic book through and through,' generated from 'a process of memorizing while strolling around'; 'each street', Benjamin concludes, 'is a vertiginous experience', the city, 'a mnemonic for the . . . walker' (*SW2* 262). Nowhere is this felt to be more authentic than in those moments where the past erupts from the pavements of London, as in the narrative of Todgers's. What engages the narrative effect above all is the idea of London, and the condition of re-presenting that idea as an infinite task involving the labour of memory and figuration. Such an idea, which coincides with the Kantian notion of the Idea, is 'an idea *of* infinity' (Kates 2008, 147). As such – this will explain much about the modalities of the Dickensian architecture of re-presentation – 'London' can never be presented directly or as such, in totality; it is only ever available to that subjective experience indirectly, in every singular situation, for the idea 'can never be conceived as presenting its subject matter' directly (Kates 2008, 147). As 'an idea of infinity, the object at which this idea aims necessarily overflows the consciousness of this idea' (Kates 2008, 147), as a result of which one only grasps the subject's apprehension of London, if at all, in the frustration of representation, mapped here as the inability to locate location. London is only known in its 'nonappearance and nonpresentation' (Kates 2008, 147).

Admitting the past, with its promise to return the multiplicities of London, its memories, situations, subjects and tales, the narrator turns back to 'Todgers's itself', limiting for the moment presentation by engaging to speak 'of it only as a house in that neighbourhood'. Involved in this turn of focus is an attempted delimitation of the image through negation: 'As to Todgers's itself—speaking of it only as a house in that neighbourhood, and making no reference to its merits as a commercial boarding establishment—it was worthy to stand where it did.' To say that the sentence appears to say nothing would be to state the obvious. The evaluation of worthiness seems grounded in the doxa of tradition, which empasises the the inoperability of a staircase window, whether regarding its being opened or being transparent:

> There was one staircase-window in it; at the side of the house, on the ground-floor; which tradition said had not been opened for a hundred years at least, and which, abutting on an always-dirty lane, was so begrimed and coated with a century's mud, that no pane of glass could possibly fall out, though all were cracked and broken twenty times.

The window no longer functions as a window. Its uselessness is paired with the 'mystery' of the cellarage, an enigma echoing that of the area itself ('the mystery was known but to a chosen few'), and of which no one knows or cares anything. While narrative in the form of rumour surrounds it, 'indifference' is the mood, the mode or affect directed towards it. Moreover, it has nothing to do with Todgers's, being the property of another, apparently. The cellar's most striking aspect is that no one knows anything about it, or has any memory about its purpose or precise ownership. The inutility, coupled with that pervasive defeat of any positive knowledge, reiterates the epistemological negativity, along with other denials or comparative dismissals (no sound, no activity, nothing worthy of the name of street, no-thoroughfare), with which the chapter had begun, and continued ('Surely there never was . . . You couldn't walk about in Todgers's neighbourhood, as you could in any other neighbourhood . . . never once . . . Nobody had ever found Todgers on a verbal direction'). We have moved around and around the neighbourhood, without purpose or sense of direction, or being able to orient ourselves. We have witnessed strangers, our epistemological *doppelgängers*, equally lost, thwarted as to goal or destination. Yet, we, you, the stranger find ourselves *at* Todgers's, the sense and knowledge of which is equally purposeless. Indeed, given that we have arrived as if by accident, without knowing how we got there, without being able to observe how we made our way, Todgers's appears before us as if it were some mystical lodestone or keystone, centring and determining the occluded identity of place.

At the house, you are taken to the top, on to the roof. Clotheslines no longer work, having rotted, and plants have been forgotten, their withered condition transforming them. The promise of seeing anything is almost immediately negated on arriving on the roof, the prospective observer having been mildly concussed, then choked. If these trials are survived, however, *you* finally have both a perspective – on the condition of fine weather – and a point of orientation:

> there were things to gaze at from the top of Todgers's, well worth your seeing too. For first and foremost, if the day were bright, you observed upon

the house-tops, stretching far away, a long dark path: the shadow of the Monument: and turning round, the tall original was close beside you, with every hair erect upon his golden head, as if the doings of the city frightened him. Then there were steeples, towers, belfreys, shining vanes, and masts of ships: a very forest. Gables, housetops, garret-windows, wilderness upon wilderness. Smoke and noise enough for all the world at once.

Below, in the streets nothing is to be seen clearly; clearly, nothing is what is to be seen, on the roof, all one can do is list in the face of the spectacle before the senses. The impression coalesces into the collective metaphor of a forest, which, in turn, transforms into 'wilderness upon wilderness', with smoke and noise, the assault on the senses virtually complete, being 'enough for all the world at once'. Before the iterable leading to a loss of focus – the world blurs into an endlessness of similar phenomena – optical, olfactory and aural senses are immersed, subsumed. More than representation, it is the subject's perception, his or her situation vis-à-vis the world, in the situation that is given the subject, and which grounds subjectivity's consciousness. Within the empirical are the symbols of the subject's being-there in the 'world' of nineteenth-century London. The novelty of the sensuous overload is such that it is only indirectly apprehensible through the natural analogy.

This is London as if for a first time. In this, Dickens's text mediates between classical and modern, in pictorial terms; for the passage suspends the subject between the world and the subject's senses. The view from the roof is not merely about seeing London. It is concerned with showing the reader how the subject sees London, if at all, at a given moment. And in order to make the reader see and sense in a manner appropriate to the modern urban subject's genesis, so that reading might have the chance to experience the memory of perception touched by the truth of its historicity, the narrator-effect circumscribes vision, constructing a 'representation in which each thing ceases to call the whole of vision to itself' (Merleau-Ponty 1964a, 49), but works to recall the subject's situatedness. Everything in the phenomenological flow tends towards a reflection on subjectivity; concomitantly, perception of 'reality in itself and as it truly is' (Henry 2008, 26) for someone, whether you, I the narrator, the stranger, or whoever.

It should not be forgotten that whatever the reality revealed, however authentic the sense of that reality and the resonance of its material and sensory experience, this is nevertheless mediated through re-presentation, in a language of indirection tending towards the apprehension of impression and image. That this involved formulation *is* forgotten has tended to the assumption of the mimetic and objective, the merely aesthetic on the one hand, and the semi-transparency of the medium supposedly in the service of the historical, of context or whatever, as the justification for a critical reading, on the other. But the literary has as much, if not more in common with painting and other visual arts than it does with 'history', in the functions of its representations. If we do not see the subject, neither do we see the city; hence the constant motion of analogy, the rhythms of negation, and all those other devices of indirection by which the passage in its detail and its entirety gives us to apprehend. What the passage from the rooftop gives us to understand is that we do not see the city, any more than we do a landscape; we see, instead, through that circumscription already acknowledged, all that which makes up a city; description forms a narrative surface, tending to the interminable and the infinite. The impression, the condition of apperception – the subject feels the 'whole' of the city's reality only through the intimacy and density of detail – demonstrates indirectly that which, in the text of Dickens concerning the modernity of the city and the subjectivity engendered, is always informed by the experience of the aporetic; hence negation, doubt, hesitation, the expression of limit, the passive suffering, the *resignation*. For re-presentation, we read, and learn from the reading / writing of London in Dickens, in its endlessly aporetic condition of 'no-thoroughfare', 'encompasses the infiniteness of singular difference, the infiniteness of reality'. There is, for the reader, as for the subject, what Louis Marin calls a 'loss in excess', a 'vertigo' (Marin 2001, 249). Of such images, I may have to say, following Marin's argument, this is London, or '"it is a city, a landscape"'; but we are at least able to conceptualise, from that which London gives to be read in the mediated impression and experience of the text of Dickens, 'the infinite difference of reality ['you observed upon the house-tops, stretching far away, a long dark path . . . steeples, towers, belfreys, shining vanes, and masts of ships: a very forest. Gables, housetops, garret-windows, wilderness upon wilderness'] without ever being able to express or represent it' directly or in full (Marin 2001, 248). As subject, entering into and resigning ourselves to a subjectivity not our own, neither ours nor of our time, our perception is as of a 'vertiginous experience: the eye loses itself in the surface where representations of things definitively' disappear in the 'words that designate and identify them' (Marin 2001, 249).

You arrive, therefore, at the conclusion of this extract, which begins, ironically, with the observation that

> After the first glance, there were slight features in the midst of this crowd of objects, which sprung out from the mass without any reason, as it were, and took hold of the attention whether the spectator would or no. Thus, the revolving chimney-pots on one great stack of buildings, seemed to be turning gravely to each other every now and then, and whispering the result of their

separate observation of what was going on below. Others, of a crook-backed shape, appeared to be maliciously holding themselves askew, that they might shut the prospect out and baffle Todgers's.

Clearly, particular elements and objects determine what is to be noticed, and how one is to see, with no volition on the part of the resigned subject, whose gaze 'finds itself prescribed', the city's potential impression 'pre-written' (Marin 2001, 257) in the image of quasi-animate architectural details. This strangely vital architecture speaks or remains silent, it sees and communicates what it witnesses, or otherwise remains silent. Then, you happen to have your eye drawn towards someone:

> The man who was mending a pen at an upper window over the way, became of paramount importance in the scene, and made a blank in it, ridiculously disproportionate in its extent, when he retired. The gambols of a piece of cloth upon the dyer's pole had far more interest for the moment than all the changing motion of the crowd. Yet even while the looker-on felt angry with himself for this, and wondered how it was, the tumult swelled into a roar; the host of objects seemed to thicken and expand a hundredfold; and after gazing, round him, quite scared, he turned to Todgers's again, much more rapidly than he came out; and ten to one he told M. Todgers's afterwards that if he hadn't done so, he would certainly have come into the street by the shortest cut: that is to say, head-foremost.

Who might the man in the window be? Why has he paused in the middle of writing? Is this no one in particular? Or might it be the artist in the mind's eye, placing himself in the field of vision, not in a self-portrait but, instead, in the manner of Velázquez, peering out from behind the canvas, as he paints the painting in which you see him, *Las Meninas*. This figure, appearing briefly, then retires. You are reminded that, if you see London, someone authorises that vision; becoming subjects of the text, subject to the text and the figures of the city from which it is composed, our perspective is positioned. You are invited to reflect on the perception of perspective, coming to consciousness reflectively of your having been situated. This moment is brief, however, the writer's retreat leaving a blank, as with a page remaining to be filled, or as a reminder that there is no image without a subject. And with that disappearance, the tumultuous phenomenal revenance visually and audibly of the mass of the city returns, to disorient and intimidate. Too much uncontrollable vision is awful, the figural vertiginousness threatening to become real, the stranger, or you, transformed into the looker-on, quickly withdrawing from the scene. This is not just a question of falling from the roof. It is also a question of resigning: *from* the perception itself, from its presentation, from living in memory through the experience of encountering London. Infinity is too much; the abyss cannot be comprehended. There 'can be sensation only on condition that it exists for a central and unique *I*' (Merleau-Ponty 1962, 219). However, the event of modernity revealing that there is no pure subjectivity but that the self is always situated, the 'reflective *I* . . . [comes to find that it] is not [pure] consciousness or pure being' (Merleau-Ponty 1962, 219); such an illusion is pre-modern. The reflective *I*, situated in resignation to the time and place of London in the early nineteenth century, is 'experience, in other words the communication of a finite subject with an opaque being from which it emerges' (Merleau-Ponty 1962, 219). London gives us to read a radical subjectivity in Dickens' reading / writing the city and its experience or perception of the world, which is revealed 'as an open totality the synthesis of which is inexhaustible', and 'indivisibly demolished and remade by the course of time' (Merleau-Ponty 1962, 219).

Were I tempted to give a name to the mode of phenomenal production and its situation of a subject signed by the historicity of its perception that is on display in the text of Dickens, it might be *apophatic hypotyposis*: the vivid representation of scene or event, brought before the mind's eye as if I were subject in close proximity to the experience, but produced through negation and indirection. Dickens gives us the possibility to see truthfully through a textual mnemotechnic that creates perception as if it were a new revelation. This is achieved through what might be thought initially to be paradoxical. Eschewing the pretence of mimetic transparency and yet offering the figuration of all that is there, the text of the city constructs and projects kaleidoscopic, fragmentary, iterable and protean impressions of itself. It achieves this through 'a reflexive or presentative opacity' (Marin 2001, 257) that is capable, if we resign ourselves to a patient, attentive, *resigned* and exhausted reading not driven by any purpose, goal, direction or teleologically desired meaning, by 'making the most of the representative transparency of descriptive discourse [that is a roof, this is a door] through its opaque boundaries' (Marin 2001, 257). We cannot find Todgers's because there is no map, no overview. Todgers's is not to be found, not because it does not exist but because it is everywhere; and everywhere *and* nowhere, once again, is where subjectivity finds itself when attempting to come to terms with London, foolishly seeking an authoritative perspective, a controlling and controllable point of view, rather than falling into the resignation of the passive perception, that involves one more intimately.

Spring Evenings • London

Our Mutual Friend

That mysterious paper currency which circulates in London when the wind blows, gyrated here and there and everywhere. Whence can it come, whither can it go? It hangs on every bush, flutters in every tree, is caught flying by the electric wires, haunts every enclosure, drinks at every pump, cowers at every grating, shudders upon every plot of grass, seeks rest in vain behind the legions of iron rails. [. . .]

The wind sawed, and the sawdust whirled. The shrubs wrung their many hands, bemoaning that they had been over-persuaded by the sun to bud; the young leaves pined; the sparrows repented of their early marriages, like men and women; the colours of the rainbow were discernible, not in floral spring, but in the faces of the people whom it nibbled and pinched. And ever the wind sawed, and the sawdust whirled.

When the spring evenings are too long and light to shut out, and such weather is rife, the city which Mr Podsnap so explanatorily called London, Londres, London, is at its worst. Such a black shrill city, combining the qualities of a smoky house and a scolding wife; such a gritty city; such a hopeless city, with no rent in the leaden canopy of its sky; such a beleaguered city, invested by the great Marsh Forces of Essex and Kent. (*OMF* 147)

Returning to certain fundamentals concerning expression and perception, the subject and the world that gives itself in re-presentation, it is useful to remind ourselves of how the subject and, consequently, the reader come to find themselves oriented, once one suspends the everyday habit of what might be called 'unseeing' observation.

The modernity of the urban text of Dickens resides in its implicit apprehension that the self is always oriented in its 'relation' to the world. There is unfolded in every figuration of urban place a transcendence constituted through 'disposition, projection, and comportment' (Patocka 1996, 48) of the subject vis-à-vis the world of London. The revelation of a modernity is not made manifest, however, either wholly in a direct manner, or solely through the realisation of this transcendent affirmation of concatenation. Relationship, where this is this, where it may come to be traced belatedly, takes place in language. There is a modernity to be read here therefore, in the privilege of language as being, on the one hand, the expression of being, and on the other, as the inescapable play that constitutes a subject as the place of the world's traces and their role through the medium of expression in constituting subjectivity as belonging to the world, and inextricably bound to it. What is brought to light is relation as such, wherein the text of Dickens unveils the apprehension that the world 'as Kant was the first to say, is neither a thing nor an aggregate of experienced things' because 'it is given in the wholeness of transcendence, in this "original history"' (Patocka 1996, 48). Inasmuch as there is no transcendent determination of London, therefore, the question of transcendence is always one of this originary historicity, which speaks in every articulation of the modern self in its place, realised in a given place and taking place as the event of conscious perception and re-presentation. No ultimate transcendence, therefore, only the quasi-transcendental event of singular revelation, iterable in memory and subsequently haunting the act of reading to come.

While what I explore concerning the nature of expression and its literary modalities in following Merleau-Ponty's consideration of the linguistic closely has a general import for any reading of literature beyond what takes place in the text of Dickens, it is important to bear in mind that it is in the modality of presentation or giving whereby transcendence comes to light as that which gives to the text of Dickens its singular condition, and the privilege in the revelation of an urban modernity and subjectivity that is traced throughout the present volume. Being is 'uncovered', to use Patocka's word (1996, 49), in such a way that, in every subject's disposition towards the world of London in the novels, there is revealed a responsibility to the historicity of place. The history of urban modernity is *there* in the expression of the subject. Subjectivity, the subjectivity of the other, is *there* and at this moment, when I read, in my repetition of the subject-position, as the modern city appears to me, as if – once more – I were *there* in the place of the subject, the place of the other. In those movements of reading and writing, reading into writing, which return a reading from the subjective perspective of the other as the motions map, retrace and construct a London, successive London places in the imaginary, as if perceived for a first time every time I read, the text of Dickens does more than any other to re-present the unique experience and expression of the subject's involvement in urban space.

> We believe expression is most complete when it points unequivocally to events, to states of objects, to ideas or relations, for, in these instances,

expression leaves nothing more to be desired, contains nothing which it does not reveal, and thus sweeps us toward the object which it designates.

Thus, Merleau-Ponty on the mistaken yet persistent belief in the transparency of language. He continues to summarise this position in the following manner: 'expression involves nothing more than replacing a perception or an idea with a conventional sign that announces, evokes, or abridges it' (Merleau-Ponty 1981, 3). He then responds, posing the question: 'how could language achieve this if what is new were not composed of old elements already experienced – that is, if new relations were not entirely definable through the vocabulary and syntactical relations of the conventional language?' (Merleau-Ponty 1981, 3). If language 'channels all our experiences into the system of initial correspondences between a particular sign and the particular signification we acquired when learning the language' (Merleau-Ponty 1981, 4), then that process of channelling, in order to 'invent' re-presentation of experience and perception in, and through, the medium of language, must translate. This is a given. What is less immediately grasped though is that translation of this order is a re-presentation of the material conditions of experience between the subject and the world. Language, Merleau-Ponty argues, 'is the double of being' (Merleau-Ponty 1981, 5), the world made discourse, the subject the page, or screen, on which the world becomes word and retransmitted. We 'cannot conceive of an idea that comes into the world without words' (Merleau-Ponty 1981, 5–6).

So far, so general: it is necessary, though, to stay patiently and with some attention to the minutiae of the Merleau-Ponty's argument in order that the complexity of Dickensian urban figuring be apprehended in its own right. That the image of London on a spring evening 'in these times of ours' is an image for someone; that it is expressed at a given moment thereby revealing in the process of being expressed an originary historicity, is inescapable. The image constituted takes place in a language that causes one to apperceive a vision that is markedly counter-picturesque, but which, in being available only through this language belonging to this moment and to someone: here, being is doubled phantasmically.

Staying with Merleau-Ponty, then: when a writer, or the phantasmal subject the writer imagines, approaches the act of re-presenting experience or perception in language – even if that perception is fictional, to the extent that its linguistic articulation concerns, or rather involves, a subject who, though not dissimilar from myself, has never existed – there is still the initial silence of the writer, before narrative begins, before re-presentation and representation come about, the writer being at first silent, the page or screen blank awaiting that which he is going to say, in order to arrive. When it does arrive, it is as if only those words will do; it is as if they have always been there; it is as if, through the medium of the writer narrative, gives place to a projection for some subject of the world, and a world 'around me', at that, 'which already speaks' (Merleau-Ponty 1981, 6–7). Language is thus a 'specter' for Merleau-Ponty, as the title of the essay from which I have cited has it; it is a mode of communication, in which we are given to apprehend that communication is appearance (to reiterate a phrase quoted elsewhere in this volume). Communication causes the appearance to make itself visible, as it is, and in no other manner. To communicate the city at evening in spring as just this experience and no other, at this time and at no other, in this place and in no other, fiction must make the scene, not only seen, but felt with an impossible immediacy.

The peculiarity of such an appearance, a constellated phenomenon through which things appear to view, coming to show themselves in a singular manner distinct from any other as though that were the truth of the world, is what has to be grasped in order to apprehend the presentation of London in the text of Dickens, as distinct from the general argument concerning perception, presentation and the role of language within the subject–world relation. This being so, it remains the case that 'the book [and by extension any text] would not interest me so much if it only told me about things I already know. It makes use of everything . . . in order to carry me beyond it' (Merleau-Ponty 1981, 11). The 'ordinary meaning of the signs' (Merleau-Ponty 1981, 12) is varied in such a way that conventional signification gives way 'toward [an] other meaning with which I am going to connect' (Merleau-Ponty 1981, 12). It is in that experience of proximity, intimacy, of becoming insistently the urban subject formed within, experiencing and responding to the act of reading / writing London, which gives to Dickens's London its especial, haunting singularity. In that 'appreciation' of whirling, sawing, shrill, smoky, scolding phenomena, which cause the leadenness imminent in accents that bemoan; and also in that general, shared sense of being beleaguered, London's sensibility imagined sympathetically as this predominantly, at this moment, in this very place and no other; in that sympathetic reception of the emotional condition of birds and buds – in each of these, quotidian discourse gives way, representation evaporating in the subjective nearness imposed through that re-presentation, as the meaning, the experience of the other.

As a result, 'everything happens as though in effect language had not existed' (Merleau-Ponty 1981, 13). This, once more, is a general principle belonging to the experience of literature. What can be acknowledged, though, is that 'through the complicity of speech and its echo', between ourselves and the text, and the place which gives place for the text to come, with its subject, into being, there remain 'relations of spirit to spirit' (Merleau-Ponty 1981, 13). I am, Merleau-Ponty insists, 'brought within the imaginary self' (1981, 12). In this, a rapport is created between myself and a 'strange expressive organism' (1981, 14). That organism is already there, before the book is written, however. It is always before Dickens, and before each of the subjects to whom it speaks, and who in turn perceive its expressions. The 'phenomenon of expression' belonging, as Merleau-Ponty acknowledges, not only to the study of language but also 'to that of literary experience', the play of re-presentation in expression is our only recourse to the 'lived experience of expression' (1981, 15), the expression of an other, even or especially perhaps when that other is a phantasm, construct and performative projection. (This might just be why, if it matters, literature does matter.) This comes to be apprehended, fleetingly, in the uncanny life of paper, a 'currency' that circulates, simultaneously intimating both economic motion and the flow of the city's life-blood. No longer just a metaphor, the circulation suggests London as assuming the appearance of an animate force. There is in this passage a quality of 'lively confusion', as Robert Douglas-Fairhurst describes it, which is 'central to Dickens's imagination', and which has 'usually made his critics uneasy' (Douglas-Fairhurst 2011, 58) – or some of them at least. Such confusion is usually defined through the blurring of boundaries between 'people's insides and outsides', though here it is in the excess of multiple significations that there is given a strange 'spirit', a vivification in re-presentation that is more than mere life. It is all the more uncanny in that there is little of the human, save for the city which is a human production and projection: in short, a phenomenon of expression. And to risk a strong reading, that uncanny, frenzied motion of paper, its being both blood and money, its being that which gives expression to the city, to its subjects and to the subjective realisation of place and the relation between subject and city, is *the* figure of Dickens's text itself.

If, therefore, the twenty-two-year-old Henry James was correct in his review of *Our Mutual Friend* that Dickens's 'genius [is] not to see beneath the surface of things', thereby making Dickens 'the greatest of superficial novelists', he is only partly correct (James 1971, 481). Or rather he is right, but for the wrong reasons. For if James desired to see into the 'superfine textures of human life' (Douglas-Fairhurst 2011, 59), this was only to remain on another surface, one maintained by choosing psychologism over any phenomenological inquiry (whether it was called this or not). Psychologism is merely the hypothesised – and, in James's case, quite possibly hypostasised – 'beyond', the 'inside' that one attempts to read from the signs of the 'outside' of any human being. In this – and there is nothing wrong with this – James remains more the writer, if not the painter, of nineteenth-century life, than Dickens, while Dickens's disinterest in psychology frees him, after a fashion, to consider being from the perspective of the 'chronicler who recites events without distinguishing between major and minor ones in accordance with the . . . truth [that] nothing that has ever happened should be regarded as lost for history' (Benjamin 1969, 254). The psychology of a character is merely a quaint and somewhat dated interest by contrast, when compared with the modernity of that image of the past, which is 'seized only as an image which flashes up at the instant when it can be recognized and is never seen again' (Benjamin 1969, 255). Against James the *fin de siècle* psychologist, there remains Dickens the historical materialist, in the Benjaminian sense; only through an understanding of that rapport between subject and the 'strange expressive organism' of Merleau-Ponty is this grasped. The being which 'speaks', or who reads and writes the city, reveals the city as it comes to be given, as its appearance determines expression in its materiality and historicity. In this process of speaking, reading, writing and, with all due acknowledgement to the complex temporalities, relays, delays, echoes and deferrals which inform the belatedness of any re-presentation, any memory of perception, the subject also appears, but on this condition: the being, the subject 'is what he is talking about' (Merleau-Ponty 1981, 15); being is always a becoming, a taking place, the locus of an originary and singular expression of historicity embedded in, produced from out of the materiality and historicity of place, whereby he 'finds himself in' or 'finds himself involved in' that appearance of place, to recall variations of reiterated formulae in the Dickens text.

Such involvement identifies the ineluctable and inescapable relation between subject and world. Language is not 'over here', 'with me', and the world 'over there', somehow separate from the 'I speak' or 'I think', even when it appears that there is no 'I' in the expression, as in the passage above. And while this recognition of the inescapable connection and proximity may well be general, what is peculiar to the text of Dickens, I would argue, is that narrative suspension, whereby the grammar of London demands it be figured in the articulation of perception, which gathers its intensity through those modalities of presentation involving grammatical and syntactical reiteration. The expression of the urban world assumes a material form through the materiality of the text that, through iterability and modulation of form, variations on theme, insists in the structural apprehension. We witness, but also, importantly, in or *through* reading, find ourselves involved in, a 'renewal and recovery' of the world 'which unites me [and *us*] with myself [*ourselves*] and others', and thus assume the subject position of a 'consciousness *in* the hazards of language' (Merleau-Ponty 1981, 17), for the time of reading. The urban text in both its ostensible forms – the one built and experienced, perceived, on the one hand, and the one read / written, re-presented, appearing to memory, on the other – illuminates 'modalities of the system of embodied [and therefore material and his-torial] subjects' (Merleau-Ponty 1981, 18). Dickens's discourse of the modern city operates in the singular manner that it does – this, I would argue, is a fundamental aspect of its modernity – through a double gesture. Breaking with narrative motion to reflect on the experience of London for its always hypostasised subject, for a subjectivity always already hypostasised in its intimate enfolding with the city's phenomena and forms as they communicate through appearance, Dickens's urban language 'envelops and inhabits' (Merleau-Ponty 1981, 19) subjectivity without distancing the subject position through reflection until the habi-tation, the being-involved, announces itself from within the non-reflec-tive apparition of London. Subject-position and, through that, modern urban subjectivity returns in reading, in my reading, in the other's expression in me, for me, and this revenance, which is always already that of the city for someone, is always capable of being 'rebuilt again by the other person . . . by others who may come along [each and every other reader], and in principle by anyone . . . This transcendence arises the moment I refuse to content myself with the established language' (Merleau-Ponty 1981, 20).

Moreover, language, Merleau-Ponty continues, is not, 'while it is functioning, the simple product of the past it carries with it' (1981, 22). To recall an earlier comment, coming back to that circulation of paper: when I read the opening sentences of the extract I enter into that moment, as if I were there, as if the phenomena of the event in this instance arrive to re-present themselves, give themselves phantasmally through the material medium of the language. Never just a constative observation distinct from what it represents, the language is performa-tive inasmuch as we move through the assonant echo from my*ster*i*ou*s to cur*ren*cy, to *cir*culates, and from within this the internal aural oscillation between *cur*rency and *cir*culation. In turn, the susurration and motion of the paper in the wind marks itself through '*wh*en *th*e [there is a phonic and phonemic after-echo of the wind's motion here] *wi*nd', with that slight vowel modulation, the sound engaged again in the performative 'blo*ws*', the latest sonority repeating that earlier sibilance. And while the sonic repetition is not exact, its variations are markedly, decidedly there, in a chiastic play, 'circulating' through partial and whole alliterative

Whitechapel

devices, and in consonance as well as assonance ('w-' / '<u>s</u>awe<u>d</u>' / '<u>s</u>awd-', 'wh-'), extending to further consonance in the final sound of 'whirled'. The wind blows through the sentence as it blows the paper through and around London – *in London*, as the fulcrum of the sentence states it. The erratic motions of the paper are then performed in the second clause of the first sentence in the tonal modulations and rhythmic play of *here, there and everywhere*, the figure of gyration anticipating the motion whilst also picking up the susurrating assonance and sibilance of the first part of the sentence. The wind in London is the wind I hear, I feel in the reading / writing of the London atmospheric current, and in my perception, the insistence and propinquity that performativity intensifies to present a consciousness to me, as if the questions that follow are mine, as if I am the subject in the moment, at that particular place, experiencing the unpleasant qualities of a London spring evening. In the present that the communication and the appearance of London, the wind and the evening figure collectively, a phantom present in the expression crosses from the 'period when it was written'. In this apparition for me, the 'inalienable subjectivity of my speech enables me to understand those extinct subjectivities [and, in addition, those phantasmal subjectivities belonging to those who have never existed as such, through the haunting agency of the literary] of which objective history gives me only traces' (Merleau-Ponty 1981, 24–5). History is thus revealed as 'not just a series of events external to one another and external to us' (Merleau-Ponty 1981, 25). As a result, the 'radical awareness of subjectivity enables me to rediscover other subjectivities and thereby the truth of the linguistic past' (Merleau-Ponty 1981, 25) and, with that, the authenticity of the re-presentation of the perception of the event, the place and the subject's historicity. Though no subject is there as such, the insistence of the moment presses on me as if it were my perception, and I am made subject to this vision of a spring evening in London.

Time • The City, Coram's Fields

No Thoroughfare

Day of the month and year, November the thirtieth, one thousand eight hundred and thirty-five. London Time by the great clock of Saint Paul's, ten at night. All the lesser London churches strain their metallic throats. Some, flippantly begin before the heavy bell of the great cathedral; some, tardily begin three, four, half a dozen, strokes behind it; all are in sufficiently near accord, to leave a resonance in the air, as if the winged father who devours his children, had made a sounding sweep with his gigantic scythe in flying over the city.

What is this clock lower than most of the rest, and nearer to the ear, that lags so far behind to-night as to strike into the vibration alone? This is the clock of the Hospital for Foundling Children. Time was, when the Foundlings were received without question in a cradle at the gate. Time is, when inquiries are made respecting them, and they are taken as by favour from the mothers who relinquish all natural knowledge of them and claim to them for evermore. (*NT* 1)

There is no one time in Dickens, no single temporal measure. Clock time, cosmic or 'natural' temporal flows, motions, circulations, time in a linear motion, time as the marker of haunting memory, the different times of narrative movement, the times of reading, the *époché* called into existence through temporal suspension – and, inevitably, the temporal given prosopopoeic form. Before coming to the personification of Time, we might pause to consider the relation in the text of Dickens between certain temporal motions, the 'natural' world and Being. Associated with flow, Time is figured in the image of the Thames, as in the opening nocturnal moments of *Our Mutual Friend* (*OMF* 13), which further situates temporal flow topographically through the river's flow between the 'future', implied in the iron bridge at Westminster, and the past, signified in the stone of London Bridge. The time of the Thames is the time of work, getting a 'living', but also that of the reminder of the end of time, in the dead bodies by which that living is earned. Time and the

Thames are again invoked in *Our Mutual Friend*, though in a markedly different manner:

> Mr. Mortimer Lightwood and Mr. Eugene Wrayburn . . . had taken a bachelor cottage near Hampton, on the brink of the Thames, with a lawn, and a boat-house, and all things fitting, and were to float with the stream through the summer and the Long Vacation. (*OMF* 147)

Here the motion of time and river, on which desultory human existence is borne, is perceived, if not as one, then at least synonymous or analogous, through the implied logic of zeugma, which serves as a rhetorical undercurrent. Human time is carried on the tidal and seasonal flow – indeed, the temporality of Being is a flow – even as, in the novel's inaugural passage, the riverine time brings a living through the death of others, as has been acknowledged. Most significantly, time, presented as sound, 'paves the way for a new matrix of perception' (Danius 2002, 15) – and this can be of great importance in London, when on so many occasions vision is hindered, sight limited, the visible occluded.

To Time's personification, which ultimately here intimates the merest moment of a weak messianism (on which I shall conclude): *No Thoroughfare* starts factually enough, dating itself. Against this date – 30 November 1835 – a clock strikes, that of St Paul's, to announce our entrance into the narrative, and also to fix momentarily the precise time of day – 10 p.m. – on 30 November. This is not any time; it is London time. Such nomination is significant in relation to the year, Greenwich Mean Time not being adopted globally until 1884, and not nationally until 1847, with a necessary standardisation known as 'railway time' (though not without legal challenge as late as 1858). At the time of London time in which our story begins, therefore, local mean time or sundial time was still the standard. There is thus, already, in *No Thoroughfare*, written more than thirty years after the time of its setting, a temporal localisation: a disordering also perhaps, at least rhetorically, and as something of an *après-coup*, given the 'national' fact of date situated in distinction from the 'regional' temporal record.

The temporal discordance is then exaggerated in the irregular, if not 'anachronistic' sounding of the bells belonging to various London churches, which set up a dissonant 'resonance in the air', some chiming before, some after 'the great clock of St Paul's. The initiation of prosopopoeic manifestation takes place through this collective resonance, inasmuch as the bells are heard to strain their 'metallic throats', completing time's initial apparition in that grotesque figure of a flying, cannibalistic Father Time, whose scythe executes the sound in the 'sweep . . . over the city'. If Being is always, in some measure, temporal, Being experienced as a temporal experience of the world, and so available to reflection through temporal awareness in anticipation, memory, the different times of experience and the experience of temporal flow, then it is, too, inescapably, in its endless becoming, a Being towards death. More radically, though, as these opening lines intimate, time *is* death; we are given in the analogical apperception the consciousness that death haunts us in time, it is there as the temporal apprehension of that which moves towards us, which maintains the inexorable movement. 'London time', then, is the sound of death, as well as life, the one within the other. But the sound of London, the passage intimates, however quietly, is that which calls up the apparition of Death. As in a number of other places, London is realised nocturnally through the aural, rather than the visual image. Equally, as I have argued, such an auscultatory impression gives a more immediate sense of closeness to one in this perception of sound rather than sight.

The apprehension of immediacy must also be thought regarding the relation between time and sound, in the temporal and resonant re-presentation of the nocturnal cityscape. That 'Dickens's works constitute an important touchstone for Victorian sound' is undeniable (Picker 2003, 11). Equally undeniable is the sense in this passage, as elsewhere, that, when it comes to the sounding of time, such reverberation is older than the nineteenth century; but also, in its purposeful deployment as the medium of the vision that breaks the bounds of realism from the very outset, exceeding the merely mimetically faithful, the figural excess provides for perception a sense of a modernity. The very idea of a 'London time' is thus out of time with itself, and in more than the simple fact of the off-kilter church bells sounding ten o'clock. In moments such as this, the archaic and modern engulf the idea of the Victorian in that perception of the auratic by which London is *known* rather than just *seen*, apprehended without being represented in an associational economy, rather than one which is rational or realistic. But this revelation of aura works precisely through that yoking of the sensate apprehension with the hallucinatory vision of the pre-modern figure of Father Time.

If, in 'the Kantian-Coleridgean conception, the imagination is the means by which we can gain insight into those transcendental truths that lie beyond the limits of our ordinary experience' (Craig 2007, 55), here imagination that so often makes itself known in the text of Dickens offers a truth in that auratic experience of London, which it makes available. Such truth as it is, is in the arrival of the perceptual awareness of that which the city gives to be known. The fixities of temporal order undone, this, the image informs us, *is* London, even if what we are given as its subjects can only be apperceived in a sensory epiphany, not expressed in other words. The 'real' of the city, 'that can only be discovered in and through the imagination is . . . dissolved into what we know can only be a "fiction", a series of associations held together, like the mind, in "a heap or collection of different perceptions . . ."' (Hume cit. Craig 2007, 205); but is recovered in the perception of aura, in that sensory revelation, the instance of the epiphanic – not for everyone, not even for a group, but for one subject, here and there, in this or in other ways.

Sound, arguably, can effect this with greater and more unexpected force than the visual, for sound can take me unawares. The visible can shock, affront, overwhelm, move me to laughter or to tears. In sight, though, the desire to read takes hold in a counter-gesture to that which is unexpectedly before my sight, and I subsume it into the habitual, by which reality reasserts itself, and I distance myself from the effect, the phenomenal in the vision, by appealing, on conscious reflection, to questions of the aesthetic. To risk a hypothesis, therefore, returning in the process to this extract from *No Thoroughfare*: time, although 'managed' through its mechanical and technological control, understood as just another technology in the service of industry and economy – though largely attributed to Benjamin Franklin, 'time is money' seems a peculiarly Victorian epithet – its audible rhythm the illusion of assurance that humans control time, rather than the other way around; when 'freed' by the imagination, Time appears as that transcendently authentic figure, over which there is no human control. That the extract – indeed, the story – starts from a statement of 'facts' and numbers, the first sentence being without commentary other than the bare record, is itself a reflection on the human desire to control, fix time, register it as 'history', keeping time in place by affixing it with numerical place holders. Such registration re-enforces the illusion of the empirical, the objective; sound, on the other hand, can only be received subjectively. Dating and the 'truth' of time, as historical statement, is the frame that opens on to the image of the narrative, but which, through the agency of sound, is broken, admitting the auratic and allegorical, the impression and perception.

And it is through the perception of a lower sound that Time's other figure appears to the subject. Time being double, as already inferred: life and death. Here Time expresses itself differently, in a different voice. It is not only lower, more difficult to catch in the midst of the discordant cacophony; it is also nearer, and much behind the other chimes. So far behind, it appears as if it were solitary, this figure that resonates from the clock of the Foundling Hospital, at Coram's Fields. The narrator pauses to reflect on the difference of times from themselves, in the locution 'time was . . . time is . . .'. Once more, one might perceive a shift in the different markers of past and present, in that the first of the two phrases is idiomatic, conventional, the second opening from within that to shift one's temporal perspective. It is in the specific perception of the times of temporal register that the specific subject is announced, for through that a reflection is made on the hospital's practices. Time affords the subject meditation, and so gives access to the articulation of the distinction. Time is thus apprehended as being of the city, London Time, inasmuch as it has no single, or universal, form or appearance. It is only understood in the event of its sounding. In the reading of such differences and the difference that makes possible the reading / writing of London times, there is the acknowledgement of a difference in apprehension between the sensible and the intelligible, which this extract opens, at the level of the sensible itself.

What is 'made visible' in this is the '*birth* of correlation between consciousness' and the world, re-presented as a unity of the phenomenon, 'whose double sense, at once "subjective" and "objective", is thus revealed' (Dastur 2000, 26–7). In this, in the Times of the city, the senses of modernity affirm themselves. Encouraging us to hear the low, near voice, almost indistinct save for its being out of time with all those other clamorous calls, sound, in the absence of sight, opens for us a vision of the difference of times, which survives in the face of Death. That subjectivity which hears, instead of simply seeing (and therefore remaining blind), opens itself to the last 'not-yet reified sense' (Danius 2002, 89); as a consequence, it does not admit to a rationalisation and the otherwise 'growing reification of reality' (Adorno 1991b, 102). In the sound of London's Time, the passage suggests, hearing the other of time and the temporality of the other, we might be saved from Death. There is still time. There is always another time – if we listen, and if we learn to perceive differently.

Unfinished • Stagg's Gardens, Camden Town

Dombey and Son

Houses were knocked down; streets broken through and stopped; deep pits and trenches dug in the ground; enormous heaps of earth and clay thrown up; buildings that were undermined and shaking, propped by great beams of wood. Here, a chaos of carts, overthrown and jumbled together, lay topsy-turvy at the bottom of a steep unnatural hill; there, confused treasures of iron soaked and rusted in something that had accidentally become a pond. Everywhere were bridges that led nowhere; thoroughfares that were wholly impassable; Babel towers of chimneys, wanting half their height; temporary wooden houses and enclosures, in the most unlikely situations; carcases of ragged tenements, and fragments of unfinished walls and arches, and piles of scaffolding, and wildernesses of bricks, and giant forms of cranes, and tripods straddling above nothing. There were a hundred thousand shapes and substances of incompleteness, wildly mingled out of their places, upside down, burrowing in the earth, aspiring in the air, mouldering in the water, and unintelligible as any dream. (*DS* 79)

Voice • Brentford, the Borough

Our Mutual Friend / The Pickwick Papers

'For I ain't, you must know,' said Betty, 'much of a hand at reading writing-hand, though I can read my Bible and most print. And I do love a newspaper. You mightn't think it, but Sloppy is a beautiful reader of a newspaper. He do the Police in different voices.' (*OMF* Ch. 16)

'Don't call me Valker; my name's Veller; you know that vell enough. What have you got to say to me?' (*PP* Ch. 23)

V is for voice and for . . .

. . . Weller, pronounced Veller, Sam or Samuel – Samivel to his father – Weller. We know that 'vell' enough. Boz 'corrects' the pronunciation and, of course, the spelling of the proper name and other words in which there sounds the W / V change, save for those moments of phonetic fidelity when Sam or his father, Tony, speak. The reader cannot but hear and see the difference between one voice and that of another. The other speaks, thereby requiring our response, if only in the simple act of attending to that voice, and by extension those voices of the other that inform the London scene. London has more than one voice, then; Sloppy is aware of this. 'Doing' the 'Police in different voices', he is the medium of the capital's polyvocal sounds and rhythms, as these have already been transcribed, reported, converted into a written record. Bringing back the voices, Sloppy admits to an ear for the other; in his vocal mimicry, his is a medium's role, a performance, but, like his creator, he is a resurrectionist. Voice, therefore, always announces and affirms the other. It gives place to the presentation and re-presentation, and through these a ghostly experience, of London, other Londons, cities of times past, which have left their traces, to be replayed or reanimated, as soon as there is a subject to hear.

The voice is always grounded, as well as opening a place, from which it speaks.[29] Sloppy, presenting himself principally as 'voice', as inarticulate vocalisation through the wide-open mouth and roar of laughter, followed by a furious 'mangling', which defeats the speech of 'gentlefolk' (*OMF* 198), lives, with Betty Higden and her charges, in an 'abode' that is not 'easy to find' in the 'complicated back settlements of muddy Brentford', on the north bank of the Thames, opposite its more genteel neighbour, Kew, in what is now the London borough of Hounslow. Sam, when first encountered, works at the White Hart, one of those 'half-dozen old inns' that still survived in the late 1820s in the Borough, south of the Thames, across from St Paul's Cathedral and the City, 'Old London Bridge', as various Dickensian narrators refer to it, joining the City and the Borough. Both the Borough and Brentford present working-class voices, voices belonging to London's riverside communities. Hearing, and thus receiving, the voice of the other, we hear them in their own words, ventriloquised in turn through the medium of narration's reiteration. Weller's well-known reversal of *v* and *w* is the most immediate and memorable example. Used elsewhere in Dickens as a phonic approximation of working-class London voice in the first decades of the nineteenth century, it intrudes repeatedly enough to make this other 'Samuel' heard, over the supposed authority of his master, Samuel Pickwick. If, as Kevin McLaughlin has argued, Sam (Weller's) language in the form of the 'Walentine' is a sign of the 'unavoidability of an artificial, "poetic" moment' (McLaughlin 1995, 116), such artifice, and with it the implication of performance and persona, presents the reader with the perception that 'voice' is staged, provisional, rather than essential. At least, this is admitted through Weller. The city, appearing through its voices, is a place of provisional identity, unstable meanings and shifting appearances; there is no 'natural' language for London.

Yet it is the human sound of one aspect of London, and one manifestation of 'the Londoner' in the voice of Sam, that registers so indelibly in the reader. We come to be inhabited by that voice, for the moment of its enunciation, and in this there takes place 'a taking up of others' thought through speech, a reflection in others, an ability to think *according to others*, which enriches our own thoughts' (Merleau-Ponty 1962, 179), and our apprehension of those London subjects. We do not, of course, sense all of London; nor should we. Such an apprehension is impossible, no more imaginable than a full representation of London through a single image. But what we receive through this given voice, in this experience, is working-class humour and subversion of authority. An image appears for me, of a subjectivity greater than that of the individual who speaks, for through voice, accent and idiom, a world of difference emerges to my apprehension. More than the individual subject's voice, I hear in this a trace of one image of the city; for in that matter of accent, delivery, rhythm, idiom, in the 'trace of a voice, phonetic writing' that which is heard 'is also linked to drawing (contour); what one sees is linked to what is de-scribed. Rhythm, as a consequence, is thus produced by an interaction between voice and the visual' (Louvel 2011, 180). Voice 'textualises' the image, the image an apparition in the trace of the voice. This textualisation, which is also the opening to the visualisation, does not present London in its entirety, to stress the point once more. It does, however, through the voice and figure of Samuel Weller, imagine the working-class male Londoner in a comic, affirmative fashion; it also situates that figure in a place that, once opened, cannot be close but leads to different perceptions of the world. Moreover, what we receive is one figure of working-class south London at a singular temporal instance. For there is 'no essence, no idea, that does not adhere to a domain of history and of geography. Not that it is *confined* there and inaccessible [though not everyone receives the transmission] . . ., but because . . . the space and time of a culture is not surveyable from above' (Merleau-Ponty 1968, 115). Whoever 'Dickens' was, Dickens understood this like no other. We only experience London in the singular, through the particular voice; while voices might sound the same, we do not hear if we do not attend to what is singular in the voice, in its moment, and in its projection as a presentation to be differentiated from those other voices of the city that initially sound the same.

Additionally, if voice is always grounded, formed and informed, equally voice says, 'there is', it announces and affirms the *there*, the place of the body, and the otherness of the experience in the place of another, to which the body gives form, which I experience through perception that is both visual and auditory. Sloppy and Sam are not simply voices, they 'exist' for me as corporeal figures, texts given shape and rhythm, but which, importantly, remain inanimate until the voice, its rhythms, punctuation, timbre are imagined and take place. While this is necessarily true of any character in any fiction, the general truth does not negate what remains particular to both Sam and Sloppy: it is their voices which are that which leaves the most indelible trace on the reader of the Dickensian text, in speaking for, in the place of working-class London subjects, their histories and cultures. Yet, as both figures admit, though the voice is *there*, a trace of urban location, it is provisional, once again. Voice returns as a contingent, performative, inessential interruption in order and representation. Whether it is Sloppy's corporeal disorder ('Of an ungainly make was Sloppy'; *OMF* 199) or what McLaughlin calls the disorder of Samivel Veller's similes, dispersed at random throughout the novel, like chance encounters, which refuse the formal equivalence on which such speech acts rely by convention (McLaughlin 1995, 113–14), the other of London disrupts in order to call attention to the absence of any 'natural' perspective or authoritative voice. More than one voice, less than a voice: London, Londres, London (to recollect Mr Podsnap's futile, bilingual attempt at nomination and definition) – a performative, 'radically dispersed' (McLaughlin 1995, 113) series of rhythms, pulses, fluxes, traces and phenomena, coalescing as the experience and perceptions of its subjects, and returning in each singular encounter, or the voice that is received, 'a performative moment that calls attention to itself as such' (McLaughlin 1995, 115). And the modernity of the voice as both trace and phenomenon of the city, signalled in that shift from one Sam(uel) to the other, signals also the transformation from representation to re-presentation, from empirical observation, collection and ordering (Pickwick), to phenomenal perception, chance association, and endless, iterable motion and random energy (Veller). The transition in *Pickwick* is also one of narrative form, genre and ideology. Through Sam Weller's voice, the city arrives and the picaresque retires, making way for the sound of the nineteenth century.

Walking • St Martin's Court, Covent Garden

The Old Curiosity Shop

Night is generally my time for walking ... I have fallen insensibly into this habit, both because it favours my infirmity and because it affords me greater opportunity of speculating on the characters and occupations of those who fill the streets. The glare and hurry of broad noon are not adapted to idle pursuits like mine; a glimpse of passing faces caught by the light of a street lamp or a shop window is often better for my purpose than their full revelation in the daylight, and, if I must add the truth, night is kinder in this respect than day, which too often destroys an air-built castle at the moment of its completion, without the smallest ceremony or remorse.

That constant pacing too and fro, that never-ending remorselessness, that incessant tread of feet wearing the rough stones smooth and glossy—is it not a wonder how the dwellers in narrow ways can bear to hear it! Think of the sick man in such a place as Saint Martin's Court, listening to the footsteps, and in the midst of pain and weariness obliged, despite himself (as though it were a task he must perform) to detect the child's step from the man's, the slipshod beggar from the booted exquisite, the lounging from the busy, the dull heel of the sauntering outcast from the quick tread of an expectant pleasure-seeker—think of the hum and noise being always present to his senses, and of the stream of life that will not stop, pouring on, on, on, through all his endless dreams, as if he were condemned to lie dead but conscious, in a noisy churchyard, and had no hope of rest for centuries to come.

Then the crowds for ever passing and repassing on the bridges (on those which are free of toll at least) where many stop on fine evenings looking listlessly down upon the water with some vague idea that by-and-by it runs between green banks which grow wider and wider until at last it joins the broad vast sea—where some halt to rest from heavy loads and think as they look over the parapet that to smoke and lounge away one's life, and lie sleeping in the sun upon a hot tarpaulin, in a dull slow sluggish barge, must be happiness unalloyed—and where some, and a very different class, pause with heavier loads than they, remembering to have heard or read in some old time that drowning was not a hard death, but of all means of suicide the easiest and best.

Covent Garden Market at Sunrise too, in the spring or summer, when the fragrance of sweet flowers is in the air, overpowering even the unwholesome steams of last night's debauchery, and driving the dusky thrush, whose cage has hung outside a garret window all night long, half mad with joy! Poor bird! the only neighbouring thing at all akin to the other little captives, some of whom, shrinking from the hot hands of drunken purchasers, lie drooping on the path already, while others, saddened by close contact, await the time when they shall be watered and freshened up to please more sober company, and make old clerks who pass them on their road to business, wonder what has filled their breasts with visions of the country. (*OCS* 9–10)

When Master Humphrey walks through St Martin's Court, around Covent Garden, that walk translated through perception as the phenomenal apparition of place, and the experience of one who walks in that world transmitted also, this is there, for us to experience, as if we were there, in that place. Dickens's narrator in *The Old Curiosity Shop* is Master Humphrey, as is known. His initial appearance is defined through nocturnal *flânerie*, seeing and experiencing the streets at night, from which motion and reflective consciousness develops the image. Night in London dictates the mode of understanding through the phenomena that persist, and insist in the subject's response, aurality rather than the visual being inevitably foregrounded, though not exclusively so. But from sound, and the fleeting images half-glimpsed and reflected, come imaginative, if not visionary possibilities, as a result of which the passage is, equally and in turns, both materially grounded and given over to the speculative and fanciful. Here is the city through the lens of the Romantic imagination, rather than a sketch of the Victorian urban world, disinterestedly observed.

The passage assumes a motion between from the interior world of the solitary walker to the external world of the city, and also from the outer world of the night's inhabitants and their occupations to the inner world of both the walker's meditations and those of an imagined 'sick man'. With such transference, the 'translation' of phenomena into the traces inscribed in the subjective apprehension, comes a movement from out the self of Master Humphrey into the crowds, whose 'never-ending' pacing takes up and amplifies his own. And there is also an echo between Master Humphrey's 'infirmity' to the undisclosed ailment of the inhabitant of St Martin's Court, who cannot choose but listen, it would seem, being unable to sleep. Such parallelisms hint at the phenomenal sensibility, and with this, the uncanny similarity between the world of the mind and the world of the streets, their motions being not dissimilar, and each iterating the other's workings. Thus a play unfolds from interior to exterior, involving the world in the subject, the subject in the world.

Movement complicates any relationship between self and other in the reading / writing of the city. The other is only and always there in the self's experience of the other. This is fundamental to understanding why the narrator in the text of Dickens mediates our experience of the city and its re-presentation in what is, initially, a self-reflexive way, and with that sense of intimacy and proximity. The narrator puts himself *in* the city even as he narrates its representation, recalling its events and its experiences. These are always experiences *for someone*. And such reflection on experience causes perception of and empathy with another, so that one's own experience is analogous with the experience of the other, as if the other were in some way 'in' the self.

It might be asked how the other enters into the subject's experience, beyond the immediate formal and aesthetic device of the first-person narrator or narrator-effect, by which the 'I' of another enters me as I read, and, reciprocally, it is as if I come to stand in the place of the other? In no small measure, experience of the city and re-presentation of that experience is, if not exactly available for sharing, then at least open through the force of analogy to the transference of perception, in which transport one is admitted to the singularity of another's apprehension, as place registers on self, the act of reading the text standing in the place of reading location and event. One observation that arises here is that 'seeing' is equivocal, if not enigmatic, and that this question of 'seeing' is not merely a theoretical question but one written into the passage from *The Old Curiosity Shop* by which Master Humphrey introduces the novel and the city, and so insinuates himself through the act of walking into the space between reader and place. In that to-and-fro of perception (and there is no neutral 'observation' not already perceptual in its translating force here, to which a matter of duration, of different times and velocities of perception also attests) two distinct modes of 'seeing' emerge – two at least: on the one hand, the visual; on the other, phenomenal insight.

X Marks the Spot • St Mary Axe

Our Mutual Friend

It was a foggy day in London, and the fog was heavy and dark. Animate London, with smarting eyes and irritated lungs, was blinking, wheezing, and choking; inanimate London was a sooty spectre, divided in purpose between being visible and invisible, and so being wholly neither. Gaslights flared in the shops with a haggard and unblest air, as knowing themselves to be night-creatures that had no business abroad under the sun; while the sun itself when it was for a few moments dimly indicated through circling eddies of fog, showed as if it had gone out and were collapsing flat and cold. Even in the surrounding country it was a foggy day, but there the fog was grey, whereas in London it was, at about the boundary line, dark yellow, and a little within it brown, and then browner, and then browner, until at the heart of the City—which call Saint Mary Axe—it was rusty-black. From any point of the high ridge of land northward, it might have been discerned that the loftiest buildings made an occasional struggle to get their heads above the foggy sea, and especially that the great dome of Saint Paul's seemed to die hard; but this was not perceivable in the streets at their feet, where the whole metropolis was a heap of vapour charged with muffled sound of wheels, and enfolding a gigantic catarrh.

At nine o'clock on such a morning, the place of business of Pubsey and Co. was not the liveliest object even in Saint Mary Axe—which is not a very lively spot—with a sobbing gaslight in the counting-house window, and a burglarious stream of fog creeping in to strangle it through the keyhole of the main door. But the light went out, and the main door opened, and Riah came forth with a bag under his arm.

Almost in the act of coming out at the door, Riah went into the fog, and was lost to the eyes of Saint Mary Axe. But the eyes of this history can follow him westward, by Cornhill, Cheapside, Fleet Street, and the Strand, to Piccadilly and the Albany. Thither he went at his grave and measured pace, staff in hand, skirt at heel; and more than one head, turning to look back at his venerable figure already lost in the mist, supposed it to be some ordinary figure indistinctly seen, which fancy and the fog had worked into that passing likeness. (*OMF* 417)

If X is a secret, not to be located, St Mary Axe might be one possible figure, where, like the chiasmus, 'lines meet at a point and continue, never to meet again' (Bennington 2000, 76), an occasional point then, of convergence, between subject and city, between reading and writing, between perception and memory, the visible and invisible. One might say, *aXe* marks the spot, this being that X which, for Kant, identifies the experience beyond or before any conceptualisation.

> All our representations [Kant reflects] are in fact related to some object through the understanding, and, since appearances are nothing but represen-tations, the understanding thus relates them to a **something**, as the object of sensible intuition . . . (1997, A250)

However, he continues, in a move towards that bracketing of the habit-ual, which opens the necessary phenomenological reduction, 'If I take all thinking (through categories) away from an empirical cognition',

> then no cognition of any object at all remains; for through mere intuition nothing at all is thought, and that this affection of sensibility is in me does not constitute any relation of such representation to any object at all. But if, on the contrary, I leave out all intuition, then there still remains the form of thinking . . . (A253–4)

St Mary Axe is, then, not represented as *something*, but instead is imag-ined immediately as the visible figure for the 'heart' of the city; or this is the convenient fiction at least – for the sake of naming the heart, when no heart might otherwise be found, no centre discerned, that parish called St Mary Axe, long since deprived of its parish church even in Dickens's times, 'these times of ours, though concerning the exact year there is no need to be precise'.

There is no need to be 'exact'; we will call, and agree to call, the heart of the city St Mary Axe. Intuition informed through perception grounds itself in, through place, yoking subjective consciousness and its particular representation in the singular event to the spot. After all, in the Kantian schema, 'a something = X' (1997, A250), that X being that of which we know nothing, but which situates itself in this singular instance in the place as organ, as metaphor in a series of substitutions behind which remains, always, the unknowability of London, its disap-pearance into some fog before the effort at any final representation. Thus, *aXe* marks the singular spot, given between subject and place in the event of experience, where *aXe* 'is not itself', to borrow from Kant once more, 'an object of knowledge, but only [a figure for] the represen-tation of appearances under the concept of an object in general'.

Admittedly, the idea that *aXe marks the spot* is a fanciful conceit, but no more so than suggesting place as the heart of the City, or indeed, this place as more than any other. The narrative conceit imagines place as an organ, a pump, an organic image, which is, at this moment, secreted, hidden from plain sight. A 'heavy and dark' fog, which circles and eddies, limits visibility. Eyes smart, lungs are irritated; London, the larger organism for which St Mary Axe chances to serve as the location of the heart, blinks, wheezes and chokes, whilst its ghostly double, 'inanimate London', hovers between visibility and invisibility. London is haunted by and haunts its other self, inhabiting and being the environment for dwelling in a liminal space, made all the more unreal, its materiality dissolving in the fog.

The city can neither see nor be seen. Phantasmagorical, London is punctuated by the uncanny presentation of gaslights become 'night-creatures', but which also, as supplements to sight, take on the function of eyes inasmuch as they are said to sob. The fog, a double itself of spectral London, becomes denser, darker, heavier, the closer it gathers around the 'heart', until it becomes 'rusty-black'. What we 'see', therefore, what we apprehend within the invisibility and extremely limited perspective, is analogous – today – to an X-ray; for we see inside the unhealthy, diseased body, the miasma crossing the corporeal boundaries to encompass the heart. All that is solid is dissolved, not into air, but as a 'heap of vapour', which enfolds 'a gigantic catarrh'.

The narrating subject, never more spectral in the text of Dickens than in this disquieting urban vision, gives access to the otherwise invisible, allowing the reader to 'see'. Such sight is both limited and yet transcendent after a fashion. The 'eyes of this history' can see into the fog, where the eyes of St Mary Axe cannot, to follow Riah into the fog. The narrative subject's vision therefore offers insight, it penetrates, revealing the hidden; the eyes of the narrating subject are the eyes of the 'history', capable of moving beyond what is only 'indistinctly seen', misperceived through the confluence and influence of 'fancy and fog'. At once animate and inanimate, narrative agency is spectral and technological. There is, to be precise, a narrative technology: the idea of the narrating subject, at once human and inhuman – we read narration conventionally as a 'voice', a human agency, even though we know this to be convention, the idea of the 'narrator' being merely a fiction to give presence to acts of writing – which has a 'spectral' power. Not simply, fancifully, a ghost, the technology, or technicity (from *tekhné*, 'art' or 'craft'), of narration causes the image to appear, even as it makes possible its gaze. It sees and gives us access to an equally spectral sight. Invisible to those it places under its surveillance, it 'sees' into the invisible.

Though obviously the X-ray was not discovered until 1895, my analogy being therefore admittedly, wilfully anachronistic, X is that which traditionally announces what cannot be said, what is not available to comprehension or knowledge. The symbol of unknown quantities ever since Descartes wrote his *Géométrie* in 1637, X has served to signify the principal axis for any given set of co-ordinates – the 'heart' of the City – but also situates the chiasmus, which in this extract is figured by both the 'heart' and the name 'St Mary Axe': for this is the heart, at the heart, and thus provides the axis for the chiasmus that puts into disordering play the animate and inanimate, the living and dead, the visible and invisible, day and night, the familiar and uncanny, the light and dark, as those figures of inverted and displaced parallelism, by which London both reveals and hides itself through the narrative technicity of spectral vision. We thus come to grasp, however indirectly, that we see nothing so much as a phenomenology of perception at work here. In drawing attention to the limits and impossibilities of full vision, in moving between visible and invisible, this movement replicated in the movement of the linguistic consciousness through its chiasmic folds and tropes, perception of the city *is* also perception of the condition of perception, and its technical extension in narrative.

Through this, the city as 'hallucination' is 'made flesh and concrete . . . an immense area of . . . signs that mediate the city to the individual and that individual to the city' (Barber 1995, 7); through the visual apprehension of the perceiving sensibility by which the phenomena of the city are traced, and so returned to the reader, our mental 'eyes' find themselves, in reading the text-image at the limits of visibility 'in a process of visual suffusion, compacting a multiplicity of gestures and movements into the act of seeing the city' (Barber 1995, 7). All narration gives us to see what is not there as such; here the text of Dickens gives access to a vision of the invisible, and thus unveils the modern subject's power of visualisation, in that very place where conventions of representation founder, perspective is ruined, the panorama impossible. This is the modern world, this 'mesh of space and time [confused, displaced, deferred, disordered], which itself transmits the history and experience of the' city (Barber 1995, 7). This is London 'performing its dense projection of vision into the eyes of its spectators', if they know how to perceive, how to read. It is envisioned, projected, by the unknown, unnamed stranger, the *flâneur*, that phantom figure of the narrator who is also, perpetually, the 'modern inhabitant . . . [and] participant entangled utterly in the visible, susceptible to an infinity of aural and visual acts' (Barber 1995, 7).

Wherever this figure is, *there* X marks the spot: for the subject brings the city into focus, in one place, at one time, every time, all that passes from the invisible to the visible, for our perception, in the narrated form of the 'phenomenal appearance we intuit' *as if* we were there (Bennington 2000, 85). Perception as the perception of experience

St Mary Axe

marks the place of the subject. X, the heart of the vision, the cross-hairs by which perception comes into focus, marks also a 'necessary convergence towards a unity . . . [a] unity of consciousness which cannot be an object of experience' (Bennington 2000, 85), but which communicates and so makes possible through the text of Dickens our act of reading / writing the multiplicities of London.

Dickens, Our Contemporary

> I refer once more to Heidegger who says that 'odos,' the way, is not 'métho-dos,' that there is a way which cannot be reduced to the definition of method.
>
> Jacques Derrida

I. Dickens, To Begin With

Before Benjamin; before Kafka; before Proust; before Husserl; before Joyce: there was Dickens; and before Dickens, before Boz (before there could be a 'Boz'), so, as a consequence, before the reader, always *before* the reader and remaining to come – *there* was London. London, Londres, London (*OMF* 135).

London (*BH* 13). But it was London (*NN* 489). What might the priority I assign Dickens, with regard to how we are invited to *see* a city, suggest, not least about notions of modernity, the subject and, of course, Dickens? What are the senses of modernity to be read, what perceptions are re-presented, in those places where, narrative suspended, the city steps before us? Whether taken for the moment as a subject of early nineteenth-century London, and produced in part by the experience, perception and subsequent memory of the various encounters, or whether understood as the writer of that city in its manifestations from the 1820s and 1830s, and its subsequent revisions in succeeding decades, Dickens is our contemporary.

Reading the Dickens text as presenting a phenomenology of London, the city being *the* exemplary and protean figure – motif *and* trope – for modernity vis-à-vis subjectivity and the inextricability of the subject from the world perceived, the contemporaneity of the text, its abiding relevance to readers in the twenty-first century, resides in its power to make legible the experience of the subject who finds himself *there* before the place, and whose perception, already a transformation of the experience of being involved, becomes transferred, transmitted to us. More than this, the text of London in the writing of Dickens presents the relation between subject and place in such a manner that, more than merely describing or representing, the text performs place for the reader in such a way that it creates in us the sense of being there, of a phantasmal proximity. Thus representation is replaced with so many acts of re-presentation. If understood as a properly and authentically historical index of place, reading and writing the city as the registration and revelation of London's historicity at given moments, Dickens's images of London-past 'may achieve legibility only in a determined moment of their history. It is in our ability', Giorgio Agamben writes at the conclusion of an essay on contemporaneity, 'to respond to this exigency and *to this shadow*, to be contemporaries not only of our century and the "now" but also of its figures in the texts and documents of the past' (Agamben 2011, 19; emphasis added). Dickens is our contemporary on the unconditional condition that we read him correctly, that we apprehend, and take responsibility for, the urban vision and its memory. If, as Agamben argues, the 'contemporary is not only the one who, perceiving the darkness of the present, grasps a light that can never reach its destiny; the contemporary is also the one who, dividing and interpolating time, is capable of transforming it and putting it in relation to other times', thereby reading 'history in unforeseen ways' (2011, 18), then Dickens is that contemporary inasmuch as he transforms the urban world, and our apprehension of how it was perceived by giving it to be seen through the eyes of an urban subject, into whose position we become subsumed, if we read aright.

Reading in this manner, throughout *Dickens's London*, then, I have sought (somewhat in the spirit, if not the manner, and however reduced in scope or simplified in execution, of Walter Benjamin's *Arcades Project*) to apprehend Charles Dickens's critical engagement with, and re-presentation of, London. The sequence of readings throughout the present volume constitute in part a topoanalysis, or rather series of topoanalyses, in that they start, and always start over again, from a critical engagement with passages that, in engaging, seeks to remain open to those passages as the reader's consciousness receives them. The topoanalysis is always that reading where place and subject are read in relation to one another, as place becomes meaningful and, in turn, determines subjectivity and, often, the meaning of being, and what it means to dwell. In this, the signs of the subject's historicity come to be acknowledged, through the reading of the subject's perception of place. Each reading has to do with, while being anchored by, the idea of place and particular places in the city, whether these be streets, neighbourhoods, squares or buildings in recognisable locales. The analysis examines the rendering of the materiality of place, along with its sensible 'mood', into the materiality of the letter, and, in doing so, considers the extent to which the Dickensian urban project, if there is one, is less an empirical, mimetically faithful, realist project than it is a serial registration in a phenomenological manner of the ways in which the city writes itself on, and comes to be traced in, the urban subject, as that subject's perception and apprehension are then given voice in the form of narrative, and the poetics and rhetoric of the Dickensian topoanalysis and architexture. Thus, as this last sentence implies, my topoanalysis finds itself situated as a tracing – the invention – of what, in coming to consciousness, is taken as being already inscribed, reiterated and translated in Dickens's own act of reading / writing the city; or taking, as it were, the city's dictation, his being its transcriber, or the medium through which London in the nearly forty years of Dickens's professional life comes – and returns – to impose itself, demanding a response and, with that, inevitably, the act of bearing witness to the phenomenon of London in all its material historicity.

Dickens is no mere, faithful copyist of the city. He is, instead, its most astute materialist historiographer, to use Benjamin's phrase from 'Theses on the Philosophy of History'; and he is this to the extent that he has no 'theoretical armature' or method (Benjamin 1969, 263). Rather, he operates, as Benjamin argues the materialist historiographer should, by basing the act of representation on a 'constructive principle', even as that exceeds the merely mimetic or that in description subservient to an empirical or realist verisimilitude, and the fatal historicism implicit in such forms of representation that remains content to trade in causality, teleology and universalism in which time comes to a halt. In this, Dickens traces the city through its flows and energies, as well as its proper nouns and recognisable forms, which in turn arrives through the play of flow and its arrest in 'a configuration pregnant with tensions [; in this] it gives that configuration a shock, by which it crystalizes into a monad' (Benjamin 1969, 262–3). At the same time, though, in exceeding mimetic and related modes of representation, Dickens's topoanalysis also succeeds in making available to the reader the subject's experience translated into the archival memory work of language and, with this, the return of the auratic experience for the subject recorded for the anticipation of its iterability in the reader, on the condition that the reader remains open to this chance of the other's coming.

The coming of the other, its arrival and return, hints at the spectral condition of Dickens's London. Already by the 1850s and 1860s, the London of the texts explicitly referring to, or re-presenting, the 1820s and 1830s (*Boz*, *Pickwick*, *Nickleby*, *Copperfield*, *Great Expectations*,

Little Dorrit, to name only those most obvious texts that bring back an earlier London on the cusp of the Victorian epoch) had begun to be replaced: not simply disrupted by the arrival of the railways, but torn down (Old London Bridge) or altered extensively (the Adelphi) in the names of 'improvement' or 'modernisation'. Dickens's Londons survive from the beginning, as it were, 'only as phantasms'. If cities, and the languages that figure and trace them, survive only in this manner, 'then only those who have understood these most intimate and most familiar deeds, only those [such as Dickens, and the Dickens-subject, the narrator-effect] who recite and record the discarnate words and stones, will perhaps be able one day to reopen that breach in which history – in which life – suddenly fulfils its promise' (Agamben 2011, 42).

This effort to remain open to the other that is London, and also the other in London, is a vital aspect of the singularity of the narrators in the Dickensian text, whether Boz, Master Humphrey, the Uncommercial Traveller, Esther Summerson, David Copperfield or Pip. I shall turn later here to make the distinction between 'author' and 'narrator' as functions of reading / writing. For the moment, however, the idea of being open as a mode of perception and reception serves initially, if not as an explanation, then as a means of comprehending the presence of the Dickensian text, albeit at a remove, in its relatively few appearances in Walter Benjamin's *Arcades Project* (2002a).[30] Although Benjamin barely cites or comments directly on Dickens, he records, approvingly, the commentaries of others – mostly G. K. Chesterton – on Dickens's affinity for the city, its streets, noises, and the event of London in general as a force in composition and invention. Benjamin's annotations in the direction of Dickens are not the only aspects of his critical discourse that are pertinent here, or throughout. However, given that there are just ten such mentions, and these, moreover, are filtered through the critical perspective of others, it is not without interest that Dickens serves as a touchstone of sorts for Benjamin, in his capacity as reader and writer of the modern urban project.

II. Reading Benjamin Reading (Others Reading) Dickens

Like some attractive, if enigmatic, wanderer in the streets whom one has seen and then catches glimpses of on other occasions, Dickens turns up intermittently in the labyrinth of notes and allusions that comprise Benjamin's unfinished work. It is worth mapping schematically the indirect manifestations of Dickens. He appears, in the words of others, in the following convolutes and in the following sources, and with reference to the following novels: **A:** Arcades (*AP* 57: Chesterton, *Dickens*; *The Old*

Curiosity Shop); **H**: The Collector (*AP* 208: Wiesengrund, Unpublished Essay, *The Old Curiosity Shop*); **J**: Baudelaire (*AP* 233–4: two references, the first to the 'allegorical element', the second to 'Dickens and stenography', both from Chesterton, *Dickens*); **M**: The Flâneur (*AP* 426: Franz Mehring, 'Charles Dickens'; *Dombey and Son*; *AP* 436: Edmond Jaloux, 'Le Dernier Flâneur'; *AP* 437–8: Chesterton, *Dickens*, first on Dickens's relation to the street and then to 'Dickens as a child'); **Q**: Panorama (*AP* 532: Dickens, *The Old Curiosity Shop*; *AP* 535: Chesterton, *Dickens*); **d** Literary History, Hugo (*AP* 770: Chesterton, *Dickens*; *AP* 774: Chesterton, *Dickens*).

A dozen citations in ten locations, eight of which are transcribed from the French translation of G. K. Chesterton's *Charles Dickens: A Critical Study* (1906). Of the others, only one alludes to Dickens directly, while the remaining three are from essays by, in turn, Theodor Adorno ('Wiesengrund'), socialist historian Franz Mehring, and French novelist and essayist Edmond Jaloux. Just two novels are mentioned, *Dombey and Son* once, *The Old Curiosity Shop* three times, while the remaining notes address aspects of Dickens's life, work habits or urban interests.

Taking the passages in order – and there seems no reason not to, certainly there being no justification for reading them in any sequence by which one might construct a narrative of one's own – we find the following discussions: Chesterton ponders on the relation between title and tale, raising the rhetorical question in order to respond by observing how streets and shops, the most obvious details of what are at once the most neutral and prosaic aspects of urban life and experience in the nineteenth century, in order to read in these, and in shops particularly ('the most poetical of all things'), as object shades into metaphor and synecdoche, through the metaphorical agency of a 'key to the whole Dickens romance', becoming 'the door of romance', through which the reader, following Dickens, has his or her 'fancy' set 'galloping' (*AP* 57). Chesterton likes to imagine a text of the city never written by Dickens, a 'huge serial scheme' and an 'endless periodical called *The Street*' divided into shops, one narrative after another beginning with a title, like the entrance to both shop and story, being the generic type of store. Clearly, when Chesterton reads Dickens, his own 'fancy' or phantasy comes to life, from the most mundane of circumstances, and in this, the reader in the Dickensian text and the reader of the Dickensian text merge for a time, as the quotidian dissolves into, opening itself on to the romantic and fantastic. One's own reading of Dickens might confirm such an experience, whether we consider David Copperfield's various musings, Master Humphrey's visit to the clock mechanism of St Paul's or the various 'keys' and allusions to fairy tale or the fantastic in *Dombey and Son*.

Of course, this is only to address Chesterton's reading. In a sense, though Walter Benjamin cites this passage in the context of gathering commentaries on shops and arcades, we can say little for sure about Benjamin's reasons for citing this passage. Is it merely to do with shops, or does the Dickensian motion from reality to the imaginary that is staged symbolically by the passage over the commercial threshold, have a greater interest for Benjamin? While part of the agenda for the *Arcades Project* is to make available a critique of the nineteenth-century capitalist commodification of the exotic, in this instance, such a critique is found wanting, for the reason that Dickens's narratives, those at least beginning from the doorways of shops, deconstruct the opposition of materialism and phantasy in that movement by which, on entering various stores (Mr Venus's taxidermist's emporium in *Our Mutual Friend*, Solomon Gill's shop in *Dombey and Son*), one becomes engaged through the agency of the narrative in the imaginary forces suggested by the objects and phenomena rather than by any desire for the commodities contained therein. More ambiguous sites, such as pawnbrokers (*Martin Chuzzlewit*) or Krook's rag and bottle shop in *Bleak House*, trouble the motion or transference, but even in this disturbance the dialectical tension raised calls into question the surety of ontological definition or purpose at the heart of any materialist or commercial enterprise, unveiling in the process its hitherto mystified purposes, and estranging the reader's unthought relation to such commercial urban spaces.

The second of Benjamin's quotations (*AP* 208) is taken from an, at the time, unpublished essay by Adorno, which touches on the dialectical tensions between materialism and 'the possibility of transition and dialectical rescue' (Adorno 1992, 171–8). As Adorno understands it, Dickens's texts express the other of the capitalist world, a non-place glimpsed *within* the phenomena and objects – 'poor useless things' – of this world, more acutely than 'Romantic nature-worship was ever able to do' (1992, 172).[31] Moving from this to two further comments taken from Chesterton, Benjamin offers on the first a minimal observation concerning the 'allegorical element' in the biographer's account of Dickens's recollection of a coffee shop in St Martin's Lane, which, for Dickens, returns with something akin to traumatic force every time he enters a 'very different kind of coffee room now', reading reversed on the glass the words COFFEE ROOM seen as MOOR EEFFOC (*AP* 233). Even as the streets, and shops, had generated the idea of writing, and of the city as textuality in that earlier passage from Chesterton (*AP* 57), so, here, there is the shock of inscription which links through memory the past and present of Dickens, with the frisson added by having been able to cross the threshold of the shop, being, as it were, on the 'inside' of society, rather than on the outside, as he recalls himself being as a child. With inclusion comes estrangement, estrangement from, and recognition or apprehension, at least, of oneself as an other. The city thus gives to one the experience of and encounter with modes of encryption that reveal one's otherness to one, as a condition not simply of the work of memory, but of memory in relation to place. What, for Adorno, is the oscillation within a given object that touches one intimately, such resonance for Chesterton is to be apprehended in place in relation to an act of reading / writing; the self writes itself, reading in the encryption the trace of its other self, seen from the other side. This leads Benjamin to yet another extract from Chesterton, this time having to do with stenography. Here, the biographer relays Dickens's apparent horror in the face of the arbitrariness of the shorthand code, the individual marks of which are taken as 'despotic characters' (*AP* 233). There is a doubleness to this phrase, the idea of character implying both the inscription and a fictional being, which remains unstable, transforming itself from a cobweb into a skyrocket, by which the former signifies 'expectation' and the latter admitting a condition of being 'disadvantageous'.

Two commentaries from Convolute M, 'The Flâneur', are next, if not as a consequence of argumentative logic, then as a result of the *Arcades*' ordering. If the previously considered citation on the apparently daunting task of learning stenography had focused exclusively on writing, both passages in Convolute M return to writing in relation to London, specifically the impossibility, or difficulty, of the former, without the presence or proximity of the latter. Franz Mehring's article (*AP* 426) relates Dickens's reiterated epistolary complaint during a European journey in the mid-1840s. London, according to Dickens, is a 'magic lantern', that Victorian curiosity, a hybrid of technology and phantasmagoria; the city seems to 'supply' something to the writer's imagination, 'set[ting] him up' and 'start[ing] me'. He expresses the opinion, in writing, that 'I can't express how much I want' the streets of the capital. Saying what one cannot say and that one cannot say it is, of course, a way of saying precisely that, albeit indirectly. It is a mode of apophatic proclamation, of what lies the other side of silence, so to speak, of what is other, and remains so, remaining to come. A drug and a desire, London is, in the letters Mehring cites, that which writes on Dickens, his subjectivity being the *tabula rasa* for its mystic inscription. Implicit in this conceit is the image of the author as automaton, writing machine, to be 'set up' and 'started going'. There is clearly something uncanny about writing the city, and London is, unequivocally, always already a textual phenomenon, demanding reading, transcription and translation, in order that what is not said comes to be articulated, however indirectly. Walking the streets anticipates writing, writing being in retrospect a tracing of the topography felt and perceived in the walk. This is confirmed in the second of the two passages, Edmond Jaloux supplanting and supplementing, thereby confirming, Mehring's reading of the letters. Dickens, Jaloux affirms, 'needed the immense labyrinth of London streets where he could prowl about continuously'; and this, as Benjamin edits Jaloux's commentary, connects Dickens to Thomas De Quincey, about whom the French essayist cites Baudelaire, Benjamin's touchstone for the *Arcades Project*. De Quincey, Benjamin notes, citing Jaloux quoting Baudelaire, was '"a sort of peripatetic, a street philosopher pondering his way endlessly through the vortex of the great city"' (*AP* 436). Backward then, in what is both a historical retrospect but also the unfolding of layer on layer, palimpsest on palimpsest of textual interrelation, thus: Benjamin–Jaloux–Baudelaire–Dickens–De Quincy, the linearity of which obscures the irregular interanimation, as well as the labyrinthine textile weave of writing / reading threads determined by the urban-text, always and only available as a vast *architexture*.

This is not to suggest that I see London 'not as an object, nor "history or "reality"', nor that I omit 'to discuss that which in London requires writers to contest it' (Tambling 2009, 307 n.2; I wonder whether 'contest' is the most appropriate word to describe what writers do when confronted by the demands London might be read as making on the imagination); rather, it is to see the London of writers in general, and Dickens in particular, as being received, if at all, indirectly and through an otherwise ungovernable totality of traces, which specific formations are always already countersigned by the historicity of their constitution, and come into being, as the reading / writing of the material event and experience. Whether this amounts to a contest for Dickens or not, there is always a struggle determined by the resistance to ungovernability or inexpressibility *in toto* and concomitantly either a resignation, an incomprehensibility or confession of giving oneself up to place and, along with that, an admission that one simply does not know and cannot say. London, in the face of this, requires the invention of an other mode of apprehension, perception and representation, one which escapes the merely mimetic, or a form of reading /writing faithful to verisimilitude; one, in short, which endlessly and ineluctably estranges and destabilises through the play between the real and the imaginary, the mundane and the exotic, where the latter interrupts or erupts from the former. London, understood thus, also requires a reading / writing faithful to the forces of interruption and eruption, displacement, fragmentation and ruin, and to seemingly illogical or incommensurate concatenations, as the registration of chance, whereby objects, phenomena and qualities or modes of determination, otherwise alien to one another, come into proximity through the subject or narrator's encounter with, or experience of them. Hence, in the convolute dedicated to 'Panorama', Walter Benjamin's one direct citation from Dickens (*The Old Curiosity Shop*), where he takes down the phrase used to describe a waxwork's 'character', its 'unchanging air of coldness *and* gentility' (*AP* 532). It is in the apparently incongruous yoking of nouns that one finds expressed what, throughout Dickens's novels, becomes a recurrent process of registration: a relation in non-relation, which remains faithful to incongruity, incompatibility, heterogeneity, and avoids the falsification of aesthetic harmony through ontological wholeness, in the maintenance of ruin and fragmentation that affirms more than can be said, that admits a significance other than that which is available to expression.

It is perhaps for this reason that Benjamin refrains from all but the most cursory commentary on Dickens, the most minimal remarks serving only as place-holders. It is perhaps also for this reason, that, with the exception of the citation from Adorno, in one way or another, each of the passages excerpted by Benjamin has to do with Dickens's relation to writing, and this most pertinently, most insistently, regarding the visionary reading / writing of London. Thus, Chesterton's 'return' in Convolute Q: 'There floated before him a vision of a monstrous magazine . . . an Arabian Nights of London' (*AP* 535). The city becomes or is envisioned as an endless serial publication, nothing other than serialism itself, labyrinth after labyrinth of passage, page on page of event, each the supplement of every other, and yet all remaining, in their serial supplementarity, other from one another, whilst being written in the name of London. This might be said to culminate for Benjamin in a comparison he risks between Dickens and Victor Hugo, through, once more, a passage of Chesterton's. In this, the claim is made that Dickens was the literary voice of 'the community', and that the author's desires and those of 'the people' were the same (*AP* 770). In this, Dickens might be said to be the *genius* of London, but a *genius loci*, whose inventions of London are manifestations of both the spirit of place and its *Zeitgeist* also. Dickens is the medium of the spirit of London, his name a shorthand for a kind of technology of memory and witness, a recording device, by which the 'more than one voice in a voice' has the chance of arriving and being received. 'Dickens' names a polyology, to recall J. Hillis Miller's neologism from the Preface. But, this being so, the proper name announces a mode of polyology that is simultaneously an *apopolyography*, a more-than-one-writing in any inscription that can only trace the city indirectly, and otherwise than mimetico-ontological modes of representation and comprehension dependent on totalisation, organisation, verisimilitude and homogeneity. If Charles Dickens was the 'old Radical' Chesterton calls him in the final of Benjamin's extracts (*AP* 774), he was also the first modern, if by modernity we can suggest a modality of re-presentation (to imply the Husserlian definition [of which more in the fourth section, below]) as opposed to representation that is phenomenological rather than empirical; which, furthermore, can be apprehended as such in the shaping of narrative presentation in response to the city. And what is strikingly modern about Dickens is that, like Victor Hugo – and here I borrow from Benjamin, quoting this time Albert Béguin – the English author

> transports all that he takes up – and which could appear pure foolishness were reason alone to judge – into his mythology ... But his vengeance will be to become, himself, the myth of an age devoid of all mythic meaning ... Every great spirit carries on in his life two works: the work of the living person and the work of the phantom ... The writer-specter sees the phantom ideas. Words take fright, sentences shiver ... (*AP* 775–6)

In light of this, I would propose that if a spectre is haunting London – the spectre of Dickens – then a spectre haunts Dickens: that of the city.

III. Reading Tambling Reading Benjamin (Reading etc . . .)

There have been a small number of prompts, signs indicating the directions in which we will head. Chiefly, these will gather around the notion of Dickens's London as phenomenological in its narration. Although there is, most specifically in the idea of the auratic but also elsewhere, a reading of Benjamin, which might gesture towards Benjamin as phenomenological materialist, this is not the place to develop such a hint. What I have sought to sketch instead is a reading of the fundamentally textual nature of London, through a commentary on those places in the *Arcades Project* where Walter Benjamin nods in the direction of Dickens, as the way through to that presentation of Dickensian phenomenology. Before turning fully to this, however, it is important to consider another's critical intervention on similar subjects. Jeremy Tambling has already responded to Benjamin's various Dickensian prompts, with some telling and astute observations (2009, 7–10). These anticipate to a degree both my own commentary on Benjamin's quotations and, to a lesser degree, particular dimensions of my readings of Dickens. It will be necessary therefore to consider Tambling alongside Benjamin, as we all follow in the wake of 'the Inimitable', pursuing his inventions of the city, tracing his steps through its streets and looking through his – or rather his narrators' – eyes.

Considering Tambling principally on the question of the 'allegorical element', this being Benjamin's prompt: the critic cites a passage from Chesterton, quoted approvingly by Benjamin for treating what the latter calls the 'allegorical element' (*AP* 233; Tambling 2009, 8). Tambling has already observed of Benjamin that he 'wrote when criticism, as opposed to appreciation of Dickens, was still comparatively new, relying on G. K. Chesterton' (2009, 7). Tambling takes Benjamin at his word, asking '[w]hat does it mean to think of Dickens in "allegorical" terms, even when he is being autobiographical? It obviously means seeing the world in reverse. And as disconnected and yet organised' (2009, 78). Though Tambling appears to be apologising, in part at least, for Benjamin's paucity of sources, and those lacking necessary critical rigour because still novel, he none the less takes up Benjamin's term, which 'obviously' means in a certain way. The figure of allegory is maintained after another of Chesterton's commentaries, which Tambling argues, 'has the potential to make the city a text, *with a system and a defiance of any system of reading built into it*. While compelling reading to become allegorical, seeing that which is 'other', it makes the writer produce a script from which he is *alienated*' (2009, 9; emphases added). I would note here that, in remaining on the side of an historicist criticism, one determined by the appreciable separation of text from context and the maintenance of that distinction, Tambling's consideration has something odd about it, moving between the 'allegorical' and the 'theoretical', as this latter critical language is encoded in notions of 'textuality' and 'otherness'. Arguably, to read the anachronism from a different perspective, the quality that Tambling reads is already at work in Chesterton's text – and is precisely what Benjamin apprehends in the English commentator – and which is already immanent in Dickens's text, at least as this regards the reading and writing of London.

I am not faulting Tambling's reading here; but, instead, I am attempting to trace a certain process of relay, and with that an unfolding and reformulating of the act of reading / writing the city at work in, and making possible, the Dickensian text from the outset. There is no Dickensian city *before* the text, no simple material correlative that precedes its imaginative reading and writing. If allegory is read by Benjamin, this is not yet to be fully aware of the surface of the text, and to assume a subterranean semantic level, rather than seeing the extent to which Dickens, already aware of the city as text, and unavailable to the modern subject in any other way, does not so much 'realise' the city as having the potential for becoming textual; but, instead, that he apprehends a radical textuality already at work for the subject, and in the subject's response, which must learn an alternative reading and writing. That all is surface is the case, but there is no causality, no logic in what is seen and how it might be read. More than this, the radical perception, towards which Benjamin is moving but at which Dickens has already arrived – this being a question of London and not Paris, and therefore impervious to order and regularity – is that, all being rhizomic surface, there is – *there*, over there, before the subject, unassimilable in any totalising reading, and thus already replete with the subject's exhaustion, incomprehension or defeat, in principle – that which is given to be read / written, but, paradoxically, that which sets reading at defiance and which affirms that which cannot be expressed; except, to recall Dickens's own words, that which can only be expressed as that which cannot be expressed.

To take the inverse script and its mirror image, seen in the present of the writer but conjuring the writer's other, past self, MOOR EEFFOC : COFFEE ROOM. All is surface, this is not a 'code to be deciphered', as Tambling suggests (2009, 9). There is nothing to be decrypted, everything is there, whether in Dickens's own words, and prior to that before his eyes, or before the reader. Time and depth, visible and hidden: these are the modular pairings which motivate Tambling's observation. Turning back to Dickens's letter, however, we read:

> I only recollect that it [the coffee room in St Martin's Lane] stood near the church, and that in the door there was an oval glass plate with coffee room painted on it, addressed towards the street. If ever I find myself in a very different kind of coffee room now, but where there is such an inscription on glass, and read it backwards on the wrong side, moor eeffoc (as I often used to do then in a dismal reverie), a shock goes through my blood. (*AP* 233; Chesterton 1942, 36)

That which the author *only* remembers, or says he only remembers – for he remembers both street name and, therefore, location, and proximity to an adjacent building – is the oval glass plate in the door, with the shop's definition. Writing, inscribed on the subject, always already read, in conjunction with architecture and site, are inextricably bound together in memory; so much so, in fact, that they are part of the subject, as the subject comes to be defined by this pivotal, not to say traumatic, remembrance. The Dickensian subject – in this example just happening to be Dickens, or one Dickens fictionalising another Dickens, or even two; the subject fragments even as he multiplies – reads the self as an other, in an abyssal staging of selfhood at home and homeless, either side of the glass, never at home with himself. This is what, for Dickens, it means to dwell in London, dwelling on one's own estrangement, and one's phantom *doppelgänger* as the revenant souvenir of the subject and place; and with this the displacement of the subject as a condition of an uncanny modernity.

More than this, what Benjamin, and Tambling after, appear to fail to read is precisely what Chesterton notes, following his observation – the last remark cited by Benjamin in this particular extract – that 'effective realism' comes down to a 'principle that the most fantastic thing of all is the precise fact' (1942, 36). While Chesterton's purpose here is more causal, more biographical and more anchored in a sense of authorial intent than my own interests, he pinpoints nevertheless the relation between the real and the fantastic, or phantastic, reading, as he does, the excess, the exotic, in verisimilitude, in the everyday. In short, Chesterton reads that which Dickens reads: the other within the self-same, Dickens being the name for a reading that becomes transformed into a writing of the other, which opens the other, and remains open to the other, rather than seeking to master or control that. What is at work here, what Dickens puts into play, is not, therefore, a question of the allegorical, but a more radical subject-effect historically and materially enabled by modernity, if not a phenomenologically inflected proto-modernism.

Without departing too far from the current path of inquiry, it is arguable that Chesterton notices in the formal play of Dickens's acts of reading / writing London that which subsequent commentators, usually of a historicist bent, have lost sight of to a degree, if not completely. For all the many problems or limits of Chesterton's analysis, there remains none the less a sympathetic apprehension in his analysis, a resonance between the Dickensian text and his reading (however couched in authorial and biographical terms), which is a sign of Chesterton's own historicity. A near contemporary of Ford Madox Ford, E. M. Forster and Arnold Bennett (he worked with Ford, Belloc and Bennett, amongst others, for the War Propaganda Bureau during the First World War), Chesterton's appreciation of Dickens is marked, at moments such as that just cited, or in the image of Dickens having the key to the street (which the latter possessed, according to Chesterton, in a phrase not picked up by Benjamin, 'in the most sacred and serious sense of the term'; 1942, 34–5), with that kind of sensate quasi-mystical 'channelling' of London that marks Ford's *The Soul of London*. In the example of the key trope, there is even a move from the mundane to the messianic: 'He [Dickens] did not look at Charing Cross to improve his mind or count the lamp-posts in Holborn to practise his arithmetic . . . He walked in darkness under the lamps of Holborn, and was crucified at Charing Cross.' Importantly, for our understanding of that which Chesterton catches in

Dickens, the former continues: 'our memory never fixes the facts which we have merely observed . . . the scenes we see [in recollection] are the scenes at which we did not look at all – the scenes in which we walked when we were thinking about something else. . .'.

> We can see the background now because we did not see it then . . . Herein is the whole secret of that eerie realism with which Dickens could always vitalize some dark or dull corner of London. There are details in the Dickens descriptions – a window, or a railing, or the keyhole of a door – which he endows with demoniac life. The things seem more actual than things really are. Indeed, that degree of realism does not exist in reality: it is the unbearable realism of a dream. (1942, 35–6)

From this, Chesterton, employing this seemingly paradoxical mode of reasoning that is to be found in his non-fictional writings, turns to the mnemotechnic of the coffee room glass. Certainly, the idea of 'eerie realism' touches closely on that uncanny power of evoking a sense of place that has, in Dickens, the power to make one feel and see in the sense accorded these terms by Joseph Conrad.

Thus, returning to Jeremy Tambling's reading of Benjamin's citations, the notion of 'allegory' does not quite work, at least not without modification – or radicalisation – with regard to historicity and origin. Benjamin employs the idea of allegory elsewhere in his writings, to be sure. But I would like to suggest a turn here to the question, for Benjamin, of the constitution of authenticity in the experience of the historical. For Benjamin, the 'hallmark of origin in phenomena' is authenticity; and the discovery of this authentic and phenomenal 'origin' takes place 'in a unique way with the process of recognition' of what comes to be discovered 'in the most singular and eccentric of phenomena' (1998, 46). From these remarks it should be plain that 'origin' is not synonymous with a material or historical source, or that its location is necessarily teleologically prior to the phenomena in question, or discernible in some strictly linear construct. What, then, is meant by 'origin' in Walter Benjamin's use? As that which is unveiled as, or mediated by, the perception of 'authenticity', 'origin', in being recognised, neither depends on nor serves 'to construct a unity' from a 'sequence of historical formulations', even though it 'absorbs' such a sequence (1998, 46). Benjaminian authenticity and origin are then available as sensible apprehensions that, in singular conditions, reveal to the subject facets of a phenomenon's historicity, without being just the causal outcome of historical events. They are, if you will, what haunt the phenomenon, and which spectral force is given to return, as if for a first time, in completely chance circumstances, which, as Benjamin expresses it, is the experience of the virtual; and 'Virtually, because that which is comprehended in the idea of origin still has history, in the sense of content, but not in the sense of a set of occurrences which have befallen it. Its history is inward in character ... something related to essential being' (1998, 47). To dis-cover or re-member the revenant spirit in a given phenomenon or constellated matrix of phenomena is, then, to be open to the other, and read what one is given to read, in order that the 'redeemed state of being in the idea' comes to light (Benjamin 1998, 47). It might just be that what Chesterton calls the 'eerie realism' or 'demoniac life' of the Dickensian text is *just* that authentic historicity revealing itself. In that inversion of the glass, MOOR EEFFOC : COFFEE ROOM, the structure that is made available is not one of the surface and subterranean, but rather a mode of contemplation founded on a 'dialectic [that] shows singularity and repetition to be condition by one another in all essentials' (1998, 46).

Allegory might well, from this vantage, be a term for, or else serve in touching on, that which is analogous to the subjective experience of the auratic, or merely, with an eye to the literary text, an analogical form for that produced in the expression of memory, given material form through language, but which is traced by, as it traces, its historicity. Here is Benjamin, from a fragment in his archive: 'Language has unmistakably made plain that memory is not an instrument for exploring the past, but rather a medium.' Benjamin continues:

> It is the medium of that which is experienced ... the 'matter itself' is no more than the strata ... [in memory, which] yield those images ... for authentic memories, it is far less important that the investigator report on them than that he mark, quite precisely, the site where he gained possession of them. Epic and rhapsodic in the strictest sense, genuine memory must therefore yield an image of the person who remembers. (*SW2*, 576)

There is an affinity here between Chesterton and Benjamin – and, by extension, the Dickensian text. The text as mnemotechnic, formed from memory and the inscription of, and on, the subject, of the site, as memory of place and place of memory have become intimately enfolded, is not 'allegorical' so much as it is a key to a phenomenology of reading / writing the city. Thus, despite this word, when Tambling concludes his initial consideration of Benjamin by observing that 'seeing', in the Dickensian sense as noted by Chesterton, 'is not the beholding what is in front of the eyes but seeing differently, other' (2009, 9), this is precisely so. To suggest, however, as Tambling goes on to do, that 'there is no agency here' misses the mark. For, while it may be the case for Chesterton's reading of Dickens that 'mind and places change places, the mind [being] full of places which the memory cannot necessarily remember seeing, and places meet the subject with memories of earlier looking', those modes of reading herein implied, by which the subject comes to be formed and informed by the trace of the site, then becomes transformed, translated, in the process, by which a reading becomes what it is immanently: a writing. For, as Benjamin notes above, apropos memory of place: the subject must 'mark, quite precisely, the site' where memory became possessed. It is this archiving habit which marks out the ragpicker and poet, and the relation between them, for, as Benjamin quotes Baudelaire approvingly in seeking an extended metaphor for the work of bearing witness to the poetics of the city, but in an observation equally applicable to Dickens and London:

> 'Here we have a man whose job it is to gather the day's refuse in the capital. Everything that the big city has thrown away, everything it has lost, every-thing it has scorned, everything it has crushed underfoot he catalogues and collects. He collates the annals of intemperance, the capharnaum of waste. He sorts things out and selects judiciously: he collects like a miser guard-ing objects between the jaws of the goddess of industry.' This description is one extended metaphor for the poetic method, as Baudelaire practised it. Ragpicker and poet: both are concerned with refuse. (*SW*4, 48)

Or, as Dickens might have said, not having any method but merely seeking the way, a way that London maps before him, 'Noddy Boffin, *c'est moi*'.

IV. The Dickens-machine: phenomenality and the Subject

If Charles Dickens *is* – or might be, in any given parallel universe – Noddy Boffin according to the Baudelairean definition of the city-poet, then he is also several, diverse others. Sloppy is not alone in 'doing the police' in different voices, therefore. As is well known, doing the police in different voices is a quality attributed to Sloppy's ability to read newspapers by Betty Higden (*OMF* 198), thereby allowing the voices, the 'more than one voice in a voice', to arrive through him in the act of reading. As a good reader, Sloppy, it can be argued, opens himself to the other, his interpretation and channelling being that process by which reading takes place, becoming a writing. But Dickens does not restrict himself. He not only does the police, significantly, he does the *polis* as well. Dickensian narrative – its rhetoric and poetics, and all the other technologies of invention – gives form to the city; and through this the state and the body politic, as these find themselves coming to singular articulation in the 'London particular' (*BH* 42) of Dickensian narrative in its various symptoms, materialisations and presentations. Of course, a 'London particular' is the name for a fog, as anyone having read *Bleak House* will know. But given that fog is, itself, not simply fog, but metaphor and singular trope for the law and one aspect of the city,[32] 'fog' names, arguably, a London resistant to order and full comprehension or representation. There is, we might wish to argue, the reading / writing of a *Realpolitik* that finds itself given form in London narrative. With that, there takes place repeatedly the manifestation, tracing and mediation of London subjectivity in its historicity and the various forces that inform and deform the subject, reified in turn through the Dickensian topoanalysis of London, its inhabitants, flows, rhythms, territorialisations and deterritorialisations. If such a formula for comprehending the Dickens city-text is permissible, then Dickens's narratives, with their inflection of singularity and repetition or – to move Benjamin towards a Derridean turn – singularity and iterability, give a place not only to polyvocality but a heterovocality irreducible to a single, coherent subject. The subject, whether 'Dickens' or Sloppy, is, through the act of reading, rendered a passive agent. Though this might sound paradoxical, agency is there in the shaping of re-presentation, but only insomuch as what is shaped arrives and demands that there be a witness to what takes place in the name of London. Hence, the question of voice, and the 'more than one voice in a voice'.

To approach this differently: when I speak of 'Charles Dickens' or 'Dickens', this is not to refer either to the author as particular source or origin of texts, or to the private individual whose life overlaps with that of the celebrity author who that individual became. It is, instead, to identify and give provisional location to a narrating technology or machine. It is to speak of a recording, translating device that serves in the re-presentation of the city and its voices and places in a particular manner. 'Dickens' names also a phantom subject, the projection of the narrating-machine, whose purpose is to experience the city, to bear witness to its events, to read the interactions of characters and location, and to write and tell those. 'Voice' is just a trace, therefore, a mode of inscription, rather than being a living vocalisation behind which is implied a presence. There is no narrator 'there' as such. There is no *there* for a narrator, save the haunting and haunted place of performativity in our imaginations when we read. Narrative, narrating, these are modes of production. From this understanding, 'Dickens' is, in any of the commentaries or analyses that follow, an apparitional effect in addition to being a technology of narrative; or, to recall the words of Walter Benjamin, the 'medium of that which is experienced' and which yields through processing the images of authentic memory. Such a phantasm, itself no more than a medium, is, on various occasions, displaced through various non-synonymous substitutions such as 'Boz' (the Boz of the *Sketches* and that of *Pickwick, Oliver Twist* and *Nicholas Nickleby* should not be thought of as being exactly the same, there being differences in register), 'David Copperfield', 'Esther Summerson', 'Master Humphrey', 'Dr Marigold' or any other ghostly figure, the apparition coming into being through tropological play, who steps forward in order to structure and reveal virtually the provisionally 'essential being' of a subject, a place or an event's historicity (often all three in conjunction).

'Dickens' names a reading / writing process grounded in history. Properly historical, it not only responds to the material conditions of a historical moment, but also bears the trace of historicity in its inscription, and this is shaped in turn by the material conditions and phenomena to which it attests. It does not bear witness to events and experiences directly, however, but unveils the past as virtual space, giving form to memory, thereby making possible the chance for 'evocation' and an authentic re-presentation of experience as translated in memory. In this, 'history' is not merely empirical fact or context; it is of the essence of language and memory – hence 'e-vocation', that which is called out from something, some moment, some time, but equally that which calls out from the other. If there appears to be formal repetition in the Dickens reading / writing, this is not the limitation of imagination, but the response to the force of memory and history, which demands of the reading / writing subject a fidelity to the enormity of the material experience. For, as Walter Benjamin would have it, memory is a 'fan', which, once opened, reveals itself as having 'no end of its segments' for the subject. 'No image satisfies' the reading subject, argues Benjamin in the apprehension of a figure whose insatiability is not dissimilar to Dickens, 'for he has seen that it can be unfolded, and only in its folds does the truth reside—'

> that image, that taste, that touch for whose sake all this has been unfurled and dissected: and now remembrance progresses from small to smallest details, from the smallest to the infinitesimal, while that which encounters in these microcosms grows ever mightier. (*SW2* 597)

Once having been apprehended in one detail, nothing about London satisfies the Dickens-machine, and so the reading / writing technology increases productivity, speed, intensity, acquisition and recording. Image, taste and touch (Benjamin's terms) signal the sensible nature of the subject's experience, which, become traces of memory, must be rendered in some translatable form; and which, though given in other words, makes available to the reader to come a phenomenal experience, *as if* the reader were standing in the place of the phantom subject who narrates. It is this phenomenal condition – that which drives and feeds the very insatiability it has created – at the heart of, and so disclosing what Benjamin calls 'essential being', that which the Dickens-machine opens, and which the Dickensian subject has had unveiled to him or her by his or her encounter with the urban. So as Dickens registers, reads and writes detail after detail, London 'grows ever mightier' through memory of the phenomenal experience transcribed.

The problem – and there is one for some readers – is that we confuse things and phenomena. That there is a city called London, that it exists materially and has a history: none of these 'facts' is in question. However, there is a fundamental and radical difference, an order of reading and not reading, the gap between which appears incommensurable for some in terms of a true or authentic (to use that Benjaminian word once more) comprehension. This difference amounts to a statement, the baldness of which might appear staggering in its wilful simplicity. The 'real' London is one thing, the London one reads on the pages of a novel by Charles Dickens is another. The latter may be a translation of the former, it may be inspired by aspects or experiences of the former; but as soon as transcription and memory take place, even in the experience by which memory becomes encoded with experience, there is already an opening of the gap between the two Londons. In turn, in principle, and in effect, this opens the place for innumerable other Londons to be given. The difficulty for some is in the inability to recognise that which puts the difference to work, which is this: we must apprehend, as Gilles Deleuze argues following Kant, the truth of the relation between the given and the subject; we must even, necessarily, work through the relation between the one and the other, in order to arrive at the truth and so avoid a confusion between 'the essential and the accidental' (1991, 70). London is just such a given; the narrator is such a subject, as reader / writer of the city. However 'the given is not a thing in itself, but rather a set of phenomena, a set that can be presented as a nature only by means of an *a priori* synthesis. The latter', Deleuze continues, 'renders possible a rule of representations within the empirical imagination only on the condition that it first constitutes a rule of phenomena within nature itself' (1991, 111).

To take the question step by step: prior to any synthesis, before also what Gaston Bachelard terms 'the immense domain of the imagination' (1994, 212), there is the material ground to be considered. As Paul de Man argues though, materiality is irreducible to a single concept. There are three materialities: 'the materiality of history, the materiality of inscription, and the materiality of what the eye sees prior to perception and cognition' (Miller 2001, 187; see de Man 1996, 119–28). Thus, J. Hillis Miller, whose summary of one of de Man's 'most difficult and

obscure' considerations from *Aesthetic Ideology* captures with a suc-
cinctness and adroit precision the stakes of a sustained challenge to
the notion of 'realism', a challenge which hegemonic forms of critical
materialism and historicism fail, in the main, to grasp, this failure often
being allied to certain formal and aesthetic dismissals of Dickens over
the question of being 'properly historical'. Understanding this, one can
observe of Dickens (to make specific the de Manian critique) that what
is otherwise reduced to the aesthetic dimension of representation fails
to appreciate the work of 'cognition and [the] deep complicity with the
phenomenalist epistemology of realism' (de Man 1996, 120), wherein
an authentic historicity might be given to read.

That said, returning to the question of materialities, and, in particular,
the third materiality – this being perhaps the most significant apropos
the matter of the narrating subject and its relation to place; once the
materiality that the eye receives prior to perception undergoes that synthesis spoken of by Deleuze, the given is no longer available as 'thing', as
such. It is, to reiterate Deleuze's words, a *set of phenomena* that *renders
possible a rule of representations*. Such 'representations' for the subject,
once perceived and reflected on – and thereby synthesised or mediated
through 'memorial consciousness' in some fashion in order that the 'perception of the event' or experience comes to correspond, or be analogous, with 'an (actual or possible) memory of this perception' (Husserl
2005, 248) – are apprehended as the phantasmic figures projected by the
work of memory. In this way, the past returns as apparition, as spectral
or virtual presence or present. In turn, perception, 'somehow', to cite
Edmund Husserl, 'becomes modified into re-presentation of what was
received' (2005, 248). Not representation, not simple mimetic manifestation, but re-presentation, memory as the mediated trace through
which past becomes space, and the subject's relation to thing, to place
and event, is structured. Therefore, whatever London there is, as a
there distinguished from the I whose perception gives place to form and
form to place, this London or these Londons that we read the Dickens-
machine reading / writing are (obviously) already processed through
various filters and layers, maintaining any 'historically' real London at
a further remove. It does not matter that we can visit streets, look at
shop fronts and details of architecture, take photographs and so on, as
if, in doing so, we were to close a gap between a now and then, when
the *then* of the text was never a *there* available in any unmediated way.
All such activity would be only to attempt to reconstruct, and so invent
once again, making real the phantasmal re-presentation of the phenomenal experience of the Dickensian subject. Such activity amounts to a
misunderstanding, thereby confusing, once more, the essential and the

accidental, the phenomenal and the empirical, and avoiding or seeking to hold at bay, downplay, marginalise or deny 'a phenomenology of inner experience' (de Man 1996, 123) – for which reading is one name.

The Dickens-machine places its subject in a given place so as to read, write and relay an architectonic vision and a sense of the world expressing the subject-memory of place. In the presentation of the subject-memory, the technology of narration produces the image in the reader of location as if the reader were in that place, before that site, but having sight of place as *over there*, *not-I*: in short, as other. Thus I receive in phantasmal form a sense of the world, and through this the apprehension that the '"sense of the world" does not designate the world as a factual given', to borrow Jean-Luc Nancy's formulation, but 'as the constitutive *sense* of the fact that there is world' (1997, 54–5). This brings me back to the Husserlian term 're-presentation', despite the reservations that Nancy has regarding phenomenology's being closed off, or attempting to close itself off, from a 'letting-come', as he puts it (and there is an implicit and sustained answer to this problem in the work of Jean-Luc Marion, particularly *Being Given*), and with that a concomitant 'surprising of sense, and also . . . its letting-go' (1997, 36). The reader as subject in the Dickens text is all too aware of the surprising of sense, and of letting go, becoming passive in the face of what can always arrive or arise, to become in the process lost in reflection on the city, or on a particular vision or location.

Inasmuch as this *letting-come* takes place repeatedly in Dickens, or that there arrives that impression of London taking the senses by surprise (pleasantly or unpleasantly, traumatically or uncannily), the Dickensian text might be read as anticipating and overcoming a particular limit in Husserlian phenomenology. It is important that we remember in particular the recollection of the coffee shop, and from there think the connection between journalistic and fictional narratives in terms of the play of 'more than one voice in a voice' by which the city comes, keeping in mind the play of memory that is essential. The image I receive as memory of my past subjectivity and the site that gives ground to my memory of my past self is, in its apprehension, a 'phantasy presentation'. It is this '"image" appearance', according to Husserl, which returns to me the earlier perception of an experience. In the distinction made here between perception – I perceive at a given moment, which is the *now* of my perception – and memory, the image of that perception returns as '"image" re-presentation of the earlier perception', which, in turn, is doubly constituted: on the one hand, it is the constellated image of particular phenomena, events and experiences; on the other hand, 'its appearance is the image of the earlier perceptual appearance'

(Husserl 2005, 233). In the temporal distinction between perception and re-presentation, memory and the constitution of the subject take on – perhaps *make visible* is the more appropriate phrase – the poetics of re-presentation; that is to say, specifically a form, an architectonic construct or invention, of the *there is* arrives, and, with that, the subject for whom there is the *there is*, both *in* the re-presentation and to the subject who has consciousness of, and therefore narrates (if only to him- or herself), the memory in particular form, with particular effects and modes of apprehension.

This is seen in the example of the coffee shop memory. What arrives before any representation of the present scene is the memory as it was first perceived by the earlier Dickensian subject. This remembered event and that prior perception are what comes to shape, and so determine, the reading / writing of the subject's present narration. That Dickens utilises the shibboleth MOOR EEFFOC : COFFEE ROOM is particularly helpful here, once more. For we perceive in that graphic division and inversion an irreducible difference, as temporal as it is formal or spatial, which illuminates the force of memory in the constitution of narrative even as the revenant trace overcomes any present perception. As a result, what comes to be revealed through this is the narrated modality of the image constellation of synthesised phenomena. There is traced the reception of the sense of the world in its overcoming of the subject. With this, as a result, 'the appearance of the event in memory is an "image" of the appearance of the same event in the earlier perception' (Husserl 2005, 236), whilst remaining separate. As a result, the two times of perception and memory remain articulated through the spatial and temporal play, even as they threaten to engulf one another, through the inscription of difference – and, additionally, the *différance* – that informs re-presentation and the being of the subject whose presence is always caused to differ and defer itself from itself. And re-presentation has always already taken place, the mirror inversion of the glass script reminding the reader of an over-determining priority by which reading is underway, whether immanently or brought to the fore in an explicit awareness of memorial consciousness to itself. Indeed, it is through reading that re-presentation is opened in *and* to the subject, and from which there is no retreat, or before which there is, and can be, no sense of the world. All reading / writing amounts to such re-presentation: a 'memorial presentation', which, formulated as 'intuitive presentation of the event' (Husserl 2005, 236) through the place of the subject, takes the reader as if by surprise, as if for a first time – and thus, with the power of that authentic and originary revelation, that touches one most closely.

V. Interruptions in the field of vision

Dickens likes to get in your way, to get in your face – not to show you how the tricks are achieved, but to make you refocus, to see, as if for a first time, what you are looking at without really seeing it, and so to think about the experience of perception and the perception of experience. Whether we speak of Boz meditating on Monmouth Street, the stranger confronted with the neighbourhood of Todgers's, or Esther Summerson in the face of a London particular, we have to confront the fact that each is involved with responding to that which particular places or phenomena of London impose on them. The encounter is, must be, phenomenological. By extension, the figure we name 'narrator' is also involved in similar processes of confrontation, experience and response, by which a dynamic is put into play. There is a convergence between place and subject that is analogous with that between text and reader. That this takes place might be noted if one observes how, repeatedly throughout the Dickensian text, but with an especial intensity and gathering force giving the appearance of velocity in the fictions, sentence structure becomes increasingly attenuated or distorted. Most frequently, though not exclusively, the semi-colon assumes the formal role of distinguishing in the architectonics of re-presentation the details of place, as if each moment of punctuation announced the shift of the eye from phenomenon to phenomenon. All that can be written down is written down. That which cannot remains immanently there, unwritten but to be imagined by the reader who steps in for the narrating subject, becoming possessed in turn by that subject's re-presentation of perception.

Take this familiar passage concerning the scene from an interior, in Chapter 2 of *Our Mutual Friend*, 'The Man from Somewhere'. Here, the reader is positioned before a mirror, a 'great looking-glass'. Though the compound noun by which Dickens defines the object may be somewhat obsolete today, it was not that uncommon a phrase in the nineteenth century, as the title of Lewis Carroll's second *Alice* book suggests. There is a minor cultural history to the term's use, inasmuch as, according to the *OED*, it appeared on several occasions in book titles from the end of the sixteenth century and throughout the seventeenth century.[33] In each of several examples, the title in question would hold a 'looking-glass' not up to nature but up to England, the state of the nation. Thus, 'looking-glass' is a figure for reflecting, and causing the reader to reflect upon, social and cultural habits or blind spots, which require illumination and bringing into focus. This, in miniature, is the purpose of Dickens's 'looking-glass'. It offers a deliberately distorted composite image of a London demi-monde. Not merely reflective, therefore, exaggeration and distortion, fragmentation and iterability serve to draw the reader's attention to social phenomena, but also, importantly, to the question of how one sees, that an 'eye' or viewing mechanism is an always necessary medium in the process of looking, and with that, the idea is introduced that there is no perspective, which is not also, immediately, a perception, and that perception and perspective are, furthermore, positioned; a viewing subject, the eye of some *one*, is always implicated. There is always an 'I' who looks, and reads. The looking-glass trope – for it is the mirror that 'reflects', in the double sense of showing through a process of light refraction, on the one hand, and applying conscious thought to, and cognition of, its phenomena, on the other – functions 'blindly' in order that the reading subject might 'reflect' on how he or she 'reads' what strikes the eye, with such a rapidity as to give the illusion of instantaneity, and, with that, the illusion that one just sees, and that phenomena, uninterpreted, are simply objects, vision being mistaken as empirical.

The full effect of this paragraph can only be gauged by citing the extract at length:

> The great looking-glass above the sideboard, reflects the table and the company. Reflects the new Veneering crest, in gold and eke in silver, frosted and also thawed, a camel of all work. The Heralds' College found out a Crusading ancestor for Veneering who bore a camel on his shield (or might have done it if he had thought of it), and a caravan of camels take charge of fruits and flowers and candles, and kneel down to be loaded with salt. Reflects Veneering; forty, wavy-haired, dark, tending to corpulence, sly, mysterious, filmy—a kind of sufficiently well-looking veiled-prophet, not prophesying. Reflects Mrs. Veneering; fair, aquiline-nosed and fingered, not so much light hair as she might have, gorgeous in raiment and jewels, enthusiastic, propitiatory, conscious that a corner of her husband's veil is over herself. Reflects Podsnap; prosperously feeding, two little light-coloured wiry wings, one on either side of his else bald head, looking as like his hairbrushes as his hair, dissolving view of red beads on his forehead, large allowance of crumpled shirt-collar up behind. Reflects Mrs. Podsnap; fine woman for Professor Own, quality of bone, neck and nostrils like a rocking-horse, hard features, majestic head-dress in which Podsnap has hung golden offerings. Reflects Twemlow; grey, dry, polite, susceptible to east wind, First-Gentleman-in-Europe collar and cravat, cheeks drawn in as if he had made a great effort to retire into himself some years ago, and had got so far and had never got any farther. Reflects mature young lady; raven locks, and complexion that lights up well when well powdered—as it is—carrying on considerably in the captivation of mature young gentleman; with too much nose in his face, too much ginger in his whiskers, too much torso in his waistcoat, too much sparkle in his studs, his eyes, his buttons, his talk, and his teeth. Reflects charming old Lady Tippins on Veneering's right; with an immense obtuse drab oblong face, like a face in a tablespoon, and a dyed Long Walk up to the top of her head, as a convenient public approach to the bunch of false hair behind, pleased to patronize Mrs. Veneering opposite, who is pleased to be patronized. Reflects

a certain "Mortimer," another of Veneering's oldest friends; who never was in the house before, and appears not to want to come again, who sits disconsolate on Mrs. Veneering's left, and who was inveigled by Lady Tippins (a friend of his childhood) to come to these people's and talk, and who won't talk. Reflects Eugene, friend of Mortimer; buried alive in the back of his chair, behind a shoulder—with a powder-epaulette on it—of the mature young lady, and gloomily resorting to the champagne chalice whenever proffered by the Analytical Chemist. Lastly, the looking-glass reflects Boots and Brewer, and two other stuffed Buffers interposed between the rest of the company and possible accidents. (*OMF* 20–1)

Though neither a scene explicitly addressing London, nor one apparently engaged in memory work, this 'at home' event is important in thinking through the Dickens text as phenomenological. There is little description of the room's architecture or furnishings here. Everything concerns reflection, as we have said. The entire passage amounts to a reflection on reflection, through a number of reflections on what is reflected concerning the people in the room, who serve formally as a series of correlatives in the construction of the passage, and which use moves this extract from being merely a statement or faithful representation, to a performative and labyrinthine gesture of numerous foldings and bendings, inversions and distortions across the plane of the 'great-looking glass'. The iterable formulae serve as refractions, images of images, all of which combine in a continual modification, so that this particular, overburdened, exhaustive and exhausting paragraph serves as a reflection on reflection.

More than this, though, it engages – and engages the reader in – a mediation, a narrative transformation of the physics of reflection, which process implies indirectly a means to reflect in the reader's imagination on the ontology of society given in the phenomena perceived and thus experienced through the passive agency of the mirror. The looking-glass is passive inasmuch as it serves to focus figure after figure, drawing the reader's attention to a given image. But in the distortion of the image, where, for example, Mrs Podsnap's nostrils are distorted in order that hers come to resemble those of a rocking horse, the agency is transformed, so that the mirror becomes an active amplifier of detail. This is not the only example of the slippage from passivity to activity; indeed, the passage is nothing but this motion, and its repeated rhythms cause a concentration of amplification, everywhere one looks. The eye – as well as the 'I' – moves from the materiality of vision to cognition and consciousness of subject.

The use of present tense maintains performatively the seemingly endless reflective mode of perception, what strikes the eye in looking in the glass having already been modified. Expectation of any other purpose is frustrated by sequential iteration, as the multiplicity of relations only appears to promise to continue. Every detail, in essence, not only mirrors every other, it gives a preview of what is to come, whilst reflecting on what has already been seen. Reflection of phenomena is therefore both temporal as well as spatial. The motion of the narrative across the surface plane of the mirror, and what is reflected in that mirror, stages an abyss without depth, if such a thing is possible. In the world of the mirror, a virtual mediated world, there are only phenomena, which, in their relation to one another, foreground the coming to consciousness of the subjective experience of phenomena. In other words, the mirror – and the passage – shows and tells, albeit indirectly, the reader how reading begins, how the materiality of vision is surpassed and how narration is always phenomenological. This is borne out by the fragments of analysis to which the Veneerings and their guests are subjected, which tend towards essential rather than factual 'reflection', or which lead from the merely factual to the apprehension of essence. Authenticity of essence is arrived at through distortion and amplification. The mirror may be read, then, not as object in itself, but as self-reflexive phenomenal trope for considering how reflection's reflectedness (if I can put it like that) opens to us a *first* thinking of phenomena rather than objects, and so to reflect on the apprehension of experience as it appears to take place.

Returning once more to the textual example. We make an assumption about realist narrative – and, indeed, narrative in general – that it flows, or should flow, more or less continuously. Unless it is Lawrence Sterne, some markedly self-referential, modernist or (so-called) postmodernist author, interruptions, digressions and other formal displacements in narrative continuity are assumed to be discrete and to be subsumed, so as to be as unobtrusive or un-self-advertising as possible. In Dickens's narration of the Veneerings and their guests reflected in the looking-glass, however, the paragraph is nothing other than the constant breaking into of narrative flow and the assumption of transparency that accompanies this by virtue of the notion of reflection, given continuous fragmentary surges in the charged iteration of 'reflects'. In order for reflection to be seen, and for the literal reflection to be transformed as mental reflection, there must be some 'eye', to insist on this point. A 'narrator' is there, to be sure, as those arch comments on those reflected make clear. But, in its play of iterability, interruption and fragmentation (is the work of the mirror image analogous more with a kaleidoscope or a broken glass?), the space of reflections refuses to admit to what Merleau-Ponty calls – regarding Cézanne's refusal to follow the 'law of geometrical perspective' – a 'medium of simultaneous objects capable of being apprehended by an absolute observer' (2004, 41). Dickens's breaking of the smooth surface and the motions installed therein brings the reader into closer proximity. Such fracture and movement locate the reader as subject of, to this experience, in an intimate manner akin to how one perceives the sense of the world. To stress, once again, what is crucial here for understanding the radical nature of the Dickens-machine in its narrative modalities, the effect here is not simply 'aesthetic'. It is, far more fundamentally, concerned with showing us how we see, how we perceive, and how our sense of the world is felt through the subjective relation to the space of perception; it achieves this, moreover, in the 'normal process of seeing' (Merleau-Ponty 2004, 40), as this is connected to, and enfolded in, reading, analysis, writing and, by extension, memory.

What the mirror reveals, so to speak, is that the phenomena on which I reflect are the principal images by which I judge the world. There is an I and a *there is*.[34] But the *there is* is always a condition of my sense of the world, always announcing that place both *is* and is thought *there*, where it is. One reflection here, another there, the looking-glass offers evidence of the *there*, as the *there is*, to my senses. Each reflected image as *punctum* both implies and reflects every other point, and also both the *there* in itself *par excellence*, and evidence of the *there is* to my senses. The looking-glass is, therefore, both subject and substrate for my perception and for the reflection on the condition of my perception of the world. Dickens is never under any illusion that seeing and perception are anything other than this immediacy and proximity of relation, which, in reflection, condenses the temporality, the duration, of the gaze. In this passage, it is strikingly clear that, whether one considers matters of orientation, relation or reflections, whether in themselves or for one another: all are merely the displaced, differing and diverted phenomena connected to, and by my presence, to my experience and my perception. To extend this, each phenomenon is seen to be absolutely itself, in itself and equal to itself; but in its reflection of each and every other phenomenon, whilst remaining other, wholly other, each is in its singularity and iterability as reflection, by definition, substitutable for every other one, though given in relation only by my perception (Merleau-Ponty 1964a, 47).

Furthermore, although this immediate scene is not explicitly the exploration of the memory of the past in relation to present perception, it gives me to understand how perception always relies on memory for the validity of my sense of the world, inasmuch as the time of reflection, of the duration of the eye moving from one reflection to another, offers a spatial metaphor for the work of memory in any moment of the subject's experience and reflection on that experience.[35] It being the case, to borrow from an argument of Wolfgang Iser's in which he advocates a phenomenological approach to the act of reading, that in 'every text there is a potential time-sequence which the reader must inevitably realize'; and, moreover, that the 'reading process always involves viewing the text through a perspective that is continually on the move, linking up the different phases [or, in this case, reflections], and so constructing . . . the virtual dimension' (Iser 1972, 285), so what the Dickensian looking-glass reflects is just the temporality and modulation of such a process, involving experience, perception and the continual modification of the process. The process gives insight into the fundamental aspect of reading, most frequently, in the text of Dickens, the reading of place through the subject's search for connections between fragments, which themselves make us aware of gaps in re-presentation as they remain before us, and the narrating subject, as so many elements that will not otherwise cohere without the realisation of perception. This realisation on the part of the narrating subject closely mirrors our own experience, as 'this experience comes about through a process of continual modification . . . the reading process . . . illuminat[ing] basic patterns of real experience' (Iser 1972, 288). Nowhere is this more insistently foregrounded and experienced repeatedly than in the subject / narrator's experiences of London, the streets, locations and neighbourhoods, interiors, architectural forms, and the detailed observation of the phenomena comprising these sites. The narrating subject thus offers, in the various encounters with the city's exteriors and interiors, a process that 'mirrors' (with all the modifications, mediations, plays of shadow, moments of indistinctness, distortions, exaggerations and effects of perceptual parallax that this term implies, instead of any uncomplicated or simple reflection), in the duration of the encounter, the reading subject's own continuous striving, 'even if unconsciously, to fit everything together in a consistent pattern' (Iser 1972, 288).

An objection might be raised that this is true of any reading. Indeed, given the generality of Iser's commentary, it might be hard to see what distinguishes Dickens. Such arguments are fair enough – or would be, were I advocating here a phenomenological reading of Dickens in light of Iser's generalisations. However, what is being proposed here is not a matter of application but of explication: Dickens's narrative voices, in their presentations of the urban, and the figuring of place in relation to subject, as such re-presentations of self and site take place in narrative, are already phenomenological. To put this differently, the narrative mechanism meets the demands of reading the city and does so through a phenomenological mode of perception. This being so, the purpose here in having recourse to Iser's essay is to illuminate phenomenological processes of reading that are already underway in Dickens's text. Dickens, it might be said, is a phenomenologist of the city, *avant la lettre.* This, in another reading, might serve to explain why Dickens has such an influence on many subsequent writers of London, but, whether or no, what *does* occur in the text of Dickens through its modalities of perception and re-presentation is, for fictive narrative, a new way of seeing. Iser's generality, as this is alluded and returned to, helps offer a 'theorised' model of what is intuitively at work in Dickens, which it has been the purpose of the various essays to show.

Dickens, most insistently of any Victorian writer, repeatedly frustrates the desire to form a whole, undifferentiated image. The mechanisms of the text offer paradox, contradiction, interruption, space and the experience of the aporetic. It does so, on the one hand, with a frequency and density allied to the experience of the modern city, thereby foregrounding the question of the ontology of the city, while, on the other hand, it constantly demands how the narrating urban subject comes to terms with the modernity of place through the formation of subject positions in relation to place, the formation epistemologically of an 'I' who sees and is involved in the perception of a *there is* comprised of phenomena in such a manner that unbroken comprehension and flow of reception are no longer possible. As Iser argues in general, 'it is the very precision of the written details [as themselves traces inscribed in memory of urban phenomena] which increases the proportion' (Iser 1972, 290), if not solely of indeterminacy, as Iser has it, but also of a self-aware cognition of that which the phenomenon of London demands. Moreover, Dickensian singularity resides in a 'grouping together' of phenomenal elements for someone who stands and gives focus for the reader, which in their resistance to an interaction that appears to offer consistency and integration, presents and re-presents the city as problem. In this, there is a textual, architectonic and *architextural* 'richness' that plays on a tension between 'our awareness of this richness' and any 'configurative meaning' (Iser 1972, 290–1). The Dickens text exploits the problem of the modern subject's perception as a problem of modernity, through what is seen, experienced, and how this is then re-presented in the mnemotechnic of urban configuration. As Iser suggests, with respect to modernist writing,

> In this very act the dynamics of reading are revealed. By making his decision [the reader but also the narrating subject in the Dickens text] implicitly acknowledges the inexhaustibility of the text; at the same time it is this very inexhaustibility that forces him to make his decision. With 'traditional' texts this process was more or less unconscious, but modern texts frequently exploit it quite deliberately. They are often so fragmentary that one's attention is almost exclusively occupied with the search for connections between the fragments; the object of this is not to complicate the 'spectrum' of connections, so much as to make us aware of the nature of our own capacity

for providing links. In such cases, the text refers back directly to our own preconceptions – which are revealed by the act of interpretation that is a basic element of the reading process. (1972, 285)

What is general in Iser is particular in Dickens, historically speaking. While other texts 'unconsciously' make available a formal inexhaustibility, Dickens brings into play the inexhaustibility of the urban place as text; as the principal 'modern' writer of the city, deliberately exploiting the endlessness of London, quite explicitly in the iterable, often labyrinthine phenomena, and at the performative level of sentence structures, as convoluted as the haphazard nature of the architecture and topography. As will be seen, it is in 'seeing' the city from the position of narrative subject that London as concatenation of sensory apprehensions and phenomena comes into being for the reader. The Dickensian modality of representation works through exhausting the subject in the face of urban inexhaustibility; it challenges epistemological certainty through the ineluctability of fragmentary information allied to the rhythmic motions of the prose; it engages in a poetics of iterability, and in addition puts the reader to the task of making connections through the occasional use of poetic devices such as alliteration or a deliberate borrowing from other literary modes or genres in order to foreground the experience of form, whilst constituting the subjective experience and perception of place.

All of which tells us that we are always before the modern Babylon, even as London is always before us, returned in revenant re-presentation. We have always to begin again with Dickens, after Dickens. With Dickens and the re-presentation of the city, *as if* for a first time, again and again, we are made aware of, thereby being given to consider through the shaping of our experience and perception, the phenomenal 'origin' that gives itself in its authenticity and historicity. In this, London is re-presented to our experience as what Iser calls a 'living event' (Iser 1972, 285): if not living, then a virtual event, a revenance of evocation, the iterability of which is marked by that which in the spirit of London – as Dickens inscribes it, as the field of vision projected by the Dickens-machine generates it – remains open, remaining to be read and written. And the continuous reinscription of our proximity to the experience of the Dickensian narrator as reading / writing subject in the face of a London always remaining to be read forces us to feel, if not see ourselves *in* that experience; in its invention of the city, the Dickens-machine produces an *aide-mémoire*, if not a souvenir of the city itself, which prevents us 'both from apprehending ourselves as a pure intellect separate from things and from defining things as pure objects lacking in all human attributes' (Merleau-Ponty 2004, 51). For Dickens, London is a human awful wonder, not of God, as Blake would have it, but of our

Early Nineteenth-Century London Street

own humanity – it is the signature of an age we have not yet outgrown, and which we have yet to read. In reading / writing London, the Dickens subject illustrates how '[c]ontemporariness is . . . a singular relationship with one's own time, which adheres to it, and, at the same time, keeps a distance from it' (Agamben 2011, 11). More exactly, contemporaneity, Giorgio Agamben argues, is '*that relationship with time that adheres to it through a disjunction and an anachronism.* Those who coincide too well with the epoch . . . are not contemporaries, precisely because they do not manage to see it' (2011, 11). In Dickens, the subject sees, responds to and is formed by London, *seeing* always as if for a first time, and placing us in that place, to assume the perception anachronistically of the other. But Dickens maintains the contemporaneity in another manner also; for, in most, if not all the novels, London bears in its figures, its re-presentations, traces not only of 'times of ours', but also of that earlier epoch, before 'Boz', but calling Boz into being – the 1820s and early 1830s. This is the London in which the subject wanders, and wonders, losing himself – and, occasionally, herself – in the city. For, as the Dickensian subject knows

> —Not to find one's way around a city does not mean much. But to lose one's way in a city, as one loses one's way in a forest, requires some schooling. (*SW3* 352)

Notes

1. Read's analysis of modern painting begins in 1840, with Constable amongst others. That modernity in painting is therefore attributable to an early nineteenth-century moment in its development might serve to suggest that, apropos a reading of a Dickensian phenomenology of the urban, Dickens belongs to a broader aesthetic and philosophically inflected endeavour – not necessarily conscious or concerted, but none the less underway as the belatedly read sign of an origin, the authenticity of which, in turn, signals its historicity – to 'renew', in Read's words, 'one's sensibility toward one's environment' (xiii).

2. Constantin Guys (1802–1892) is Baudelaire's 'painter' in the essay 'The Painter of Modern Life', an artist who worked as illustrator for the *Illustrated London News* from as early as 1843. When Baudelaire, in his essay, defines Guys a man of genius, defining this quality as the ability to recover childhood 'at will' (398), and to combine the adult capacity for reasoning and analysis with an all-consuming sensibility typical of childhood, he might well be describing Dickens's powers of narrative. When Baudelaire defines the *flâneur* as the 'passionate observer . . . in the throng, in the ebb and flow, in the movement, the fugitive and the infinite' (399), this commentary is undoubtedly applicable as an appreciation of the passage on Nickleby's return to London. Here, and below, the translations have been silently modified.

3. Throughout, I have given the page of the original, followed by the translation.

4. In the translation, the grammar and syntax are changed somewhat, for the purposes of rendering the sentence in a more idiomatic English. I have restored the original here, with my own translation, as the rhythms of the argument are central to what I have to say in the final paragraphs of the present essay: 'Car je ne le regarde pas comme on regarde une chose, je ne le fixe pas en son lieu, mon regard erre en lui comme dans les nimbes de l'Être, je vois selon lui ou avec lui, plutôt que je ne le vois' ['Because I do not look (at the painting) as one looks at a thing, I cannot fix it in its place, my gaze roams in it as in the auras of Being; I see according to or with it, instead of seeing it'].

5. The question of haunting is one addressed by Merleau-Ponty in the first section of the essay (9–15 / 121–3), specifically at a juncture in the

argument where Merleau-Ponty wishes to reconnect consciousness and perception to the body, against the scientistic or intellectualised remote consciousness from which the gaze is directed towards objects, as if one's corporeality or being-in-the-world were of no relevance. (See 'Dickens, our Contemporary' on the distinction between a Husserlian phenomenology and that of Merleau-Ponty.) While scientific thinking, as Merleau-Ponty calls it, 'looks on from above', I am in the 'there is', which 'involvement' needs to be brought back to thinking inasmuch as, pre-theoretically, it precedes the separation of consciousness and world of things. (One might argue that the 'I' is only a 'there' in the there-is.) As a result of what Merleau-Ponty terms an associated corporeality (*corps associés*), there are others, I am not outside this world of association and the 'there is'; there are 'others who haunt me and whom I haunt; "others" along with whom I haunt a sole, present, and actual Being' (12–13 / 122–3).

6. If, as in the case of *David Copperfield*, narrator and subject are the same fictive persona, they remain different nevertheless by virtue of time and perspective. The former is a narrating narrator, recounting with the illusion of hindsight and memory; on which topics there might be much that has been said, and remains to be said, regarding this novel, especially given the various uncertainties that the older David professes, or those moments where he claims not to know or not to remember. But there is also the narrated narrator, that other, younger David, who, in the midst of an experience, is not yet re-presenting through the work of memory his younger self, and therefore, does not know what he does or does not know, as it were.

7. On the subject of dating the time of *David Copperfield*: although there is no direct dating in the text, some clues are available. In Chapter 11, in which David begins work at Murdstone and Grinby's at the age of ten, the older, narrating David recalls that his narrated, younger self's 'favourite lounging-place', between rising in the morning and visiting the Micawbers in the King's Bench Prison, was 'old London Bridge, where I was wont to sit in one of the stone recesses, watching the people going by, or to look over the balustrades at the sun shining in the water, and lighting up the golden flame on the top of the Monument'. In this location, the younger David would occasionally be met by the Orfling, who would tell 'some astonishing fictions respecting the wharves and the Tower'. 'Old London Bridge' refers to the medieval structure, more than 600 years old by the beginning of the nineteenth century, and was replaced by a bridge designed by John Rennie, the building of which began in 1824. King's Bench Prison, Southwark, the original buildings for which were constructed in the medieval era, remained in use until the 1860s as a debtors' prison, but had been renamed Queen's Prison in 1842.

8. Tambling helpfully reproduces the passage from *Copperfield* with Dickens's edits interpolated into the 'fictional' account. The autobiographical fragment, used by John Forster in his biography of Dickens, is appended to the Oxford World's Classics edition of the novel (856–69), the particular passage concerning Warren's Blacking Factory being 859–60. Any reference I have to this, above, is taken from here.

9. Andrew Sanders, 'Appendix A' (*DC* 856–7). Readers are also referred to Sanders's discussion of the distinction from his introduction to the Oxford edition of *David Copperfield* (vii–xx).

10. Dickens, 'Appendix A', 857.

11. In the most neutral of tones, David offers an aside at one juncture, that 'Hungerford Market [was] a very different place in those days,' referring to the time, immediately following the collapse of Betsy's finances, when David takes Mr Dick to a chandler's shop in the Market, in order to 'take possession' of a bed, 'which Mr. Peggotty had lately vacated' (*DC* 462). David remembers an old architectural feature, a 'low wooden colonnade before the door . . . which pleased Mr Dick mightily', this recollection presumably because, Hungerford Market having changed, the colonnade was no longer there at the time of David's writing. It is not enough to say that memory is always memory *of* loss, but that memory just is loss, absence, difference, or at least the trace of these effects, and the coming to mind, the apparition of such traces, by which the subject perceives itself as the subject of, produced by the trace.

12. Like the Adelphi or Old London Bridge in *David Copperfield*, the Temple Bar referred to here is the older structure, that barrier demarcating the City at the point where Fleet Street and the Strand converge. Though currently occupied by a monument erected in 1878, atop which is a griffin, the original architectural form designed by Christopher Wren was an arch, at which it was custom for any reigning monarch to halt, before being 'admitted' to the City by the Lord Mayor. The name 'Temple' comes from Temple Church, itself part of the area known as the Temple, once owned by the Knights Templar. There is thus to be read an implicit connection between fiction and history or, at least, a general, if submerged Orientalist discourse within, between or, at least, a general, if submerged Orientalist discourse within the relation between the real and the imaginary in the image, inasmuch as there is that acknowledgement of the *One Thousand and One Nights* and the idea of the Knights Templar, the Crusades and so forth. Given the convenience or accident of the architectural and topographical proximity between the Temple, Temple Bar and the idea of a Barmecide room, histories of crusading acquisition and banking practices suggest narratives of indirect relation, if not affiliation, which phantasmic analogical weave is teased further by the not unrelated image of the severed heads placed on Temple Bar. The refurbished Wren Temple Bar is now in Paternoster Square.

13. The walk would take somewhat less than twenty minutes. Noakes, we might suppose, proceeded south along what is now Gray's Inn Road, turning briefly west on High Holborn, then south again down Chancery Lane to Temple Bar where Fleet Street becomes the Strand.

14. On Dickens's time at the *True Sun*, see Slater (39, 101, 620), Douglas-Fairhurst (77, 100, 123); on the relationship between Leigh Hunt and Dickens, see Bodenheimer (42–6); on Leigh Hunt's influence on Dickens's representation of London, see Schwarzbach (36–7).

15. Hereafter, essays from the other three volumes of *Selected Writings* are referred to throughout and given as *SW*, followed by the volume number.

16. Douglas-Fairhurst observes of Dickens's time at the *True Sun* in 1832 that, working for this radical evening newspaper at the height of the 'Reform crisis', 'he would certainly have had more opportunities than before of blurring the line between "truth" and "literary work"' (77).

17. I am alluding here to Lacan's comparison of Freud's notions of *Verdichtung* (condensation) and *Verschiebung* (displacement) with Jakobson's analysis of metaphor and metonymy, which leads Lacan to his well-known observation that the unconscious is structured like a language (Lacan 1966, 47–81). Were one to pursue a psychoanalytic reading here, one might suggest that the skittles are what tumble, one knocking another down in succession until David recalls with painful immediacy his younger self.

18. For place to be given, there must be as a minimal condition of awareness, '*l'ouverture affirmative pour la venue de l'autre* [the affirmative openness for the coming of the other]' (Derrida and Steigler, *Échographies* [1996], p. 19). Thus, Jacques Derrida, but also Charles Dickens, or at least 'Charles Dickens', that machine by which memory becomes text, the city inscribed, *transcribed* from one materiality to another, and in that transcription the re-presentation of the authentic trace of historicity: on the one hand, the historicity of place, on the other, that of the subject, of that subjectivity that responds to the call of the other by giving place to the givennness of place and that which takes place in the relation between the subject and the other; this is determined by receiving, but also, importantly, perceiving place through the constellated phenomena that make it what it is, and no other, but which remains nevertheless as the remains of an untotalisable figure. The 'affirmative otherness' of which Derrida speaks, which must be the condition for the coming of the other, is written into the manner of narration, its modalities of reception and perception, in the Dickens text, the technology of which, in its reading / writing of London, not only affirms in its openness, its perception, but also remains open, to the other we call the reader, and readers to come. Yet, forcing translation, I would also like to render Derrida's remark as the 'affirmative openness for or towards, to, the venue of the other'. Venue names both place and the coming. The other's venue, then: a coming which takes place, and is thus temporal, but which also has place, which gives place to be apprehended and is apperceived in the subjectity of the subject, 'subject' being given as that mode of apprehension and orientation to the world, and which, in taking place, is *just* place, taking and giving the place in which the subject finds oneself given in the world.

This phrase 'venue of the other' or the 'other's venue': this is a double genitive of sorts. On the one hand, the phrase remarks a place where the other's arrival is possible, the other's own ground, albeit a groundless ground, a utopian topos, as it were; on the other hand, it signifies this coming, as simply other, emplacement, place and taking- or giving-place simultaneously, as my play between French and English seeks to acknowledge. There is no other, no possibility of the other, the other's arrival, coming to pass, without place, and therefore time; and so, there is no possibility of a subjectivity not subject of or to the material and the historical. In this, apprehension of the relation between subjectivity and place, in accordance with the Derridean principle of the affirmative openness, we are given to hear the necessity for the ethics of reception, described by Nietzsche's phrase, '*ungeheuer unbegrenzte Ja*' (Nietzsche, *Also Sprach Zarathustra*, in *Sämtliche Werke*, vol. 4, p. 208) – which is to say, a 'monstrous illimitable yes'. This is what is found in Dickensian subjectivity, an immense limitless yes to the coming of London – the coming of modernity, no less.

I see the world. I am in the world. I tell the world I am in, and in my act of telling, I shape through narration, through image, perspective, experience and perception, not only what I call 'the world' but also my self, the self, on the one hand, that observes and tells, and the self, on the other hand, who acts in that world, and who narrates itself as an I narrated in that world, even on the minimal condition of my receiving, perceiving, experiencing and standing before that place in which I find myself and my consciousness taking place. My perception and experience, my consciousness of material experience is not, therefore, separate from the world. Consciousness and corporeality are different, but not separate; the dualism introduced by Descartes cannot hold, even though it is a model of thought that has maintained consciousness in its separation from the body quite convincingly, perhaps so that there might be an over-intellectualisation and a retreat into theoretical 'seeing' assumed to gaze from above the world in which the body takes part and is apart. This, undoubtedly, is what has led to the persistence of an empirical misapprehension of the self and the world, or the world as world of things, distinct from the self. However, there is a correlate between the corporeality and consciousness, in the event of perception. In order that I may transmit my perception, and the memory of experience, there is language. Perception as reading becomes then narrative as writing, in order that I relay to others that which I am in and before which I stand. In order to give the image of event and experience in translated form, words come into play. They are not, however, subservient to the image, a mere mode of transference or medium of transmission. They are, instead, the medium or media that, rather than coming between, constitute the between: between then and now, self and other, consciousness and place.

Words are thus found to be analogous with the painter's brushstrokes. Patterns are formed, rhythms imposed. The image thus invented through the projection of narration in this mediated form always pertains to the body's perceptual relationship to the materiality of the world, not as undifferentiated materiality, nor as things in themselves, but as the relationship between self and the constellated phenomena of the world, as language gives the image given, in narrated form. I do not, therefore, simply receive the world. Instead, through my being in the world, through my perception and re-presentation of that world, I maintain an openness to the world, whilst refiguring that perception in an active mode, through the agency of a narration that is always invention, part shaping, part response to consciousness of what is found, or given. As narration, as image-constituting medium, language does not represent things, it re-presents perception and experience in a form both proximal and distant to the initial corporeal-perceptive consciousness of Being *in* and *with* others, a Being which I find to be given place, in-formed by the narrating, narrated response of subjectivity to the call of the other.

The 'world of perception' is, then, a phrase that does double service. On the one hand, it names all the world that there is, over there, opposed to but involving an 'I' who remains open to that world. The world, in this case, is the world I perceive. On the other hand, all that I perceive is the world, the world to me; my perception is always of some world, produced through the agency of perceptual consciousness. In thinking the world merely as objects, my 'thought' makes the fundamental mistake – or, let us say, is caught in a misapprehension, a miscognition – that my perception is just an event that takes place in the world, already made, and not subject to an endless making on the part of perception (Merleau-Ponty 1962, 207ff.). Language receives the world, of what is coming, and gives advent to the sense of the world, the sense I have of the world, and the world as received sense, that sense which is the world in which my perception is involved. Narrative is therefore always the transformation and transmission of perceptual agency and partakes primarily, not of 'history' but of memory. To speak of literature in terms of history (and, corollary to this, to fall into any facile assumption of text and context) is to fail to recognise the historicity of language, re-presentation, and memory given phantom, imaginary, apparitional form on the one hand; on the other, this is merely to seek to stabilise a certain relationship between the formal presentation of language as representation and the world misunderstood as objects rather than phenomena for consciousness. The ever-strident attempt to place literature and keep literature in its place through recourse to history is only the always increasingly desperate effort to subordinate the literary and forget the work of memory.

Literature or, let us say, with an economy that is as enigmatic as it is transparent, the *literary*, is always a singular reflection, but that singularity is always informed by condition of its having been generated at a given moment. That is to say, the singular act of the literary, a mediated form of anamnesiac or mnemotechnic re-presentation, is always already countersigned by the traces that perception receives in its openness to the world of the historicity of phenomena. The literary as memory-archive does not belong to history but is instead a 'register of imaginaries' (Huyssen 2004, 4): a register, but also a revenant belonging to other modalities of registration that include, but are not limited to, painting and photography. To read a narrative, of London, for example, is to fall into another's memory, into the memorial re-presentation of the sense of the world, and thus to enter into different temporalities and spatial apprehensions.

19. Jean-Luc Marion points to the 'invisible' matter of sight, and by extension the spectral, within the visible, and with that the phenomenality of an object (2002a, 119; see also 125, and 117, where intuition is related to vision [f. Latin: *in* + *tueri*, 'to look'].)
20. I am drawing here on Marion's argument across a number of texts already cited. Marion's project, in part, is to rethink earlier models of phenomenology – specifically Husserl and Heidegger's – because both recuperate themselves into transcendental notions of Being. Marion seeks to move beyond this by arguing for a pure givenness to phenomena.
21. Such figures of the walking subject are common in Dickensian meditations on, and mediations of, London and are, in part at least, the trace of a Romantic urban subjectivity, such as is to be found most obviously in De Quincey or Wordsworth, but also Lamb, Southey, Hazlitt and other Romantic writers.
22. See the extended discussion of language from a phenomenological, specifically Merleau-Pontyan, perspective in 'Spring Evenings', below.
23. The particular building referred to in the narrative was the second church

on the site, replaced in 1877, and subsequently rebuilt and reconsecrated in 1882, following a fire in 1880. This church was destroyed during an air raid in 1840 and was not subsequently rebuilt. The location is now the site of the Altab Ali Park.

24. The allusion to 'omnibus cads' and the comparison between them and the Commissioners serves effectively, if cryptically, to date the passage, especially as *Pickwick* is set a decade or so before its publication, in 1828–9. George Shillibeer introduced the omnibus to London on 4 July 1829, having seen similar vehicles in Paris. The cad, as many readers will be aware, was the name given to the conductor, who collected the fares from passengers. Dickens had previously written on omnibus cads in *Sketches,* Chapter 17, 'The last Cab Driver and the first Omnibus Cad' (*SB* 142–50).

25. I am borrowing here, and further down the paragraph, on an argument put forward concerning testimony and literary criticism in an as yet unpublished book by Thomas Docherty (2012). I am very grateful to Thomas not only for his insightful and acute, necessary commentary, but also for permission to cite or allude to *Confessions* prior to publication.

26. Barthes continues in this passage, significantly, to describe de-piction as the unfurling of a carpet of codes (as he has it), where code does not refer to or signify a referent but to yet another code. This is what we witness at work in Esther's description / depiction: the 'visuality' and 'verbality' (Bal 1991, 27–8) of the extract exchange places, substituting and supplementing one another.

27. To those who would make claims of anachrony, postmodernity, 'theorisation' and a lack – apparently – of historical acuity or awareness, I can only cite the words of Maurice Merleau-Ponty: 'Even when it is possible to date the emergence of a principle which exists "for itself," it is clear that the principle has been previously present in the culture as an obsession or anticipation, and that the act of consciousness which lays it down as an explicit signification is never without a residue' (1964a, 41).

28. Poulet is drawing here on Coleridge's consideration of the imagination, as discussed in Chapter 13 of *Biographia Literaria*, 'On the Imagination, or Esemplastic Power' (1983, 295–306), and figured as a motivating force in 'Dejection: an Ode' (1997, 307–11).

29. Speaking about 'voice', and in this discussion about the working-class voice, it is necessary to qualify immediately by making it clear that I am not talking about the working-class voice in general, but only that which appears in singular instances. Thus, phonetically, while Sam Weller or Sloppy might be more closely related to Rogue Riderhood, Krook or Bill Sikes, rather than the 'northern' voices of John Browdie or Sleary, the Circus Master of *Hard Times*, the chance of shared location is the only thing that connects them, making it impossible therefore to talk of, or assume, a 'generalised' working-class voice. What Sloppy and Weller share, and share with Sleary, is the ability to entertain, to engage the imagination of their audience, and from their voices to project the fictive vision. It is extremely unlikely that Sloppy would have ever heard the voices he produces. Sloppy's is an inventive and a creative act, one of the imagination, which communicates to Betty. Of course, it is inaccessible; we never have an example, nor would one be representable. But is that not the point?

In what Betty hears, the papers come alive, and that does not necessarily need to be something specific to where one comes from but by being open to reception. Weller's voice is closely tied not only to those improper anecdotal moments, but also to a general sense of comic disordering, a puncturing of the serious. He is the court jester, the one who knows more than his master and turns the world upside down, displaying in the process a story-telling ability in all its uselessness, but which interrupts 'business as usual' with its power to entertain. Krook, Riderhood and Sikes may speak similarly, but they do not 'perform' in the same way. This may explain a connection between Sloppy and Sam, but also, crossing from London to what in Dickens is a largely undifferentiated representation of the north, to Sleary. The phonetic spellings of his speech not only indicate a lisp, but an, again, undifferentiated northern, certainly regional accent. And when, towards the conclusion of *Hard Times*, he advocates the necessity for fun, magic, entertainment, the circus, and other matters of fantasy and escape which, strictly speaking, are 'useless', other than the joy they deliver, he does so by telling Gradgrind, 'you muth 'ave uth, thquire'. The positive representation in Sam, who obviously comes before the villainous and negative figures already mentioned, is perhaps the sign, historically, of Dickens's affection for a London that is passing, the London of the 1820s and 1830s, the London of Pierce Egan's Tom and Jerry, of Leigh Hunt's 'townosophy', of Joseph Grimaldi's performances.

A still significant essay on 'voice' in Dickens is P. J. Keating's, on 'The Phonetic Representation of Cockney' (1971, 246–68). An interesting if limited consideration, it is somewhat too broad in its generalisations, too sweeping to be fully attentive to function and purpose in the Dickens text. There are at least two problems throughout the assumptions and argument that are pervasive. The first is that Dickens is seeking to portray a 'true picture' (he gets co-opted into the category of the 'slum novelist', however indirectly), and that 'Cockney' is a generic London patois, which it is not. Moreover, there is the overly easy association between 'Cockney' and the 'slums'. 'Cockney' pre-exists the 'slums' and is not exclusive to them. Furthermore, Keating undercuts his own argument by stating that phonetic variants are 'rarely consistent', though he does admit that Gamp and the Wellers are consistent. Taking the Wellers and Gamp: their 'consistency' has as much to do with the purpose of speech as it does with its locale, or place of origin, and is not exclusively a London phenomenon amongst Dickens's characters. In the somewhat undifferentiated materialist attention to a lumpenproletariat, Keating does not give necessary attention to the rhetorical orientation of forms of speech, nor their gestural disposition within the novels as novels. There is no real sense in Keating that accent is, or can be, merely a medium through which a certain form of commentary can be delivered, rather than it being a 'true' presentation of working-class argot, and it is, to repeat myself, that which distinguishes Weller (and Gamp) from other working-class figures. Both Sam and Mrs Gamp are anecdotalists – one might pause to consider Gamp's tale of her husband's alcoholic wooden leg, with its own machinic life, a comic Hofmannesque moment of music hall entertainment, and a form of comic exaggeration and displacement Dickens first develops in the letters home from his first trip to the US, where person becomes object, object becomes exaggerated, and the surface, often surreal absurdity of the image (on this, see J. Hillis Miller 1970, 467–76). There is in the text of Dickens, through the agency and performance of voice, the distinction being made that the purpose is entertainment or a form of loquacious reflection that places one materially, regardless of where the character is from regionally. Often such deliveries serve as comic encomia, or are obscure, not to say allegorical, perorations. Venus and Sleary belong to this category of witty and informative discursive gesture. Characters such as Quilp, Wegg, Riderhood or Sikes are distinguished by the fact that they do not tell extended stories (or if they do, it is only rarely, and is always mendacious).

30. See 57, 208, 233–4, 426, 436, 437–8, 532, 535, 770, 774. All further references are given parenthetically as *AP*.

31. In *Minima Moralia* examples of kitsch, related 'domestic monstrosities' and the general existence of household 'trash' objects in all their ambiguous presence in our everyday lives are considered by Adorno, apropos 'Balzac or Dickens', whose 'little wights' the critic compares disturbingly with the 'polychrome garden dwarf'. For Adorno, such objects are disquieting precisely because of their auratic possibilities, their capability to echo, as he puts it, the spectral in 'the mightiest works of art' (Adorno 1974, 225). I mention this because, though tangential to the principal discussion, Dickens's placement of objects with no apparent purpose does have the power potentially, in those objects' inutility, to haunt place and page, albeit in the most evanescent of fashions, by reminding the reader that the 'souvenir' is also the material embodiment of memory, and therefore capable of escaping or exceeding the materialist realm in which it is produced. Perhaps the question is whether Dickens, in advertising and apostrophising the useless, is seeking to recuperate, for aesthetic and phenomenal purposes, that within any commodity which is otherwise unavailable to commodification. If this sounds as though Dickens might be read as anticipating Marx's concept of the commodity fetish, perhaps Dickens's spectral aestheticism comes from the other side, as it were, 'de-commodifying' or, at least, dematerialising the materiality in order to open the reader to the sensible and phenomenal. This remains speculation, of course, a hypothetical on the edge of undecidability. What may be argued not too unreasonably, however, if only so as to retreat strategically from this strong reading – in order to visit it through the specific and singular examples to be discussed in the essays of the volume, rather than to generalise too broadly here – is that Dickens's text, in its constant confrontation with the city in the nineteenth century stages in its representation of place, event, experience, object and phenomena in close relation the historicity of tensions between materialism and aesthetic or phenomenal reception. It is, perhaps, for such reasons that Benjamin refers to Dickens, confronting an experience of the aporetic in dialectical thought, without being able to resolve or pass this encounter.

32. *Polis* can signify not only the city but also the state or the body politic. Dickens often uses 'London' as a synecdoche for both.

33. Whether Dickens was aware that looking-glass was a slang synonym for chamber pot in the seventeenth century is unknown, but given his sense of humour, it is nice to think he might have been.

34. I am drawing here on formulations proposed by Merleau-Ponty (1964b/1993, 47ff./121–50).
35. See Merleau-Ponty's critique of the 'ingenuous' nature of intellectualism and its scientistic turn to empiricism. *Contra* the veiled 'theoretism' here, Merleau-Ponty insists on a pre-theoretical experience and perception, whereby 'I would not know that I possess a true idea if my memory did not enable me to relate to what is now evidence with what was evident a moment ago, and, through the medium of words, correlate my evidence with that of others' (1962, 39).

Bibliography

Ackroyd, Peter. *Dickens*. New York: HarperCollins, 1990.
—. *London: The Biography*. London: Chatto & Windus, 2000.
Adorno, Theodor W. *Minima Moralia: Reflections from Damaged Life*. Trans. E. F. N. Jephcott. London: Verso, 1974.
—. *Notes to Literature: vol. 1*. Ed. Rolf Tiedemann. Trans. Shierry Weber Nicholsen. New York: Columbia University Press, 1991a.
—. *In Search of Wagner*. Trans. Rodney Livingstone. London: Verso, 1991b.
—. *Notes to Literature: vol. 2*. Trans. Shierry Weber Nicholsen. New York: Columbia University Press, 1992.
Agacinski, Sylviane. *Time Passing: Modernity and Nostalgia*. Trans. Jody Gladding. New York: Columbia University Press, 2003.
Agamben, Giorgio. *Nudities*. Trans. David Kishik and Stefan Pedatella. Stanford: Stanford University Press, 2011.
Arsic, Branka. *The Passive Eye: Gaze and Subjectivity in Berkeley (via Beckett)*. Stanford: Stanford University Press, 2003.
Attridge, Derek. *The Singularity of Literature*. London: Routledge, 2004.
Augé, Marc. *Non-Places: Introduction to an Anthropology of Supermodernity*. Trans. John Howe. London: Verso, 1995.
Bachelard, Gaston. *The Poetics of Space*. New edn, trans. Maria Jolas. Foreword John R. Stilgoe. Boston, MA: Beacon, 1994.
Badiou, Alain. *Conditions*. Trans. Steven Corcoran. London: Continuum, 2008.
—. *Logics of Worlds: Being and Event II*. Trans. Alberto Toscano. London: Continuum, 2009.
Bal, Mieke. *Reading 'Rembrandt': Beyond the Word–Image Opposition*. Cambridge: Cambridge University Press, 1991.
Barbaras, Renaud. *Desire and Distance: Introduction to a Phenomenology of Perception*. Stanford: Stanford University Press, 2006.
Barber, Stephen. *Fragments of the European City*. London: Reaktion, 1995.
Barthes, Roland. *S / Z*. Paris: Seuil, 1970.
Baudelaire, Charles. 'What is Romanticism?' *Nineteenth-Century Theories of Art*. Ed. Joshua C. Taylor. Berkeley and Los Angeles: University of California Press, 1987, pp. 220–36.
—. 'Le Peintre de la vie moderne'. *L'Art romantique* (1869), pp. 51–114. Trans. as 'The Painter of Modern Life'. *Selected Writings on Art and Literature*. Trans. and Int. P. E. Charvet. London: Penguin, 1992, pp. 390–436.

Benjamin, Walter. *Illuminations*. Ed. and Int. Hannah Arendt. Trans. Harry Zohn. New York: Schocken, 1969.

—. *Selected Writings Volume 1 1913–1926*. Ed. Marcus Bullock and Michael W. Jennings. Cambridge, MA: Belknap, 1996.

—. *The Origin of German Tragic Drama*. Trans. John Osbourne. London: Verso, 1998.

—. *Selected Writings Volume 2 1927–1934*. Trans. Rodney Livingstone et al. Ed. Michael W. Jennings, Howard Eiland and Gary Smith. Cambridge, MA: Belknap, 1999.

—. *The Arcades Project*. Trans. Howard Eiland and Kevin McLaughlin. Cambridge, MA: Belknap, 2002a.

—. *Selected Writings Volume 3 1935–1938*. Trans. Edmund Jephcott et al. Ed. Howard Eiland and Michael W. Jennings. Cambridge, MA: Belknap, 2002b.

—. *Selected Writings Volume 4 1938–1940*. Trans. Edmund Jephcott et al. Ed. Howard Eiland and Michael W. Jennings. Cambridge, MA: Belknap, 2002c.

Bennington, Geoffrey. *Interrupting Derrida*. London: Routledge, 2000.

Bodenheimer, Rosemarie. *Knowing Dickens*. Ithaca, NY: Cornell University Press, 2011.

Budd, Dona. 'Language Couples in *Bleak House*'. *Nineteenth-Century Literature*. 49:2 (Sept. 1994), pp. 196–220.

Chesterton, G. K. *Charles Dickens, The Last of the Great Men*. Foreword Alexander Woolcott. New York: Press of the Readers Club, 1942.

Coleridge, Samuel Taylor. *Biographia Literaria*. Ed. James Engell and W. Jackson Bate. Princeton: Princeton University Press, 1983.

—. *The Complete Poems*. Ed. William Keach. London: Penguin, 1997.

Craig, Cairns. *Associationism and the Literary Imagination: From the Phantasmal Chaos*. Edinburgh: Edinburgh University Press, 2007.

Danius, Sara. *The Senses of Modernism: Technology, Perception, and Aesthetics*. Ithaca, NY: Cornell University Press, 2002.

Dastur, Françoise. *Telling Time: Sketch of a Phenomenological Chrono-logy*. Trans. Edward Bullard. London: Athlone, 2000.

de Bolla, Peter. *The Discourse of the Sublime: History, Aesthetics and the Subject*. Oxford: Basil Blackwell, 1989.

Deleuze, Gilles. *Empiricism and Subjectivity: An Essay on Hume's Theory of Human Nature*. Trans. and Int. Constantin V. Boundas. New York: Columbia University Press, 1991.

de Man, Paul. *Allegories of Reading*. New Haven, CT: Yale University Press, 1979.

—. *Aesthetic Ideology*. Ed. and Int. Andrzej Warminski. Minneapolis: University of Minnesota Press, 1996.

Derrida, Jacques. *Edmund Husserl's* Origin of Geometry: *An Introduction*. Trans., with Preface and Afterword John P. Leavey. Lincoln, NB: University of Nebraska Press, 1989.

—. *Without Alibi*. Ed. and Int. Peggy Kamuf. Stanford: Stanford University Press, 2002.

—. *Sovereignties in Question: The Poetics of Paul Celan*. Ed. Thomas Dutoit and Outi Pasanen. New York: Fordham University Press, 2005.

—, and Bernard Steigler. *Échographies*. Paris: Galilée, 1996.

de Waehlens, Alphonse. 'Merleau-Ponty: Philosopher of Painting'. Trans. Michael B. Smith. In Johnson, ed., pp. 174–92.

Docherty, Thomas. *Confessions*. London: Bloomsbury, 2012.

Douglas-Fairhurst, Robert. *Becoming Dickens: The Invention of a Novelist*. Cambridge, MA: Belknap, 2011.

Eliot, George. *The Mill on the Floss*. Ed. and Int. A. S. Byatt. London: Penguin, 1997.

Eliot, T. S. *Selected Prose of T. S. Eliot*. Ed. Frank Kermode. London: Faber & Faber, 1975.

Fielding, Henry. *Jonathan Wild the Great*. Foreword Peter Ackroyd. London: Hesperus, 2004.

Freeman, Nicholas. *Conceiving the City: London, Literature, and Art 1870–1914*. Oxford: Oxford University Press, 2007.

Gasché, Rodolphe. 'Objective Diversions: On Some Kantian Themes in Benjamin's "The Work of Art in the Age of Mechanical Reproduction"'. *Walter Benjamin's Philosophy: Destruction and Experience*. Ed. Andrew Benjamin and Peter Osborne. London: Routledge, 1994, pp. 183–204.

Guattari, Félix. *The Machinic Unconscious: Essays in Schizoanalysis*. Trans. Taylor Adkins. Los Angeles: Semiotext(e), 2011.

Hegel, G. W. F. *Phenomenology of Spirit*. Trans. A. V. Miller. Foreword J. N. Findlay. Oxford: Oxford University Press, 1977.

Henry, Michel. *Material Phenomenology*. Trans. Scott Davidson. New York: Fordham University Press, 2008.

Hotten, J. C. *Charles Dickens: The Story of His Life*. London: np, 1870.

Husserl, Edmund. *Experience and Judgment: Investigations in a Genealogy of Logic*. Rev. and ed. Ludwig Landgrebe. Trans. James S. Churchill and Karl Ameriks. Int. James S. Churchill. Afterword Lothar Eley. Evanston: Northwestern University Press, 1973.

—. *The Origin of Geometry*. In Derrida, 1989, pp. 155–80.

—. *Cartesian Meditations: An Introduction to Phenomenology*. Trans. Dorion Cairns. Dordrecht: Kluwer Academic, 1995.

—. *Phantasy, Image Consciousness, and Memory (1898–1925)*. Trans. John B. Brough. Dordrecht: Springer, 2005.

Huyssen, Andreas. *Present Pasts: Urban Palimpsests and the Politics of Memory*. Stanford: Stanford University Press, 2004.

Inwood, Stephen. *A History of London*. New York: Carroll & Graf, 1998.

Iser, Wolfgang. 'The Reading Process: A Phenomenological Approach'. *New Literary History. On Interpretation: I*. 3:2 (Winter 1972), pp. 279–99.

—. *The Implied Reader: Patterns of Communication in Prose Fiction from Bunyan to Beckett*. Baltimore: Johns Hopkins University Press, 1974.

James, Henry. Review in *The Nation*, 21 December 1865. *Dickens: The Critical Heritage*. Ed. Philip Collins. London: Routledge & Kegan Paul, 1971.

Johnson, Galen A., ed. *The Merleau-Ponty Aesthetics Reader: Philosophy and Painting*. Evanston: Northwestern University Press, 1993.

—. 'Phenomenology and Painting: "Cézanne's Doubt"'. In Johnson, ed., pp. 3–13.

Kant, Immanuel. *Critique of Pure Reason*. Trans. and ed. Paul Guyer and Allen W. Wood. Cambridge: Cambridge University Press, 1997.

—. *Critique of Judgement.* Trans. James Creed Meredith. Rev. edn, with Int. Nicholas Walker. Oxford: Oxford University Press, 2007.

—. 'Appendix: "First Introduction" to the *Critique of Judgement*'. *Critique of Judgement*, pp. 315–56.

Kates, Joshua. *Fielding Derrida: Philosophy, Literary Criticism, History, and the Work of Deconstruction.* New York: Fordham University Press, 2008.

Keating, P. J. *The Working Classes in Victorian Fiction.* London: Routledge & Kegan Paul, 1971.

Kenner, Hugh. 'The Rhetoric of Silence'. *James Joyce Quarterly.* 14:4 (Summer 1977), pp. 382–94.

Kermode, Frank. *The Genesis of Secrecy: On the Interpretation of Narrative.* Cambridge, MA: Harvard University Press, 1979.

Lacan, Jacques. 'L'Instance de la lettre dans l'inconscient ou la raison depuis Freud'. *Écrits.* Paris: Seuil, 1966, pp. 47–81.

Lefebvre, Henri. *The Production of Space.* Trans. Donald Nicholson-Smith. Oxford: Blackwell, 1991.

—. *The Urban Revolution.* Foreword Neil Smith. Trans. Robert Bonanno. Minneapolis: University of Minnesota Press, 2003.

Louvel, Liliane. 'Telling "by" Pictures: Virginia Woolf's Shorter Fiction. *Journal of the Short Story in English.* 50 (Spring 2008), pp. 2–11.

—. *Poetics of the Iconotext.* Ed. Karen Jacobs. Trans. Laurence Petit. Farnham: Ashgate, 2011.

Marin, Louis. *On Representation.* Trans. Catherine Porter. Stanford: Stanford University Press, 2001.

Marion, Jean-Luc. *Reduction and Givenness: Investigations of Husserl, Heidegger, and Phenomenology.* Trans. Thomas A. Carlson. Evanston: Northwestern University Press, 1998.

—. *In Excess: Studies in Saturated Phenomena.* Trans. Robyn Horner and Vincent Barraud. New York: Fordham University Press, 2002a.

—. *Being Given: Toward a Phenomenology of Givenness.* Trans. Jeffrey L. Kosky. Stanford: Stanford University Press, 2002b.

—. *The Crossing of the Invisible.* Stanford: Stanford University Press, 2004.

McLaughlin, Kevin. 'Losing One's Place: Displacement and Domesticity in Dickens's *Bleak House*'. *Modern Language Notes* (1993), pp. 875–90.

—. *Writing in Parts: Imitation and Exchange in Nineteenth-Century Literature.* Stanford: Stanford University Press, 1995.

Merleau-Ponty, Maurice. *Phenomenology of Perception.* Trans. Colin Smith. London: Routledge, 1962.

—. *Signs.* Trans. and Int. Richard C. McLeary. Evanston: Northwestern University Press, 1964a.

—. *L'Œil et l'esprit.* Preface Claude Lefort. Paris: Gallimard, 1964b. Trans. as 'Eye and Mind'. Johnson, ed., pp. 121–50.

—. *The Visible and the Invisible.* Ed. Claude Lefort. Trans. Alphonso Lingis. Evanston: Northwestern University Press, 1968.

—. *The Prose of the World.* Ed. Claude Lefort. Trans. John O'Neill. Evanston: Northwestern University Press, 1981.

—. *The World of Perception.* Trans. Oliver Davis. Foreword Stéphanie Ménasé. Int. Thomas Baldwin. London: Routledge, 2004.

Mighall, Robert. *A Geography of Victorian Gothic Fiction: Mapping History's Nightmares*. Oxford: Oxford University Press, 1999.

Miles, Robert. *Gothic Writing 1750–1820: A Genealogy*. London: Routledge, 1993.

Miller, J. Hillis. 'The Sources of Dickens's Comic Art: From *American Notes* to *Martin Chuzzlewit*'. *Nineteenth-Century Fiction*. 24:4. Charles Dickens Centennial (March 1970), pp. 467–76.

—. *Reading Narrative*. Norman: University of Oklahoma Press, 1998.

—. 'Paul de Man as Allergen'. *Material Events: Paul de Man and the Afterlife of Theory*. Ed. Tom Cohen et al. Minneapolis: University of Minnesota Press, 2001, pp. 183–205.

Nancy, Jean-Luc. *The Sense of the World*. Trans. and Foreword Jeffrey S. Librett. Minneapolis: University of Minnesota Press, 1997.

—. *Corpus*. Trans. Richard A. Rand. New York: Fordham University Press, 2008.

Natanson, Maurice. 'Phenomenology, Anonymity, and Alienation'. *New Literary History*. 10:3 (Spring 1979), pp. 533–46.

Nietzsche, Friedrich. *Also Sprach Zarathustra*. *Sämtliche Werke*, Kritische Studienausgabe in 15 Bänden, vol. 4. Munich: dtv, 2005.

Patocka, Jan. *Heretical Essays in the Philosophy of History*. Trans. Erazim Kohak. Ed. James Dodd. Preface Paul Ricœur. Chicago: Open Court, 1996.

Pevsner, Nikolaus. *The Buildings of England: London Volume I • The Cities of London and Westminster*. Harmondsworth: Penguin, 1957.

Picker, John M. *Victorian Soundscapes*. Oxford: Oxford University Press, 2003.

Poetzsch, Markus. *Visionary Dreariness: Readings in Romanticism's Quotidian Sublime*. London: Routledge, 2006.

Porter, Roy. *London: A Social History*. London: Hamish Hamilton, 1994.

Poulet, Georges. 'Phenomenology of Reading'. *New Literary History*. 1:1 (October 1969), pp. 53–68.

Proust, Marcel. *In Search of Lost Time Volume 6: Time Regained and a Guide to Proust*. Trans. Scott C. K. Moncrieff, Rev. Andreas Mayor and Terence Kilmartin, Rev. edn D. J. Enright; Guide comp. Terence Kilmartin, rev. Joanna Kilmartin. London: Vintage, 1996.

Punter, David. Review of Elizabeth Napier, *The Failure of the Gothic*. *Times Higher Education Supplement* (20 March 1987), p. 26.

Puttenham, George. *The Arte of English Poesie*. Menston: Scolar, 1968.

Read, Herbert. *A Concise History of Modern Painting*. London: Thames & Hudson, 1988.

Robertson, Fiona. *Scott, Gothic, and the Authorities of Fiction*. Oxford: Clarendon, 1994.

Royle, Nicholas. *Veering: A Theory of Literature*. Edinburgh: Edinburgh University Press, 2011.

Said, Edward. *The World, the Text, and the Critic*. Cambridge, MA: Harvard University Press, 1983.

Schwarzbach, F. S. *Dickens and the City*. London: Athlone, 1979.

Slater, Michael. *Charles Dickens*. New Haven, CT: Yale University Press, 2009.

Smith, James, and Horace. *Rejected Addresses: or, the New Theatrum Poetarum*. London: John Murray, 1879.

Stallybrass, Peter, and Allon White. *The Politics and Poetics of Transgression.* Ithaca, NY: Cornell University Press, 1986.

Stewart, Garrett. 'Reading Feeling and the "Transferred Life": *The Mill on the Floss. The Feeling of Reading: Affective Experience and Victorian Literature.* Ed. Rachel Ablow. Ann Arbor: University of Michigan Press, 2010, pp. 179–206.

Stow, John. *The Survey of London.* Rev. edn H. B. Wheatley. Int. Valerie Pearl. London: J. M. Dent, 1956.

Tambling, Jeremy. *Going Astray: Dickens and London.* London: Pearson Education, 2009.

Walford, Edward. *Old and New London: Volume 6.* London: Cassell, 1878.

Weber, Samuel. *Mass Mediauras: Form, Technics, Media.* Stanford: Stanford University Press, 1996.

Weinrebb, Ben, and Christopher Hibbert, eds. *The London Encyclopaedia.* Basingstoke: Macmillan, 1995.

Williams, Forrest. 'Cézanne, Phenomenology, and Merleau-Ponty'. In Johnson, ed., pp. 165–73.

Winter, Sarah. *The Pleasures of Memory: Learning to Read with Charles Dickens.* New York: Fordham University Press, 2011.

Wolfreys, Julian. *Writing London: The Trace of the Urban Text from Blake to Dickens.* Basingstoke: Macmillan, 1998.

Wordsworth, William. *The Prelude: The Four Texts.* Ed. and Int. Jonathan Wordsworth. London: Penguin, 1995.

Index of Proper Names